SOLVING PRODUCT

Reveal Gaps, Ignite Growth, and Accelerate Any Tech Product with Customer Research

Solving Product

August 2020: First Edition.

Proofreading by Joy Sellen

Cover design by Katarina Naskovski
booklerk.com

Text design by Andrew Forteath
andrewforteath.co.uk

ISBN: 978-1-7780740-6-6

Table of Contents

To my mother.
For giving me the
courage to follow my convictions.

Acknowledgement

During the writing of this book, I spoke to the world's leading experts on some of the customer research techniques discussed in this book, and many of the product leaders and entrepreneurs who use these techniques daily. The best ideas in this book are from them.

Many of the techniques and ideas covered here are detailed in full in their books, talks, and blogs, which I invite you to check out. You'll find links and references to their work at the end of the book.

Every component of this approach is well known to some particular field of research or industry. They have just never been put together into a coherent method before.

Preface

"If all you have is a hammer, everything looks like a nail.[1]"

Abraham Maslow
Psychologist

Experience is a funny thing.

The more we acquire of it, the more we become partial to doing things in certain ways.

Consciously or not, we start prioritizing the strategies and tactics that have made us successful before.

Because of this, we rarely take the time to consider all options when working on products.

If we're used to using analytics to measure how features impact customers, then we'll discount the value of learning from small groups of users.

If we're used to interviewing customers to understand their needs and reasoning, experiments and quantitative research might get neglected.

Our experience—or our team's experience—creates our blind spots, and unfortunately, blind spots are where a lot of the magic happens.

When I joined LANDR, a SaaS music mastering service, the founders and the early team had done a great job validating the need, creating valuable technology, building a brand, and attracting capital. Now growth was expected.

There were just a few problems. It wasn't clear:

- who benefited the most;
- what was valued and what wasn't;
- why users bought or didn't;
- why users stuck around or didn't; *or*
- who the users really were in the first place.

The business was growing, but blind spots were hindering its growth.

The team was already stretched thin building the product, so a key part of my role became systematically seeking out information gaps, answering questions around product use, challenging assumptions.

No stone was left unturned.

The more we learned, the faster we grew. Less than two years in, revenue had grown by 4x.

Today, well after my time at LANDR, I often speak with entrepreneurs. Too often, when I ask questions about their users or the value that their product delivers, I get fuzzy answers.

It turns out that, despite it being a proven way to grow a product[2], most businesses struggle with systematically learning about their users and customers.

I wrote *Solving Product* to share a method designed to drive new growth, step by step.

The book was written to help product teams, entrepreneurs, innovators, and marketers uncover the gaps in their business models, find new avenues for growth, and systematically overcome their next hurdles.

It covers the five stages in the life cycle of a product business:

1. **Idea**: *Is this idea worth pursuing?*
2. **Startup**: *Will it work?*
3. **Growth**: *Can it scale?*
4. **Expansion**: *How big can it get?*

5. **Maturity**: *How can we find more growth?*

No matter the stage, we're always looking for growth.

Solving Product will help you unlock that growth.

How to Use This Book

> "What is wanted is not the will to believe, but the will to find out, which is the exact opposite."
>
> Bertrand Russell
> Philosopher

Solving Product is a different kind of book.

It has been structured in a way so you can put it on your desk and thumb through it when you're facing a growth challenge for your business.

You can read it from beginning to end, or jump around as need be.

The Table of Contents and the exercises in Chapter #2 have been designed to help you navigate to the appropriate content.

I hope you enjoy this book, I really enjoyed writing it. At the end, you'll find my email address, and I'd love to hear what you thought of it.

-Étienne

Inception

1 / 26

Introduction

"Learning and innovation go hand in hand. The arrogance of success is to think that what you did yesterday will be sufficient for tomorrow."

William G. Pollard
Physicist

"It's just not working."

Julie was sitting in a dark office with her two co-founders.

She had called for an emergency, partner-only, meeting after another hectic day.

Now, well after working hours, the co-founders could hear their voices echo across Demoto's empty 30,000 square feet office.

Eight months ago, they had raised a large funding round based on their impressive growth trajectory.

Ever since the raise, the partners had spent every waking hour recruiting and hiring the best people they could find.

It seemed like they were making all the right moves—hiring, marketing, product—yet if you really looked under the hood, the business had barely grown.

Sure, they were able to acquire a lot more users than before, sales and revenue had grown significantly, but nothing they had done had really improved customer retention.

Even worse, a growing number of customers were cancelling their accounts.

At their current burn rate, and with 150 employees now on payroll, the partners knew they had to start thinking about the next round of funding. They also knew that, no matter how they positioned it, investors would see right through the issues.

For weeks, customer retention had been on their minds, but with all the new people coming in, they knew better than to sound the alarm. The last thing they wanted was for top talent and investors to get worried.

Quietly, they had asked key staff to dig into customer feedback, speak with users, research the competition, and read through years of support tickets.

To improve the product, they had also prioritized features they felt could improve retention.

The analysts had come back empty-handed. Customers loved Demoto's brand and product. Sure, there were bugs, but all products have them. It was unlikely that bugs were holding back growth this much.

The partners had met five years ago at Worktag, a now much larger technology company. They had joined early, helped the company find product/market fit (PMF), and decided to start their own business once Worktag passed $30M in revenue.

Having been through the process before, they knew that Demoto had PMF. At Worktag, however, once the company had reached PMF, it just kept on growing.

The partners were at a loss for next steps.

Hockey Stick Growth is a Lie

> "Whenever you hear anybody talk about 'growth hacks,' just mentally translate it in your mind to 'bullshit'.[3]"

Paul Graham
Y Combinator Co-Founder

There are a lot of persistent myths in the technology industry, for example:

- You can raise funding based on an idea (you can't[4]).
- The idea you choose to pursue is one of the most important factors in your success (it's not[5]).
- The best companies are started by young entrepreneurs in their early 20s (they're not[6]).
- Your business has to be based in such and such region to succeed (it doesn't[7]).
- There's such a thing as hockey stick growth.

For the past 20 years, every tech company's pitch deck has featured some variation of the hockey stick growth chart:

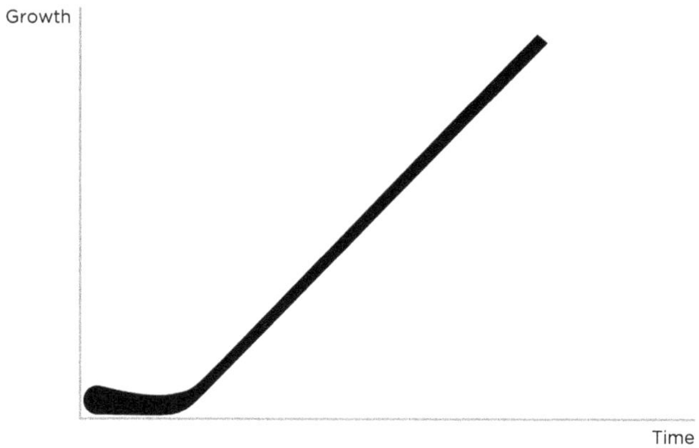

Figure 1.1 - Hockey Stick Growth

Exponential growth over time.

Don't get me wrong, I love hockey (I'm Canadian!), but this chart is more myth than reality.

Even in the rare cases where reality has matched projections, if you were to zoom in on the chart, you'd see series of tiny peaks, dips and plateaus.

Expecting never-ending growth—as Julie and her team might have—is misleading at best. Growing fast and creating predictable growth means constantly refining your growth recipe. It's rarely the result of a single action.

Why Growth Stalls

"You can only get so many quick wins before you've got to start doing the real work."

Michael Sacca
Dribbble VP of Products

There are two reasons why growth stalls:

1. The business hasn't figured out the next thing it needs to learn.
2. The business attempts to grow with a flawed, incomplete, or outdated[8] model of its product, users, market, or customers.

It *is* possible to grow (grow fast even) with a flawed, or partial understanding of your business mechanics.

Depending on the size of your market, growth can even go on for quite a while. But sooner or later, fundamental issues catch up.

If you don't figure out what makes your business *unique*, you're forced to rely on good ideas, great execution, *hacks*, emulating the competition, or any other ad-hoc tactics for growth. This can work for a time, but eventually growth will slow down and you will be left with little to no knowledge on how to truly grow your company.

All businesses are unique. They have their own cultures, founder DNAs, experiences, competitive advantages, management structures, goals, technical debts, strategies, and they compete in different markets striving to create value for different groups of humans. You can't simply copy another company's business strategy. To grow consistently, you have to figure out your own unique growth recipe.

Julie and her team's customer retention issues might have been caused by:

- misunderstanding why customers use and buy their product;
- having acquired the wrong users and customers;
- having created a product with too many unwanted features;
- all of the above; or
- something else completely.

Finding the core issue means first narrowing the list by uncovering which parts of the growth recipe are solid, and which aren't.

In the next chapter, we'll look at a way for you (and Julie's team) to assess a business.

2 / 26

Isolating the Issues

"If you search around a room with a flashlight then you're only seeing small pieces at a time. But if you replace that flashlight with a lamp, then all of a sudden you're able to see more."

Dan Touchette
Personio Group Product Manager

If you were to start painting today, you would be met with blank canvas.

Maybe you'd get inspired by an idea you had, by a memory from your childhood, or you would simply paint what's in front of you.

As you worked on some parts of the painting, it would become clear which parts needed more work, and which parts were *good enough*.

Maybe the grass doesn't look like grass. Maybe faces lack definition. Maybe there are still just rough outlines in the bottom half.

No matter your process, the painting would visually tell you which parts need more work.

A painting has its own *built-in* feedback cycle. This makes it obvious to the artist when the work is incomplete, and when it's good enough.

In some ways, businesses are like paintings. Both start with blank canvases. Both need layers of clarifications and iterations. Both are made better by the sum of their parts.

But unlike paintings, businesses don't tell you when they're incomplete, they don't show you which elements are missing, and they rarely help you find the gaps.

Worse, businesses operate under changing conditions and environments. Because of this, product teams can never really get full clarity.

If you find yourself asking strategic questions that you only have general answers to, if you're in constant reaction mode, or if your business goals are unclear or disconnected, then your business most likely has gaps that it needs to address.

How Gaps Affect Your Business

> "Facts do not cease to exist because they are ignored."
>
> Aldous Huxley
> Author of Brave New World

The five sections in this book address the key stages of the business life cycle. Although the stages and challenges within them might not entirely map back to the evolution of your business, they will provide a clear overview of the ingredients of business success.

To help figure out which stage your business is at, ask yourself:

- *Have we identified and prioritized all expansion opportunities (features, markets, products, etc)?* If so, you might be at the Maturity stage (Stage #5);
- *Have we identified our funnel's friction points, why customers buy, and the best channels to scale customer acquisition profitably?* If so, you might have reached the Expansion stage (Stage #4);
- *Have we found PMF?* If so, you might have entered the Growth stage (Stage #3);
- *Have we validated the opportunity through pre-selling?* If you did, you reached the Startup stage (Stage #2);
- If you've not reached any of those milestones, it might be a good idea to start at the Idea stage (Stage #1).

Within each of these stages, there are challenges that your team must address:

Stage 1 – Idea

- ☐ A need has been found and a customer segment identified (Chapter #4);
- ☐ A competitive advantage has been identified (Chapter #5);
- ☐ A compelling value proposition has been created (Chapter #6);
- ☐ The product concept has been validated (Chapter #7).

Stage 2 – Startup

- ☐ The product has delivered the expected benefit (Chapter #8);
- ☐ *Best fit* customers have been identified (Chapter #9);
- ☐ The product has met and exceeded customer expectations (Chapter #10);
- ☐ You've found PMF (Chapter #11).

Stage 3 – Growth

- ☐ Friction points across the entire funnel have been identified (Chapter #12);
- ☐ You know why customers have bought your product (Chapter #13);

- ☐ Users have been signing up for the same reasons that they bought and used your product (Chapter #14);
- ☐ You have found your best acquisition channels (Chapter #15).

Stage 4 – Expansion

- ☐ Engagement-increasing product improvements have been identified (Chapter #16);
- ☐ Adjacent customers segments have been identified (Chapter #17);
- ☐ Opportunities to improve customer acquisition have been identified (Chapter #18);
- ☐ Opportunities to create new products have been identified (Chapter #19).

Stage 5 – Maturity

- ☐ A rapid growth experiment process has been created (Chapter #20);
- ☐ The product's fit and effectiveness has been optimized (Chapter #21);
- ☐ Remaining acquisition opportunities have been identified (Chapter #22);
- ☐ Revenue and profitability have been optimized (Chapter #23).

Jumping ahead without properly addressing the challenges from previous stages is like trying to play professional sports without first learning the rudiments.

Whether it's premature scaling—trying to scale acquisition (Chapter #15) without clear signs of PMF (Chapter #11) —or optimizing (Chapter #12) a product without knowing if it delivers actual value (Chapter #10), growing a business without solid foundations is wasteful.

To get a sense of where your business is at, you first need to understand which aspects of your business are solid, and which aren't.

Visualizing the Gaps in Your Business

"Ignorance is never better than knowledge."

Enrico Fermi
Winner of 1938 Nobel Prize in Physics

You might be able to grow a product business that has a few gaps, but the more gaps there are, the more difficulty you'll have in pinpointing the deeper reasons why your business underperforms.

Is growth slow because you're not acquiring the right customers, or because your product doesn't have the right features, or because you're not addressing the right need?

Ultimately, every part of your business model can be positioned on a simple scale. On one end, you have *Complete Guesses* and on the other, you have *Statistically-Validated Facts*:

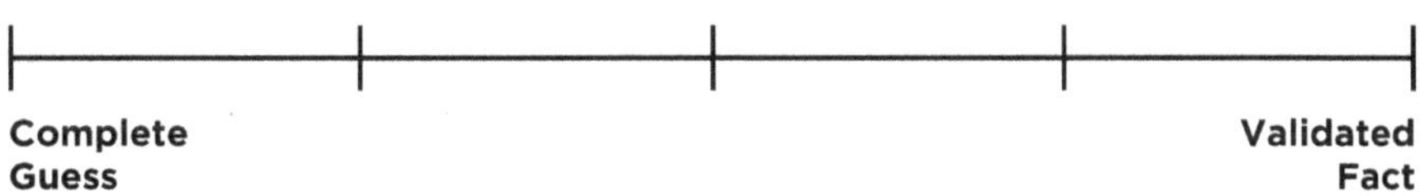

Figure 2.1 - The Certainty Scale

The difference between a guess and a statistically validated fact is the level of confidence you have in the information.

Positioning the elements of your business model on this continuum will help to reveal the gaps.

To assess confidence, *User Story Mapping* author Jeff Patton recommends thinking in terms of bets, asking how much you'd be willing to bet that the information is accurate[9].

Whenever you learn new things about your business or your product, Jeff recommends asking whether you'd be willing to bet:

> A) Your lunch; B) A day's pay; C) Your house; or D) Your retirement savings (401k).

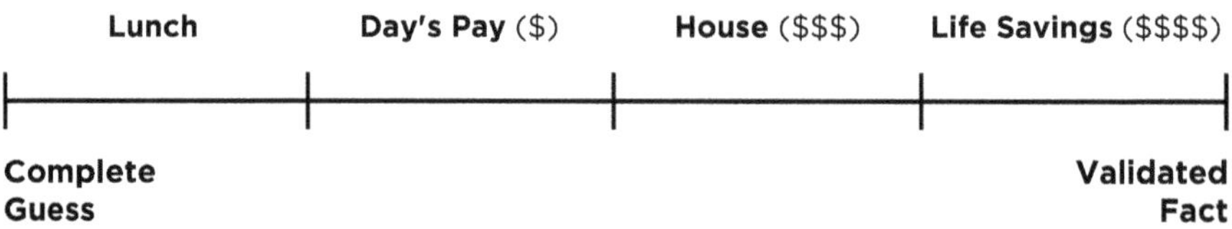

Figure 2.2 - The Certainty Scale With Bets

If you're not willing to bet more than your lunch, it's quite likely that, deep down, you know you are simply guessing. If you're willing to bet your retirement savings on an insight, you are most likely dealing with information that you can depend on.

Looking back at the 20 challenges listed above, *where would your answers fall?*

Go through the challenges one by one, and position your answers on the certainty scale.

How Clear Is Your Growth Recipe?

"People oftentimes will live in a world of assumptions, and they'll treat assumptions as facts. And without explicitly calling out those assumptions then it's really difficult to learn what the gaps are."

Dan Touchette

Focus on the challenges from the stages *before* yours: *how much confidence do you have in your answers?*

Very quickly, you should be able to uncover:

- **Assumptions**: information you accept as true with little—or insufficient—proof;
- **Gaps**: challenges from previous stages that your team might have overlooked, or that might be worth re-visiting; and
- **Validated learning**: knowledge you can *reliably* build on.

You should be able to tell which parts of your growth recipe are clear, and which need more work.

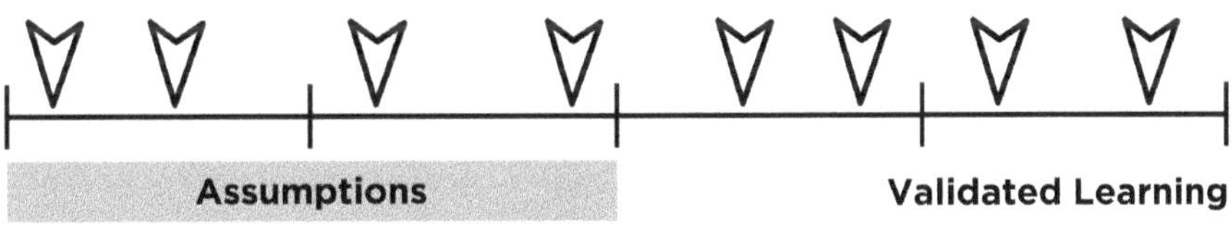

Figure 2.3 - Example of a Growth Recipe

Although your product might have reached the Maturity, Expansion, Growth, or Startup stages, it's not uncommon to still be lacking insights into key elements of your business model at those stages. If you've overlooked certain information, consider circling back to address the challenges you have skipped over.

Through this exercise, you should also be able to figure out what your next moves should be. *Where does confidence drop off? What's the next challenge on your list?*

As Peter Bevelin, author of *Seeking Wisdom* wrote: *"If we face two possible explanations which make the same predictions, the one based on the least number of unproven assumptions is preferable, until more evidence comes along."*

Rank the gaps that you've uncovered. In the next chapter, we will turn this assessment into actionable next steps.

3 / 26

Asking the Right Questions

"Research is formalized curiosity. It is poking and prying with a purpose."

Zora Neale Hurston
Author

The approach in *Solving Product* is based on five principles:

1. **There's always an answer**: You might need to get creative, but there's always a way to find the information you need to reduce the uncertainty of the decisions you need to make.
2. **The answers *almost* always come from the users**: Whether they are prospects, users, customers, or your competitors' customers, a specific segment of people will ultimately—directly or indirectly—reveal the constraints you need to overcome.
3. **You can't explore with blinders on**: Consciously or unconsciously, we tend to set limits on what we learn and how we learn it. To con-

sistently overcome the hurdles you face, you have to be able to explore broadly. As you'll notice throughout this book, sometimes this might mean getting out of your comfort zone.

4. **Learning is about making progress**: Learning for the sake of learning is a waste. Businesses always have limited time and budget. To make real progress, you have to continually focus on the core risks, gaps, and assumptions.

5. **The best way to evaluate progress is against a goal**: Feedback and learning only matter if they are related to a goal. To make progress, you need to set goals and evaluate progress against these goals.

Questions, techniques, and goals will change as your business changes.

In every chapter of this book, we discuss the factors behind goal selection, and the customer research techniques you can use to make progress.

Based on the assessment done in the previous chapter, *are there gaps you need to address?*

If so, refer to Chapter #2, and jump to the appropriate sections.

If, like Julie, you're dealing with a problem that could be caused by different challenges, you should first clarify the issue to get to the heart of the matter. Read on.

Narrowing Down the Issues

> "The scientist is not a person who gives the right answers, he is one who asks the right questions."

Claude Lévi-Strauss
Anthropologist

There are many ways to express customer retention issues: high churn, low engagement, low retention, low feature usage, low loyalty, customer downgrades, etc.

There are also many potential reasons for low retention: bad user experience, low product value, lack of funds, better solutions on the market, insufficient time to use the product, poor customer support, etc.

We can't achieve what we want if we don't understand what makes it happen. Addressing 'customer retention' means addressing a series of loosely defined problems. To make progress in addressing customer retention, first it's important to identify the core problem.

This can be done by answering the Five Ws and One H (5W1H):

- **What**: The problem. In this case, customers churn.
- **Who**: *Who is churning? What user profiles are churning?*
- **When**: *When do they churn?*
- **Where**: *Where do they churn?*
- **How**: *How do they churn?*
- **Why**: *What causes each of these user groups to churn?*

Analyzing *Who*, *When*, *Where*, and *How* helps you understand the composition of your churn rate. It will help you to decide which customer segments to focus on.

Why helps you understand what drives churn upwards or downwards for the segment you're exploring. Answering *Why* helps you generate hypotheses on how to address this problem.

Whether you're trying to reduce churn, get users to adopt a certain feature, or get them to come back more often, you should use a similar process:

1. **Narrow the issue**: Figure out exactly what you are trying to achieve.
2. **Understand the composition**: Figure out how behavior is affected by different roles and profiles.
3. **Understand causality**: Understand root causes and specific issues.

4. **Generate research and experiment ideas**: Once you know what drives the behavior, run experiments to test different solutions.

Once you know what your problem is, it becomes a lot easier to find the best techniques to solve it.

The sections in this book will help you find the best way to learn to overcome the issues your business is facing.

If the work you end up doing influences a decision of any significance, then the cost of the book and the time to study it will be paid back many times over.

Let's get started.

Stage 1:

Idea

Is This Idea Worth Pursuing?

"If you want to optimize for avoiding failure, you have to optimize for listening."

David Cancel
Serial Entrepreneur

Creating new products is exciting.

Because they're usually associated with creative freedom, and we use the word "idea" to describe the starting point of new ventures, we view the act of starting a business as a creative endeavor.

For a moment, we're Shakespeare sitting in front of blank pages. With the right inspiration, we can create Romeo and Juliet, and have our names echo into eternity.

Although there is *some* truth to this—creating new products does require inventiveness—a lot of the things that teams need to focus on in the early days contradict the idea of grand creation.

To avoid the idea graveyard (90% of startups fail[10]), you have to set up processes to structure and focus your creative efforts.

The key is to use the feedback loop to learn from a market as quickly as possible and have as many iterations as possible to figure out how wrong your original idea was. *Was it five, ten, fifty, or a full hundred percent wrong?*

No one has ever had an idea that was 100 percent on target. It has never happened. All businesses pivot.

But here's the thing, because the people who start ventures—entrepreneurs and executives—are among the people most likely to ignore facts and customer data that contradicts their theses[11], it's not as obvious as it seems.

As Steve Blank, creator of the Customer Development framework says: *"Founders see something that you don't. They see something that most of the time doesn't exist, but they're heading toward that[12]"*

The idea of 'creating' or 'inventing' new products is at the root of the failure of many new ventures. Or at least it's a key reason why, early on, entrepreneurs set out in the wrong direction.

The Challenge

> "Ideas are useful, but what's more important are behavior changes. Ideas are not enough to cause a behavior change.[13]"
>
> David Cancel

Let's take this a step further.

Imagine today I approach you with the concept for a new phone I've been working on. It's not affiliated with any of the major brands on the market, it has a brand-new operating system (OS), but it's really cool, *trust me.*

What would I have to do to convince you to get rid of your current phone, and buy a FinPhone (working name!) for $500?

Now, consider business software. How much social capital would a colleague have to put on the line to try and convince your team to change project management software? What would they need to do and demonstrate to get you to stop using Trello, a product you love, and start using their brand-new solution?

A lot, *right?*

As product creators, we tend to underestimate the effort required to get customers to adopt new products.

Getting people to buy is one thing. **Getting people to use, and keep using a product, is another**.

It has never been easier to build new products from just about anywhere in the world. As a result, markets have exploded. The Martech 5000[14], for example, now features well over 8,000 companies, more than 50 times the number it had in 2011.

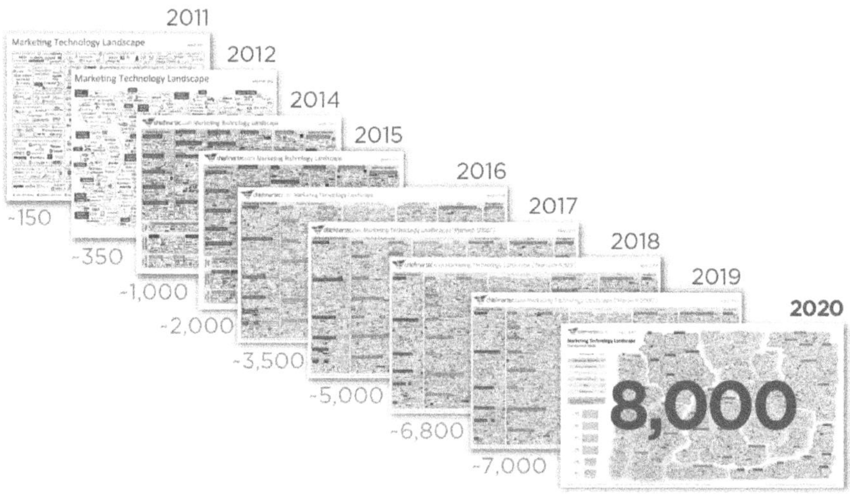

Figure II.1 - Evolution of the Marketing Technology Landscape

This means that delivering new and differentiated value with a product is more difficult than it has ever been.

To overcome the status quo and convince people to buy and replace a part of their workflow, products need to provide *must-have* value.

New products can't have feature parity, or *satisfice* by being *'good enough'*. Your product needs to add significant value to the ecosystem of products in place.

As author Rob Fitzpatrick says: *"You can't build a business on a lukewarm response"*. If you do, you'll run the risk of suffering what Andreessen Horowitz partner D'Arcy Coolican calls: *"death by a thousand shrugs*[15]*"*.

The Rubik's Cube Dilemma

> "For a brand new product, it might be harder because a lot of your decisions are based on assumptions. It's really hard for the startup to create a really solid foundation of requirements right from day one."
>
> Nick Babich
> Editor-in-Chief of UX Planet

I liken starting a business to solving a Rubik's Cube.

Figure II.2 - Rubik's Cube

When you're getting started, you have an idea of what you are trying to achieve. You might also have an idea of the strategy you'd like to use—but any plans you make ultimately depend on what happens once you flip a first row over.

For a business to succeed, a lot of things need to line up: product and market, market and channels, value and dollars.

The problem is, when you start, almost everything is unclear. The idea itself might be wrong (for 93% of new products it is[16]), but so might everything else.

It's hard to learn and adjust when everything is fuzzy.

Initially, you don't know the prospects or which questions to ask. You need to explore broadly to understand the landscape.

You also need to latch on to a first piece of the puzzle—a first piece of validated learning—to make progress.

Unfortunately, the early days of a business can also be likened to research and development (R&D): There's no guarantee that anything will work, and it almost always takes longer than anticipated.

This, in part, explains the high failure rates of new ventures.

It also explains why you need to exit the Idea stage as quickly as possible.

Laying Out the Foundations

"It's easier to make things people want than it is to make people want things.[17]"

Des Traynor
Intercom Co-Founder

So, what should that first piece of puzzle be? A market? A problem? A need? Demand?

A useful way to think about new products is to think of them as services.

If you were to start a service organization like a consulting firm, you would approach prospective customers, try to understand what they are trying to get done, find a way to help them, agree on a price for the services, deliver the work, hope for positive reviews, and over time, you'd look for ways to *productize* the service to make it more efficient with repeat customers.

This is also what you're trying to do with products:

1. Find people (a market segment);
2. Understand their goals (the Job they're trying to get done);
3. Identify gaps you could deliver value on (differentiation);
4. Provide the services (the product);
5. Iterate until clients are satisfied with your work (PMF);
6. Productize the offering (scale).

Now, whether the product uses technology or not shouldn't change what you are trying to do. Your aim is to deliver differentiated value to a clear market segment.

During the Idea phase, your goal is to align the value that you hope to deliver to the needs of the people you are delivering it to.

But prospects won't know what's possible. Most prospects won't know how to build scalable products or do road maps. It's *your* job to discover their true needs and to deliver value to them.

Because even building a Minimum Viable Product (MVP) is expensive, you should learn as much as possible pre-product, before writing even a single line of code.

In the Idea stage, we focus on:

- Finding a market and identifying a Customer Job (Chapter #4);

- Assessing the competitive landscape and finding an edge (Chapter #5);
- Creating a compelling value proposition (Chapter #6); and
- Validating our product concept (Chapter #7).

You'll be able to get out of the Idea phase once you have five to 10 preorders for your product—think Kickstarter here.

It will be a good first gut check. If you can't find four or five customers, it's very likely that the opportunity you're chasing isn't that important. It's best to find that out as early as possible.

To help simplify and explain the various concepts in this book, you'll find vignettes in each of the ensuing chapters, which detail the equivalent step in a service organization.

For example, if you were a service company, the Idea phase would be about figuring out what the market needs, why prospects should work with you, and how to land your first few customers.

Directionally Accurate

"It is better to be approximately right than to be precisely wrong."

John Maynard Keynes
Economist

One of the reasons why innovators struggle in this phase is because the information they get is ambiguous. And people, many entrepreneurs included, are uncomfortable with ambiguity.

At this stage, it's not uncommon for teams to challenge the value of customer research:

- *"It's not statistically significant".*
- *"The interpretation of the data is subjective".*

- *"The research wasn't done by 'professionals'"*.

But these reasons are mostly bogus. When your uncertainty is great, even small sample data can produce big reductions in uncertainty.

As *How to Measure Anything* author Douglas W. Hubbard says: *"The existence of all sorts of errors in an observation is not an obstacle to measurement as long as the uncertainty is less than it was before."*

Earlier on, your research won't be perfect. What matters is that you are learning forward, challenging your assumptions, and making progress.

Don't jump too far ahead or let your passion prevail. Stay disciplined.

As physicist Richard Feynman wrote: *"The first principle is that you must not fool yourself-and you are the easiest person to fool."*

Let's get started.

4 / 26

Finding a Customer Job

Early on, you're exploring ideas and markets. Use the techniques in this chapter to **find a market** and **identify a Customer Job**.

"The most successful product innovators we know start by determining what the customer values and what they are willing to pay, and then they design the products around these inputs."

Madhavan Ramanujam and Georg Tacke
Authors of Monetizing Innovation

If innovation was easy, 90% of new ventures wouldn't fail[18]. Innovation would simply be Idea > Product > Success.

Sadly, the default path for new ventures is failure.

Innovators and entrepreneurs are constantly wrong. They are always making false assumptions and wasting resources by going down the wrong paths.

To minimize *wrongness*, it's best to assume that most of your ideas are wrong, and that better answers will be uncovered along the way.

As *Lean Enterprise* co-author Trevor Owens says[19]: *"If you don't want to lose a ton of money and time, your ideas should be guilty until proven innocent."*

During the writing of my first book, *Lean B2B*, I adapted the *Double Diamond* design process by the UK Design Council[20] to highlight the importance of both exploration and confirmation phases in innovation:

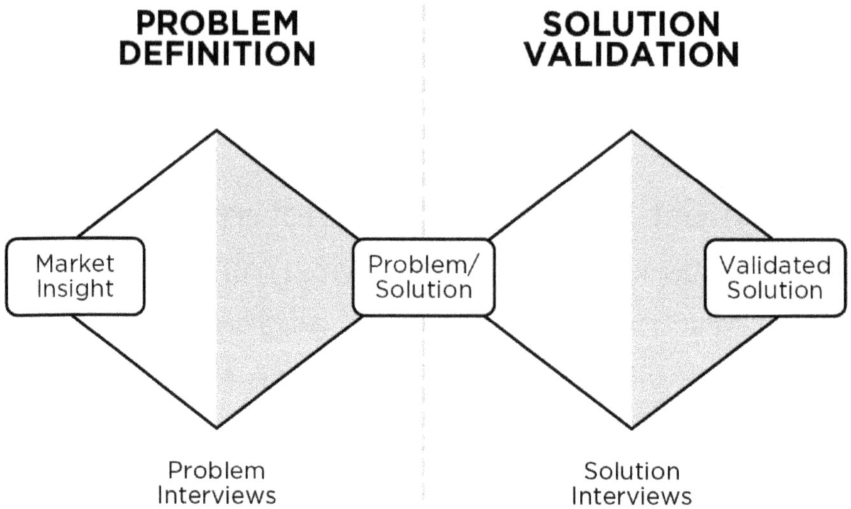

Figure 4.1 - The Double Diamond Design Process

In the early stages, your goal is to learn. You have to learn about the people you aim to serve before you attempt to define a solution for them.

You may be an expert in the industry you're targeting, but even experts fail sometimes. You need to first understand prospects' realities, independent of the innovation you have in mind.

The first question that innovators need to ask themselves is: *who are we going to learn from?*

To start learning, you need to pick a market segment that's the right size to explore. Valid markets are made up of:

- many potential customers;
- who share a pain, problem, Job, desired outcome, or an opportunity; and
- channels for people to connect, discuss, and share purchase decisions.

The market is one of the most important factors determining business growth. Choose a growing market, and you might grow fast. Pick a market on the decline, and you'll spend your time fighting to land customers.

To get started, pick a broadly defined market—like teachers, skateboarders, or the pharmaceutical industry. The more you learn, the more you'll refine your market hypotheses.

Within every market are early adopters.

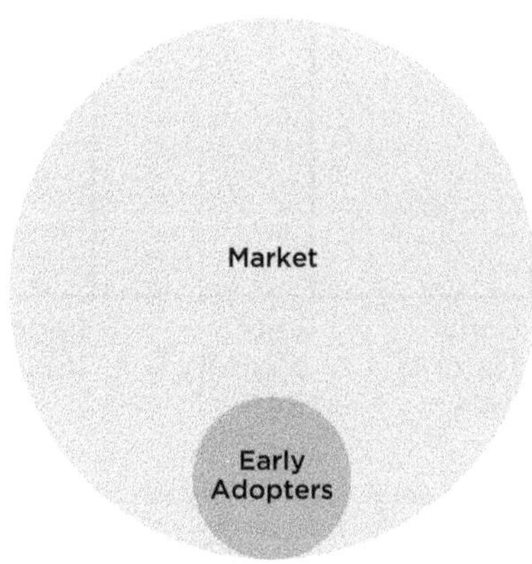

Figure 4.2 - A Market's Early Adopters

Early adopters are the people who are willing to invest to get certain competitive advantages or benefits before the rest of the market gets them. These are the people you want to find; they're the people who are going to help you co-create your product.

Early adopters share a problem, a goal, a need, or a desired outcome. They are willing to take risks because they see the strategic opportunities offered by a new product.

They can be challenging to work with and hard to please, but if you can make them successful, they'll give your product its first big break.

Early adopters are necessary, but not enough. Ultimately, there won't be enough early adopters to sustain your business. Your innovation will eventually need to attract a larger group of customers.

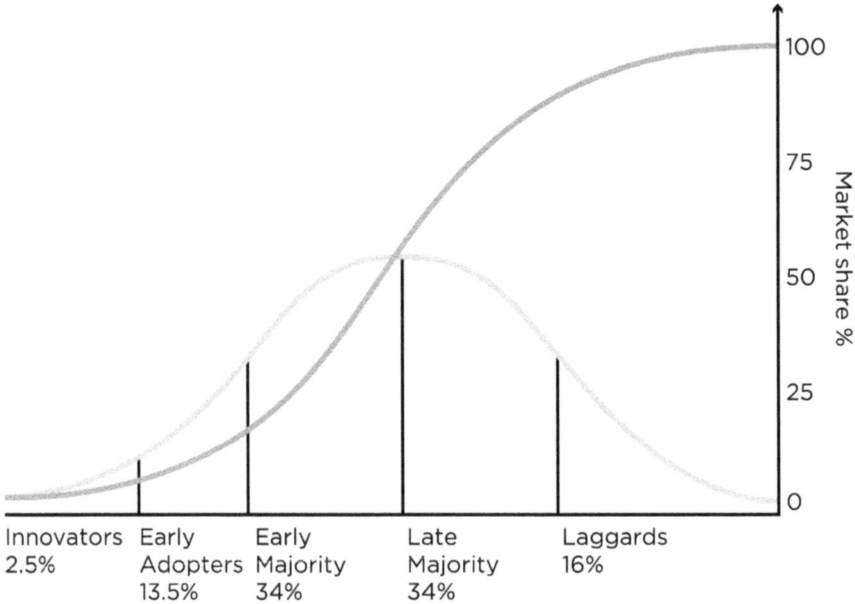

Figure 4.3 - Early Adopters' Weight in the Market

For now, however, you can use the Finding Early Adopters guide under Building Blocks to help fuel your search.

Finding a Customer Job

"The best predictor of future behavior is current behavior."

Cindy Alvarez
Author of Lean Customer Development

Once you've identified a market worth exploring, what should you be looking for: *needs, wants, solutions, problems, benefits, ideas, outcomes, or specifications?*

When you speak to prospects early on, they'll often point to problems, the challenges that they're facing, or the solutions they wished they had.

There are two main issues with problems, needs, and solutions:

1. **Problems, needs, and solutions are temporary**: They either get reprioritized, or they change in nature, whenever the environment changes;
2. **Problems, needs, and solutions are open to interpretation**: They're subjective and imprecise, which means they are difficult to evaluate clearly, and grey zones introduce risk in your innovation process.

Two people within the same team can look at the same situation and see completely different problems. As a result, each of these two people may feel that the needs of their organization are completely different. For example, in difficult economic times, one team might feel that cutting costs is the way to go, while another thinks that the company needs to change the way it sells, or to expand in new markets.

This creates major challenges for innovators. Early on, you should make sure you're building on solid ground, basing your work on the best starting premise.

The safest way to do this is to build off existing behaviors, by figuring out what people are already doing or trying to get done:

- *What are people buying today?*

- *What needs are addressed by the products they're buying?*
- *Where do they currently spend time?*
- *What have they created to solve their problems?*
- *What are they focused on today, and what will they be focused on in the near future?*

The best lens for innovation is to look for the Job to be Done (JTBD). A JTBD is a statement that describes what people are trying to accomplish in a given situation.

It's based on the JTBD theory, which states that people buy or *hire* products and services to get Jobs done. For example:

- I *hire* Mailchimp to feel like the emails I send to my subscribers are both professional and effective.
- I *hire* Ahrefs to gain a competitive edge through content marketing.
- I *hire* Twitter to feel like I'm *in the loop*.

If you help people get Jobs done faster, more conveniently, or less expensively than before, you stand a good chance of creating products customers want.

This means you need to figure out:

1. what customers want to accomplish (the JTBD);
2. who the specific actor or end user will be (the Job Performer);
3. how the Job currently gets done (the Job process);
4. how Job Performers measure or evaluate success (their Desired Outcomes); and
5. in what way you can deliver more value (the Differentiation).

Jobs aren't made up, they are discovered. If there's a *real* Job, early adopters will already be addressing it—or trying to address it—through some kind of solution; a manual process, a multi-tool solution, or a competing product.

The actual Job is independent from the solution. For example, I can use a pen, a recorder, or word processing software to take notes.

Jobs can be:

- **functional**: what customers want to get done;
- **emotional**: how customers want to feel or avoid feeling as a result of executing the functional Job; or
- **social**: how customers want to be perceived by others.

For example, when purchasing a sports car, a man may want to be able to get to work as efficiently as possible (functional Job), but he may also want to feel successful (emotional Job) and be perceived as adventurous by others (social Job).

Bain & Company's Elements of Value Pyramid[21] provides a good overview of how Job types relate to one another.

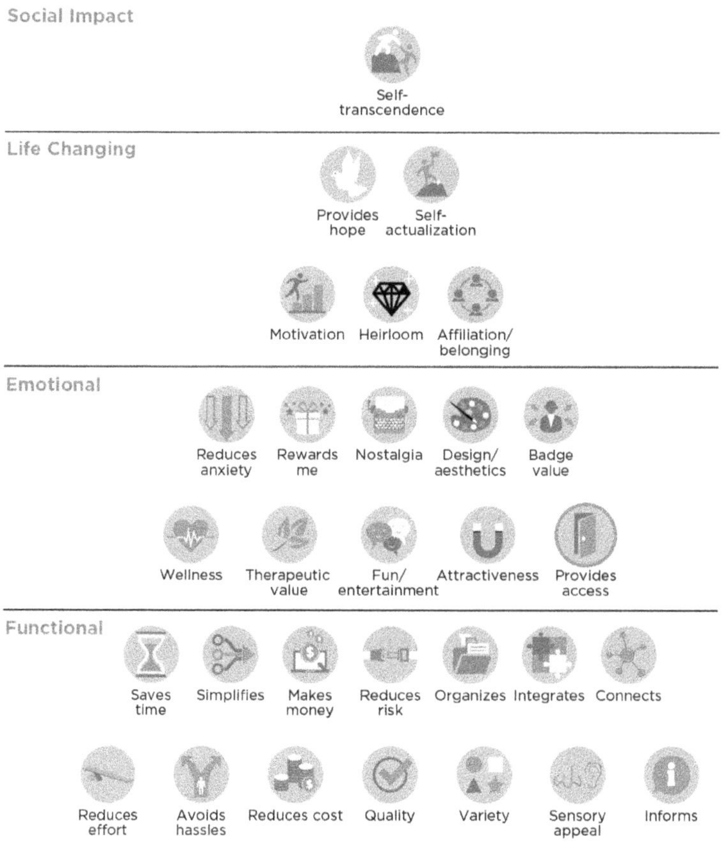

Figure 4.4 - The Elements of Value Pyramid

People use metrics or criteria to evaluate how well solutions get the Job done. These metrics are often called desired outcomes, and according to research by Strategyn, most Jobs, even simple ones, have 50 to 150 desired outcomes.

If you know how customers measure value, you can create successful innovations. So, if we sum it up:

1. Prospects want to get **Jobs** done;
2. They *hire* **products**—or other types of **solutions**—to get those Jobs done;
3. They evaluate the performance of those solutions based on how well they meet their **needs** or **desired outcomes**;
4. **Problems** and **obstacles** hinder the progress they're trying to make;
5. If you help prospects **get the Job done significantly better** based on their own evaluation criteria, they'll consider your product.

   At this stage, focusing on customer Jobs is the most reliable way to move your business forward. If you were a service company...

   This step would be about finding prospects and figuring out what key things they're trying to get done.

Techniques You Can Use

At this stage, it's important to base your innovation on real behaviors—not preferences or opinions. You can't count on prospects, executives, or other stakeholders to tell you what to build. It's your responsibility to make sure that you are addressing a real opportunity.

Used well, the three techniques covered in this chapter help reveal true customer behaviors:

- **Learning Through Sales Safaris** will be particularly useful if you intend to work on consumer products. Sales Safaris can be a good option when customer access is limited.
- **Learning Through Customer Discovery Interviews** can help you understand specific behaviors or explore customer segments. Interviews are the Swiss Army knife of customer research.

- **Learning Through Contextual Inquiries** can help you understand the customer Job at a deeper level by studying prospects in their home or work environments. It's the ideal technique when you're able to get a lot of face time with prospects.

Pick your tool carefully. The type of inputs you collect will matter more than the techniques that you use to find your opportunity.

Learning Through Sales Safaris

"Forget ideas, study a market."

Amy Hoy
Serial Entrepreneur

Sales Safari is a research technique based on ethnography developed by serial entrepreneurs Amy Hoy and Alex Hillman. In a way, the technique applies the idea of ethnography—direct observation of users in their natural environment—to the Internet.

Part of the thesis behind the technique is that the problems are already all out there. Instead of looking for new problems, you go and find problems people already have.

The technique is in part a reaction to customer interviews. Amy and Alex's reasoning is that it's better to observe conversations than to ask questions, because getting great data from interviews often means:

- trusting prospects to accurately identify their own pain points;
- believing that they remember what they do, all day, every day;
- trusting that prospects won't lie, and that they'll be open to sharing the truth; and
- assuming that people make fully rational decisions.

Alex says[22]: *"Being able to watch people talk about their problems in their natural habitat without them feeling like they're being watched means you're getting a more genuine, a more natural, and in many cases, a much richer understanding of what the problem is."*

Organizing a Sales Safari first means homing in on a market, looking for their online watering holes—places where prospects gather for pleasure or for work—to do research.

Watering holes can be found by performing searches around your target market. For example:

- "[Market] + mailing list";
- "[Market] + forum";
- "[Market] + competition".

Other keywords like Twitter, group, list, community, help, wiki, questions, meetup, list, resources, association, customers, tutorials, awards, user group, or blog can help you find watering holes. The more you can find, the better.

A good market will have several active watering holes where people share tools, knowledge, and ideas. An example could be Airliners.net, where airline geeks like my best friend spend hours each week talking about the airline industry.

Once you have found a few watering holes, dive through conversations, taking note of Jobs, pain points, beliefs, questions, complaints, products used, struggles, and desired outcomes. Amy and Alex recommend spending as much as 30 to 50 hours *listening for the nouns*[23], taking note of observations, keeping an eye out for words like "easier", "faster", "less", "more", "relief", "finally", etc.

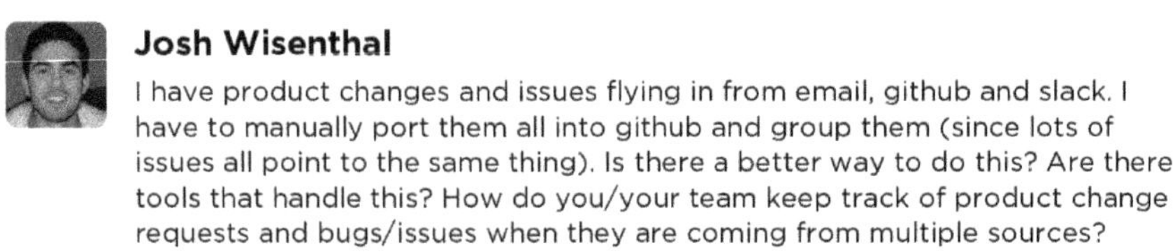

Josh Wisenthal

I have product changes and issues flying in from email, github and slack. I have to manually port them all into github and group them (since lots of issues all point to the same thing). Is there a better way to do this? Are there tools that handle this? How do you/your team keep track of product change requests and bugs/issues when they are coming from multiple sources?

Figure 4.5 - Example of a Noteworthy Comment

Although their approach focuses on finding signs of pain and opportunities to help prospects make money, the research can also be used to find customer Jobs and desired outcomes.

Amy and Alex's approach in their training, 30x500, focuses on:

1. **Pain killers**: eliminating or reducing risk, anxiety, stress, fear, uncertainty, guilt or frustration; and
2. **Money multipliers**: creating new avenues of revenue, extending customer reach, reducing costs, making it possible to increase prices, etc.

By the end of your Sales Safari, you should be able to understand the market so deeply that you can speak the prospects' language, anticipate their needs, and predict their reactions.

The information collected in watering holes will be useful later on. You can use it to flesh out your value proposition, create your marketing copy, and overcome objections.

A few questions Amy and Alex recommend answering for pain killers include:

- *What skills are they struggling with?*
- *What skills do they need to learn or get better at?*
- *What are some of the repetitive tasks they have to do over and over?*
- *What are they afraid of?*
- *What do they avoid doing that they really should be doing?*

And for money multipliers:

- *Where does their money come from?*
- *How can they increase that type of revenue?*
- *Why do their customers buy? What are their deeper needs?*
- *What's inefficient or costly?*
- *How can they create new opportunities? How can they find new customers or markets?*

- *How could they start charging more?*

A lot of successful Business-to-Consumer (B2C) products came out of Sales Safaris. The technique is easy to execute, and can be a good starting point for your business.

Learning Through Customer Discovery Interviews

> "A listening session isn't about a product, it's about peoples' purpose."
>
> Indi Young
> Author of Practical Empathy and Mental Models

It's no secret that customer interviews are key in helping innovators learn about and validate business opportunities.

Innovators always hear: *"You have to get out of the building", "Go talk to customers", "Just interview prospects!"*

Now, the problem with customer discovery—and customer interviews specifically—is that, if done wrong, they can send innovators down the wrong path fast.

To echo Amy and Alex's concerns, prospects are not skilled at identifying their own pain points and struggling moments. Nor should they be. It's your role to get the right inputs.

As innovation expert Tony Ulwick says, *"If you don't know what inputs you're looking for, then no matter what kind of interview structure you have or what kind of questions you ask, you're not going to hear the right inputs."*

To avoid spinning your wheels, you need to get to the truth. This means steering clear from lies, getting interviewees to open up, and learning about real needs and challenges.

People will lie if they think your ego is on the line. They'll give you superficial answers if they mistrust you, if the information doesn't make them look good, or if they think you plan to compete against them.

Customer interviews allow you to be very precise with your research. With interviews, you can quickly learn from a specific market segment, Job performer, or customer role.

Start by defining the market you would like to learn from. Unless you have a clear idea of the market you're targeting, it's generally a good idea to start broader, and gradually refine your segmentation as you learn.

For example, if you were looking to build an online tutoring platform, you could start by targeting teachers, and as you learn, increase precision by starting to target teaching assistants, specifically in science, or in a narrower segment.

You can use the Recruiting Prospects for Interviews guide under Building Blocks to help with recruitment.

Once you're starting to get interviews, start putting together an interview script.

Open-ended questions—questions often starting with "Why", "What", "Where", or "How"—help capture needs, opinions, stories, or feedback, while closed-ended questions—questions that can often be answered by "Yes" or "No"—help converge on relevant information.

Open-ended questions often lead to unexpected tangents and insights. Early on, your script should be as open-ended as possible. To write good open-ended questions:

- Use the words "What", "Where", "Why", and "How" to phrase your questions.
- If the question can't be phrased that way, use "Tell me about", "Explain", or "Describe."
- Create context around your questions by asking about specific situations, problems, or time frames.

- Follow up open-ended questions with prompts like "Tell me more" or "What do you mean by…".

It's a good idea to **ground your interviews in existing behaviors like a recent product purchase, a task or workflow, or an event**. This will help make sure that you're learning real facts.

You could start with what products interviewees are already buying to learn about the Jobs they need to get done:

- *Have you bought any products lately? Why?*
- *Have you switched from one product to another? When? What made you switch?*
- *Did you cancel a product recently? Why?*
- *What software do you pay for every year? Why?*
- *What goals or objectives does [Product] help you to accomplish?*
- *What problems does [Product] help you [Prevent / Resolve]?*
- *What made you choose [Product] over the competition?*

If there are no events or purchases to start from, consider exploring more broadly. Use questions like the following to get started:

- *Tell me a little about yourself and what you do?*
- *When was the last time you did [Job to be Done]?*
- *What are you trying to accomplish? What tasks are involved?*
- *What problems are you trying to prevent or resolve?*
- *How do you feel while getting the Job done?*
- *What products and services do you currently use to [Job to be Done]?*
- *How do you know you're doing the Job right?*
- *How do you feel when the Job is done?*
- *What workarounds exist in your process?*
- *What's the most annoying part? Why is it frustrating?*
- *What influences your decisions?*

- *In which situations do you act differently?*
- *What do you dread doing?*
- *What do you avoid? Why?*
- *What could be easier? Why?*
- *What else are you trying to get done?*

You can download a full interview script at **solvingproduct.com/interview** to get started fast.

When you sense emotion, follow the line of questioning. Emotion will often point you to the things that matter most.

Focus on facts and behaviors. Don't mention your idea. End the interview by asking: *"Is there anything else I should have asked?"* Similar questions often lead to interesting findings.

After two or three interviews, reevaluate. *Are the interviews pointing you in the right direction?* If you aren't finding consistent patterns, your customer segment might not be precise enough. Keep slicing your segment into smaller pieces until you do.

To improve your interviewing skills, read the interview guides in the Building Blocks section at the end of this book.

Learning Through Contextual Inquiries

"It's really interesting to go in and say, "Okay, So what do you do today? What's your process? Literally, show me what you do". And you kind of walk through that, and then you take some notes and then okay show me again, and go through that with them. You live a day in the life of your customers "

Dan DeAlmeida
LabVoice Director of Product Management

Contextual inquiries are a combination of interviews and observations on-site or in context. They can help you discover nascent behaviors and understand Jobs at a deeper level.

Since a lot of the best—and most defensible—opportunities are often difficult to get to from outside organizations, being on-site and looking at what people are doing with a fresh pair of eyes can often point to neglected opportunities. You'll notice the workarounds people use to get the Job done, and you might discover things that prospects don't even know about themselves.

As Douglas W. Hubbard says: *"If you look at how people spend their time and how they spend their money, you can infer quite a lot about their real preferences."*

The first challenge you'll face if you intend to learn through contextual inquiries will be recruiting prospects.

If you're targeting consumers, you will be able to find regular folks in malls, coffee shops, or in other public settings. By first explaining what you do, establishing rapport, and perhaps agreeing on a compensation for their time, you'll be able to get them to agree to show you their workflows.

If you're targeting businesses—unless you can do research in a public setting the way Statflo did in the upcoming case study—there will always be a fear that the information gets used competitively. For that reason, it's usually best to ask for permission before starting your research.

If you align your research around a Job or problem businesses care about, you should have a better chance of convincing them to open their doors.

Other ways to get businesses to open their doors include:

- **Leveraging existing relationships**: You'll have an easier time getting in the building if you've worked with the team before, or if a member of the management team is willing to vouch for you.

- **Building off consulting engagements**: If you have the trust of the organization, you can suggest working on site to better understand how to improve your service offering, and to start learning about other opportunities.
- **Agreeing on a pilot project**: You can set up a project with the organization, writing in requirements for on-site research. The shared desire to create meaningful innovation will motivate them to open their doors to observations.

Once an agreement has been reached, focus your observations on:

- **Time-consuming tasks**: *Why are they time-consuming? Why do those tasks matter? What are people really trying to achieve? How can the tasks be broken down? Are all steps necessary? Are there dependencies?*
- **Products used**: *What products get used? In what sequence? What triggers usage? Why did they choose the products that they're using? Are there visible limitations or frustrations?*
- **Workarounds**: *Do they use hacks? Post-it notes? Checklists? Did the prospects come up with solutions to improve their efficiency?* It's a good idea to ask prospects why they created the specific workarounds they use, focusing on the problems that led them to creating those workarounds.
- **Strapped-together solutions**: *Are there solutions they built or put together? Did they build something using Excel or a combination of no-code tools perhaps? Are there multi-tool solutions you could replace?*
- **Alternatives considered**: *Have they looked for alternate solutions? Are they not aware of the alternatives? Why can't they find an off-the-shelf solution to solve their need?*

Ask open-ended questions and explore. Getting many observations across days and prospects will help you understand the real processes and struggling moments.

Typically, the more people are affected by problems, or the more influential the people struggling are, the more likely it is that the organization will want to address the issues.

Look for patterns across roles and goals. Map out your discoveries and keep exploring.

Depending on the frequency of the problem, Job, or goals you're exploring, contextual inquiries can be very time-consuming. They can also trigger the Hawthorne (or observer) effect where, consciously or not, prospects will start behaving differently because they are being watched.

Regardless of these issues, I would argue that when you're making a critical decision—like deciding what to work on—spending a lot of time on understanding the context and the opportunities is not time wasted.

Keep exploring and find the best opportunity to address.

Making Progress

> "Very often, innovators think they are studying customers' needs – when in fact they are studying what customers don't like about the products they use today, or what customers currently expect from a product."

Alan Klement
Author of When Coffee and Kale Compete

Early on, making progress means identifying a clear functional Job in a market segment.

A Job is typically expressed as follows:

verb + object + contextual clarifier

Examples of JTBD include buy a car, listen to music while commuting to work, or plan annual vacations.

The main Job you decide to address defines your playing field and the scope of your innovation.

During your research, you'll also find related Jobs. For example, for 'buy a car', related Jobs might include 'Finance the purchase' and 'Get a parking license'. It's a good idea to understand how Jobs relate to one another before selecting a Job to focus on.

Don't define the Job too narrowly. A small Job will limit your ability to innovate. To test your Job statement, *The Jobs To Be Done Playbook* author Jim Kalbach suggests answering:

- *Does the statement reflect the Job performer's perspective?*
- *Does the Job statement begin with a verb?*
- *Is there a clear beginning and end point to the Job?*
- *Might the Job performer think, "The [Object] is [Verb]-ed"? (e.g., did the financial portfolio grow? Or was food sold on the street?);*
- *Would people have phrased the JTBD like this 50 years ago?*

A Job may have as many as 150 desired outcomes.

It's often a good idea to create a Job map—a visual depiction of the core steps of the functional Job describing what prospects are trying to get done—to make sure you are capturing desired outcomes for each step.

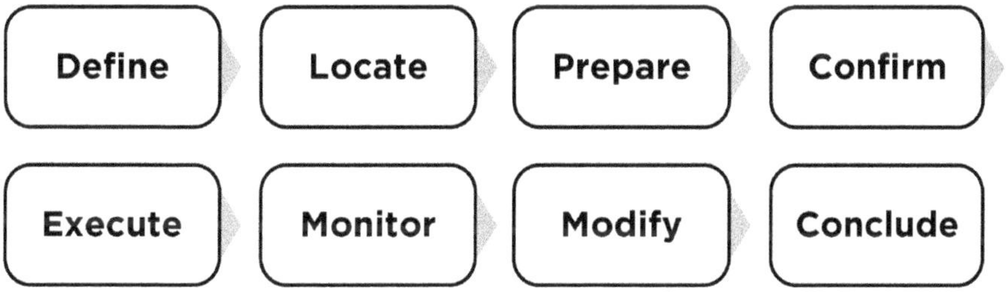

Figure 4.6 - Job Map Sequence

Through research, you should have been able to identify many of these outcomes. If you don't have a lot, consider circling back, focusing on each step of the Job map.

Desired outcomes can be expressed as:

> Direction of change + metric + object of control + contextual clarifier

Examples might be: Minimize waiting time, Decrease the likelihood of system failures, or Maximize order value.

As Tony Ulwick explains: *"Desired outcomes, typically state a direction of improvement (minimize, decrease, lower, maximize, or raise), contain a unit of measure (number, time, frequency, likelihood), and state what outcome is desired."*

Minimize the time it takes to schedule meetings while on the road

↑	↑	↑
Direction	Unit	Qualifier
Minimize	Number	
Decrease	Time	
Lower	Frequency	
Maximize	Likelihood	
Raise		

Figure 4.7 - Structure of a Desired Outcome Statement

By focusing on the functional Job and the desired outcomes of early adopters in a single market segment, you can find the real opportunity. Don't move forward unless you can find a market *and* a customer Job.

Case Study
How Statflo Found Its Opportunity

"The reaction you get to a tool is usually a result of that workplace context.[24]"

Dr. Sam Ladner
Author of Practical Ethnography and Mixed Methods

Statflo's co-founders, John Chapman and brothers Kevin and Ian Gervais, first began spending a lot of time in wireless stores when a contact of theirs informed them that stores were barely using the customer data they were collecting.

Some stores had interns turning the data into spreadsheets, printing it, highlighting information they thought was important, but overall, stores were getting little value from the abundant data at their disposal.

To make it available, the partners cleaned the data and created an online report. To Ian, this was just one of the quick apps he'd always built. He never thought this would become a business.

With the first report, store owners could see which customers were up for renewal on their cell phone contracts. Soon, they realized that the same data could be used to flag customers at risk of cancelling.

To help, the partners decided to create a second report. Once that report was ready for consumption, they were stunned by the reaction.

Not only were owners printing the report designed for online consumption, they were cutting it into tiny strips.

Hoping to understand what was going on, the partners started digging into the behavior. It turned out that store owners were handing the contact details to sales reps, asking them to focus on retaining the specific accounts.

They loved the report and were getting a lot of value from the reach-outs. Because of it, reps were no longer idle, waiting for customers to come in.

It was clear that there was a better way to do this, and that this was an important Job that Statflo could address.

In 2014, the team launched Smart Lists, a product designed to automatically point out and assign customers at risk of churning to sales reps.

The product was a hit. But, since the beginning, the pilot had been free and only a few stores were using it. It wasn't clear if it would scale.

To find out, the partners added ten stores to the pilot. Although the wireless industry is highly competitive, the response surprised them. Not only did the new stores enjoy the product, they began talking about it with other owners.

Soon, stores across Canada and in the United States were reaching out, asking to join the pilot. When Ian and the team began visiting those stores to understand if the patterns were the same, they soon realized that the product could consistently address the same need.

The co-founders knew that they had found a great business opportunity when Statflo began charging customers—and those customers were willing to pay.

Statflo was no longer just one of the quick apps that Ian had always built. It was a growing business.

By spending a lot of time in stores, observing behaviors, and being open to surprises, the partners found an opportunity for a breakout success.

Taking Action

1. Identify a market worth exploring. Consider doing a Sales Safari to evaluate different markets.
2. Use the Finding Early Adopters guide in the Building Blocks section to find prospects to learn from.
3. Pick the appropriate research technique—based on the market you chose and how accessible early adopters are.
4. Identify a functional Job and desired outcomes in a single market segment. Take note of triggers, related Jobs, and pain points.
5. Don't move forward unless you can find a clear Customer Job in a single market.
6. *Collaborating with others?* Share a PDF version of this chapter at **solvingproduct.com/chapter-4**.

5 / 26

Finding a Competitive Edge

Now you have found a Job, you're looking for a way to compete. Use the following techniques to **assess the competitive landscape** and **find an edge**.

> "If a company does not know with certainty where the market is underserved and overserved, it is more likely to make the wrong investments in new product and service development."
>
> Tony Ulwick

A common trope in technology is: ignore the competition.

Don't think about what they're doing, don't look at their features, and don't worry about them.

Instead, focus on the customer.

This is great in theory, but in reality, the competitive landscape is not what it used to be. Now that anyone, anywhere can build products to compete, markets are more competitive than they've ever been.

Competitive research is a key way to learn about the customers you aim to serve. It can teach you about their needs, their wants, their problems, and the outcomes they value.

As Hiten Shah and Marie Prokopets say[25]: *"Your job [as a product leader] is to understand your customers better than anybody else. Ignoring competitors is the same as ignoring customers."*

You need to understand the landscape and the alternatives to be able to provide *valued* differentiation. By understanding what customers would compare your solution to, you can understand how they will ultimately define "better."

Your product will live alongside the competition. Nowadays, it's almost always a good idea to think of your product alongside the competition.

So, *what is competition?*

There are four categories of competitors you can learn from:

- **Direct competitors**: Competitors addressing the same needs for the same types of customers.
- **Indirect competitors**: Competitors that don't exactly do what you intend to do. They serve the same customers and offer a solution that's similar, but not quite what you intend to build.
- **Alternative solutions**: Manual solutions that customers use to get the same Job done. The solution could be spreadsheets, books, pen and paper, checklists, consultants, conferences, etc.
- **Multi-tool solutions**: Many tools stitched together to get the Job done, for example using tools like Zapier and Airtable to automate manual processes.

Competitors are any products or solutions that deliver the same or similar value to the same customers. Value is what ultimately defines your market.

What can you learn about your future customers from the competition?

This step is about finding a way to compete, an edge on the market.

> *If you were a service company...*
>
> *This step would be about figuring out why prospects should hire you specifically.*

Techniques You Can Use

Unfortunately, as *Disciplined Entrepreneurship* author Bill Aulet says: *"If there is already a market research report out there with all the information you need, it is probably too late for your new venture."*

Learning about customers through the competition means getting creative. You can use the following techniques to learn from competitors:

- **Picnic in the Graveyard** will help you learn from the entrepreneurs who have competed in the market before. It can help you avoid some of the mistakes they've made.
- **Analyzing Product Reviews** will help you find areas of dissatisfaction or need in the market.
- **Learning from Competitive User Testing** will allow you to uncover issues with product functionalities and company road maps.
- **Learning by Selling Another Business's Product** will most likely make you uncomfortable, but it can be one of the fastest ways to understand gaps and value from the customer's perspective.
- **Learning by Speaking to the Competition** can be a bit of a Black Hat approach to learning from the competition, but it can give you in-depth insights into competitors' visions and their product strategies.

It's a good idea to use a combination of the techniques in this chapter. By digging deep, you will eventually find a way to compete.

Picnic in the Graveyard

> "Good entrepreneurs learn from their own mistakes. Great entrepreneurs learn from others' mistakes."

Dave McClure
500 Startups Co-Founder

In my first book, *Lean B2B*, I shared the story of how my previous startup, HireVoice, had failed to find a market for the employer brand monitoring solution we were building[26].

In that book I also mentioned why I felt Human Resource (HR) departments weren't a good target for technology products[27].

In the years since publication, I've been surprised by the number of readers building HR software who reached out to learn from our observations (and probably also to prove me wrong).

This, however, shouldn't have been so surprising.

Business ideas are rarely unique. Other businesses were working on similar solutions when we were building HireVoice—and chances are, others have tried to build a product like the one you might currently be thinking of building.

Before starting out, you can learn a lot from the people who have tried and failed (or succeeded) to build similar products.

This research technique—called Picnic in the Graveyard by customer development expert Sean Murphy[28]—is about figuring out which elements that should be brought back and which should be avoided if a product is going to succeed.

You can find competitors—past or present—on Crunchbase, AngelList, Product Hunt, LinkedIn, or by searching for post-mortems on Google.

For each product you want to explore, consider:

- **Exploring the product**: Try it online if it's still available. Look at the features, and try to see if there are any patterns you can uncover. Revisit past iterations of their pitch using Wayback Machine. You will be able to learn about the value propositions they tried, and the evolution of their product.
- **Contacting past customers**: You can find past customers through product reviews (more on those below), or via social media. Try to understand what product they have since switched to (if any). If their need hasn't been fully satisfied, you may even be able to land early customers.
- **Calling the founder(s)**: Since they're no longer involved in the business, they might be willing to share learnings (I was!). Figure out what worked and what didn't for them. *What would they have done differently? What advice(s) do they have for you?*

There's a lot you can learn by leveraging similar proxies. Think creatively. *How else could you get the information you need to validate your early hypotheses?*

Analyzing Product Reviews

"For any new idea I have, I make sure there are similar products out there, making money currently. Otherwise, the market may not support the executed idea.[29]"

Paul Jarvis
Entrepreneur & Author

In B2B, but also in B2C, customer reviews are playing an increasingly important role in the buying process.

Today, many prospects will do their own research, comparing products and reviews, before they engage with the product or the company's sales team. In a way, product reviews are an extension of a company's website. They are also a gold mine of competitive insights.

To analyze product reviews, you first need to get clarity around who the competitors are. For reviews, you should focus on both direct and indirect competitors.

Look for competitor reviews on sites like G2, Capterra, GetApp, TrustRadius, Software Advice, Founderkit, or even Product Hunt.

Read all reviews, positive or negative. Categorize them and analyze the results.

Note that a lack of reviews can be indicative of a company's footprint on the market. Don't assume competitors have the market when they don't.

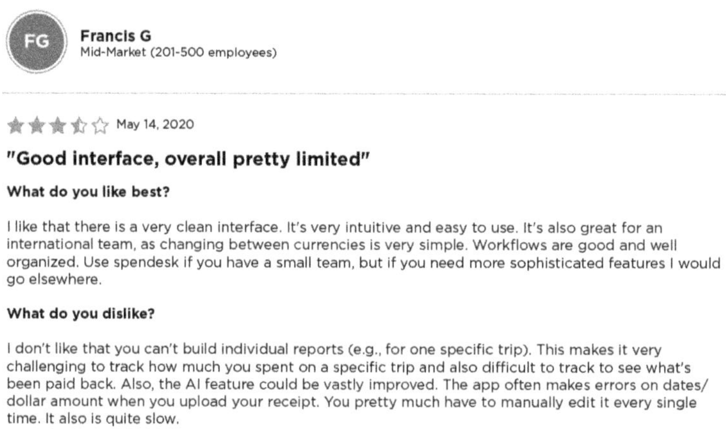
FG
Francis G
Mid-Market (201-500 employees)

May 14, 2020

"Good interface, overall pretty limited"

What do you like best?

I like that there is a very clean interface. It's very intuitive and easy to use. It's also great for an international team, as changing between currencies is very simple. Workflows are good and well organized. Use spendesk if you have a small team, but if you need more sophisticated features I would go elsewhere.

What do you dislike?

I don't like that you can't build individual reports (e.g., for one specific trip). This makes it very challenging to track how much you spent on a specific trip and also difficult to track to see what's been paid back. Also, the AI feature could be vastly improved. The app often makes errors on dates/ dollar amount when you upload your receipt. You pretty much have to manually edit it every single time. It also is quite slow.

Figure 5.1 - Example of a Noteworthy Review

Be on the lookout for important challenges, favorite features, and gaps. Look for words like "better", "easier", "faster", "less", "more", "relief", and "*finally*".

You can take this analysis a step further by diving into your prospect competitors' communities, Q&A support sites, Twitter threads, and feature request boards. To be honest, I still don't understand why businesses make request boards publicly available.

Look for unmet needs and signs of stagnation. What features have been requested often, and for a long time, but not delivered? *Could those features help differentiate your product?*

The product analytics company Amplitude got its start by copying the core features of Mixpanel—their main competitor—and addressing gaps that they had identified through support request boards[30].

Home in on opportunities by analyzing product review sites. Look for a competitive edge. Take it from there.

Learning from Competitive User Testing

"In user tests, we actually like to test our competitors. Whether it's their marketing or the actual product, that lets us learn a ton about competitors. But more importantly, it lets us learn about the customers, because we start to understand what value props resonate with customers, what do customers care about, what our customer's problems are... So whenever we look at a competitor, it's always with the lens of the customer.[31]"

Marie Prokopets

Once you're starting to get a sense of the unmet needs and the reasons why customers hire competing products, you can start to test how well those products actually meet customer expectations.

If you are on a budget, testing the products yourself (or having colleagues test the products) will help to generate learnings.

To take things further, consider doing competitive user tests.

You can use services like UserTesting or Loop11 to organize remote user testing sessions. For a fee, these platforms will recruit participants based on advanced demographic criteria.

During the test, participants will be asked a series of questions and given tasks to perform using your prospect competitors' products.

You'll be able to review videos of their actions, hear their comments as they perform the tasks, and read their answers to your questions.

To do competitive user tests:

1. Select the competitors you'd like to evaluate.
2. Define three or four tasks around the Job you identified (you can use the guide under Building Blocks at the end of this book for this).
3. Flesh out the profile of the people you'd like to test on (the proxy customers).
4. Set up the remote user testing sessions.

At this stage, two or three participants per competing product should give you enough information to go on.

The best way to identify proxy customers is to start with people that have bought the competing products by looking, for example, at product reviews: *What were the reviewers' profiles? What kind of work did they do? What were the characteristics of their organizations? Could you find more people like them?*

To further your understanding of the market and the competition, follow the user tests with open-ended questions like:

- *How do you currently [Job to be Done]?*
- *What products and services do you currently use to [Job to be Done]?*
- *How would you evaluate the product(s) you're using?*
- *Have you ever switched tools or processes? Why?*

Similar questions will help you learn the words that prospects use when they talk about the competition. You'll also learn why they choose to use those products, whether they were using them before or have switched, and what they think about the competition.

You can also follow the tests with Net Promoter Score®(NPS) surveys to learn about participants' sentiment towards those tools.

NPS is a proprietary survey with strong opponents and proponents. We will talk about this in greater detail in Chapter #12.

The basic NPS question is an 11-point scale (0 to 10) asking *"How likely is it that you would recommend [Product] to a friend or colleague?"*.

The most valuable information you can get from NPS surveys tend to be the responses to the open-ended follow up question:

> "What is the primary reason for your score?"

By combining observations from competitive user tests, NPS surveys, and open-ended answers you can get a feel for the strengths and weaknesses of each competitor. You'll also be able to identify opportunities for improvements.

Learning by Selling Another Business's Product

"You'll learn more in a day talking to customers than a week of brainstorming, a month of watching competitors, or a year of market research[32]."

Aaron Levie
Box Co-Founder & CEO

Let's take things up a notch.

Perhaps the most effective, but also the least commonly used, technique for learning about the viability of an opportunity is to pick up the phone and start selling competing products.

For this technique, pick one of the strongest competitors on the market. Look at the type of customers they have. You can do that by going through product reviews or testimonies and case studies on their website: *What segments do they serve? Could you find other prospects for them?*

If they are selling to businesses (B2B), take note of the roles and departments of the reviewers: *Are there any patterns? To whom are they selling in organizations?*

The beauty with business customers is that they're listed in the phone book. Pick the most interesting segment. Identify 10-20 other companies on the market. Make sure that those companies haven't yet bought the competitor's product.

Find the right people to sell to, get their numbers (from directories, the phonebook, or Google listings), and start calling.

The phone will be the quickest way to gauge prospect interest. Unlike email, it won't leave traces, and it also allows you to confirm information through voice intonations, and the emotions behind the words.

Avoid lying and mentioning your name for *traceability* reasons. Use the pitch from your competitor's website. Don't try to change it, and don't try to get creative.

Once you have given the prospects the basic pitch, try to close them on a demo:

> *"Is this worth looking into?"*

Very quickly, you'll learn about:

- **The company's value proposition**: *Is it a soft or a hard benefit? What words resonate? Is it easy for prospects to understand the product?*
- **The objections**: *What are the most common objections? What words do prospects use to object? What gaps do prospects point out? Are these objections showstoppers, or mild hindrances?*
- **The alternatives**: *Have they heard of the product you're selling? What other products have they considered? Why those products? What solution(s) would the product be replacing?*
- **The needs and goals**: *Why would they agree to a demo? What would be their main reason for buying? What are their evaluation criteria? What are their core needs?*

It doesn't matter if you get the appointment or not (it's not your product!). What matters is that you are learning about the market, the existing products, and the gaps.

Compare your findings with the competing product's positioning. *Are there any gaps that could be exploited?*

Learning by Speaking to the Competition

> "A big mistake people make is that they're afraid to talk to their competitors. These are literally the only people spending as much time as you are in the weeds, thinking about the same kinds of problems and customers. Yes, use discretion and don't give away all your secrets, but you'll usually learn a lot more than you'll divulge."

Alex Schiff
Occipital Product Manager

Last but not least, you can speak to prospective competitors.

Doing so can help you find positioning, understand market response, and anticipate issues.

Although it's ethically questionable to do interviews with entrepreneurs in order to learn about the inner workings of their businesses, there's no doubt that this has been done before, and has resulted in market share being stolen from the competing organizations. I'll let you work out where you stand on this approach.

A more ethical way to learn from prospect competitors is to engage with customer-facing staff (sales, customer success, support, etc.) via live chat, support channels, or face-to-face at events—making sure you avoid lies and deception.

In these situations, it can be a good idea to share some of what you have learned from the market, so that you create a fair exchange.

Founding team members and senior leadership will generally be more cautious about what information they share, so starting with customer-facing staff who are already interested in learning about the market can be more effective.

As a rule of thumb, the more value you provide, the deeper the insights you should be able to get in exchange.

Avoid crossing the line and sounding alarm bells. Think win-win here.

Making Progress

> "Product and service ideas that deliver 20 percent or more value often result in dramatic increases in market share, revenue, and profit."
>
> Tony Ulwick

Every day, the competition—or your future competition—unwittingly shares information about the market they operate in.

Be it testimonials and case studies, updates to features and benefits, updates to pricing and packaging, or homepage and landing page messaging updates, there are many signals that you can learn from.

To overcome the status quo and get prospects to switch from their current solution to yours, you need to provide at least 10 times more value for a key evaluation criterion.

This idea is based on what economist John T. Gourville calls the 9x Effect. Dr. Gourville says[33]: *"Consumers overvalue the existing benefits of an entrenched product by a factor of three, while developers overvalue the new benefits of their innovation by a factor of three. The result is a mismatch of nine to one, or 9x, between what innovators think consumers desire and what consumers really want."*

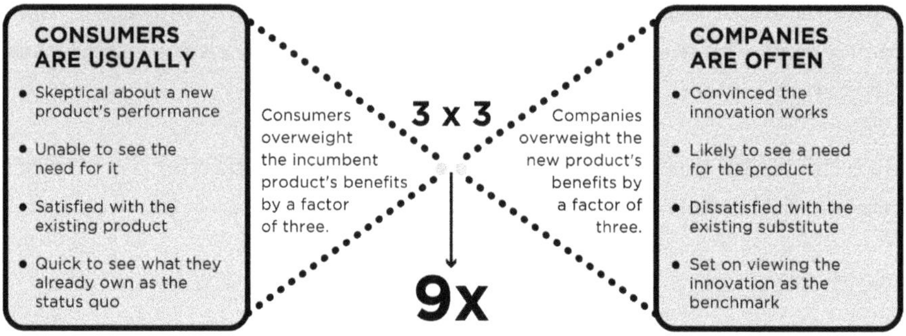

Figure 5.2 - The 9x Effect by John T. Gourville

Can you build a product that's 10 times better than the closest substitute on a key evaluation criterion? Would this be enough to get prospects to switch to your solution?

Most industries are well served at this stage. To get in the door, you need to find a way to compete. Find a wedge in the market. Focus on differentiation, first.

Case Study
How Hiten Shah and Marie Prokopets Learn from the Competition

"We found the right wedge after doing a ton of research. And it's like countless hours. You're not talking 10 or 20 hours, you're talking hundreds."

Hiten Shah

When Hiten Shah and Marie Prokopets started collaborating on the Product Habits blog and the business that would eventually become FYI, Hiten had already been through the ups and downs of startups.

His time building Kissmetrics had taught him the importance of focus, customer research, and continuous innovation[34].

Through surveys and interviews, they had realized that the biggest document management problem that they could solve was finding documents. However, they also knew that the space was extremely crowded. They would need a strong value proposition to stand out.

Instead of jumping into building a product, they decided to dive even deeper into the market, to try to understand the customers through the lens of the competition.

Hiten explains: *"[The] fastest way to understand a customer is by looking at and researching and analyzing everything that they think about, every single thing in the market."*

Through a survey of their mailing list[35] they identified the main indirect competitors for the Job (G Suite and Dropbox). They also recruited participants for customer interviews.

Through interviews, they learned which products and alternatives customers were using, whether they had switched products before, and what value they were getting out of those solutions. These interviews were followed by NPS surveys.

The NPS surveys allowed them to capture the customer sentiment towards competing tools, and also gave them tons of qualitative information about the competition. They realized that the NPS across competitors was low; customers were barely satisfied with the products they were using.

Next, they read and analyzed their competitors' websites and all the reviews they had received. This exercise helped them to understand customer targeting, the evolution of their value propositions, benefits, pricing and packaging, favorite features, gaps, and challenges.

They then took things even further by doing Switch interviews (Chapter #8)—interviews focused on understanding why customers switch from one solution to another. These interviews taught them about new products that were gaining traction, why customers were choosing certain solutions, and the value users were seeking.

Lastly, they built a quick MVP—a simple search form with basic integrations—to test the main solution that defunct competitors had tried before them. By having 20 people use the MVP over the course of a month and speaking with them weekly, they learned that search wouldn't be enough to drive daily retention.

Through all this research, Hiten and Marie began to understand customers better than anyone else. They also found a way to compete.

Taking Action

1. Identify competing solutions—Direct, Indirect, Alternative solutions, and Multi-tool solutions—prospects use to get the Job done.
2. Use several of the techniques in this chapter to understand customer choice.
3. Look for an opportunity to deliver a 10x return on a key evaluation criterion.
4. Keep searching until you find a way to compete on the market.
5. Don't jump ahead until you found a competitive edge that's valued by prospect customers.
6. *Collaborating with others?* Share a PDF version of this chapter at **solvingproduct.com/chapter-5**.

6 / 26

Framing the Value

By now you should be starting to flesh out a competitive advantage. Use the techniques in this chapter to **create a compelling value proposition**.

> "You have to look at what your competitors are doing and decide what you're not going to do and look at what your competitors aren't doing and decide what you're going to do."
>
> Thor Muller
> Get Satisfaction Co-Founder

It's common for teams to want to start defining a product or solution once they think they found an opportunity worth pursuing.

Unfortunately, when teams start thinking in terms of product and features, they often stop thinking in terms of customer value.

This, in turn, leads to wasted efforts, causes teams to fall in love with their idea or concept, and limits their ability to iterate on product value.

Your concept might change a hundred times before the business takes off. Clarifying the value independently from your solution helps make sure you really understand the value before you start designing a solution. Moving forward, it will also allow you to cleanly differentiate between product and value issues.

Find white space on the market and create a compelling value proposition before you define a solution.

> *If you were a service company...*
>
> *This step would be about learning how to communicate the value of the services you offer and your differentiation.*

Techniques You Can Use

You can't be unique if you don't know what the competition is doing. To create new value, you first need to find a positioning on the market.

Analyzing Strategic Positioning will help you compare the solutions on the market and find areas where you can compete.

Analyzing Strategic Positioning

> "Strategy is about making choices, trade-offs; it's about deliberately choosing to be different."

Michael Porter
Author of Competitive Strategy

W. Chan Kim and Renée Mauborgne, professors at INSEAD and authors of *Blue Ocean Strategy*, created The Strategy Canvas to help capture the strategic landscape for an organization.

Early-stage businesses can use this canvas to explore possible positionings for their innovation.

In its essence, the canvas helps compare how well competitors meet customer buying criteria or desired outcomes.

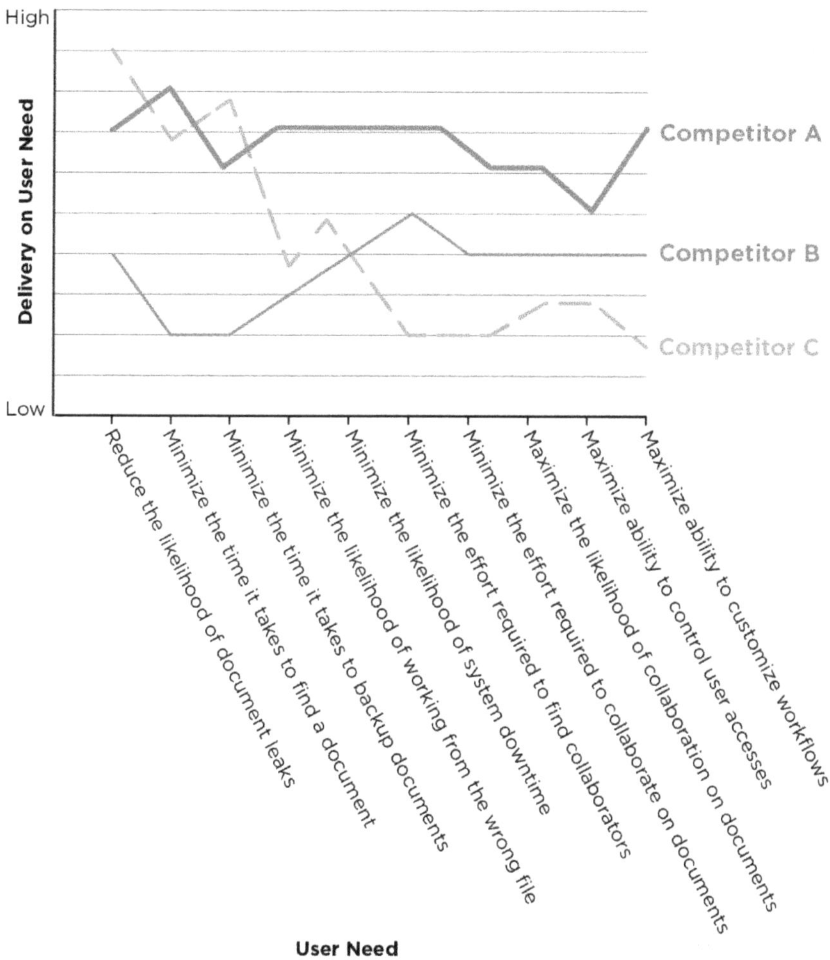

Figure 6.1 - Example of a Strategy Canvas

By this point, you should have a good idea of which desired outcomes matter most (Chapter #4), and the main competitors for the Job (Chapter #5) that you are hoping to address.

To create your own Strategy Canvas, list the 10-12 most important functional desired outcomes—or buying criteria—on the x-axis. On the y-axis, list the 3-5 most common competitors (direct, indirect, alternative solutions, and multi-tool solutions) for the Job.

To avoid going down the wrong path, only compare competitors and attributes that were uncovered through early research. Although there may be other criteria or outcomes that could help differentiate your offering, you should definitely confirm the existence of these criteria before basing your strategy on them.

Use the information collected through your competitive research to rate competitors on each criterion.

Explore alternative positionings by reducing or raising the importance of certain attributes, or by creating or completely removing other attributes.

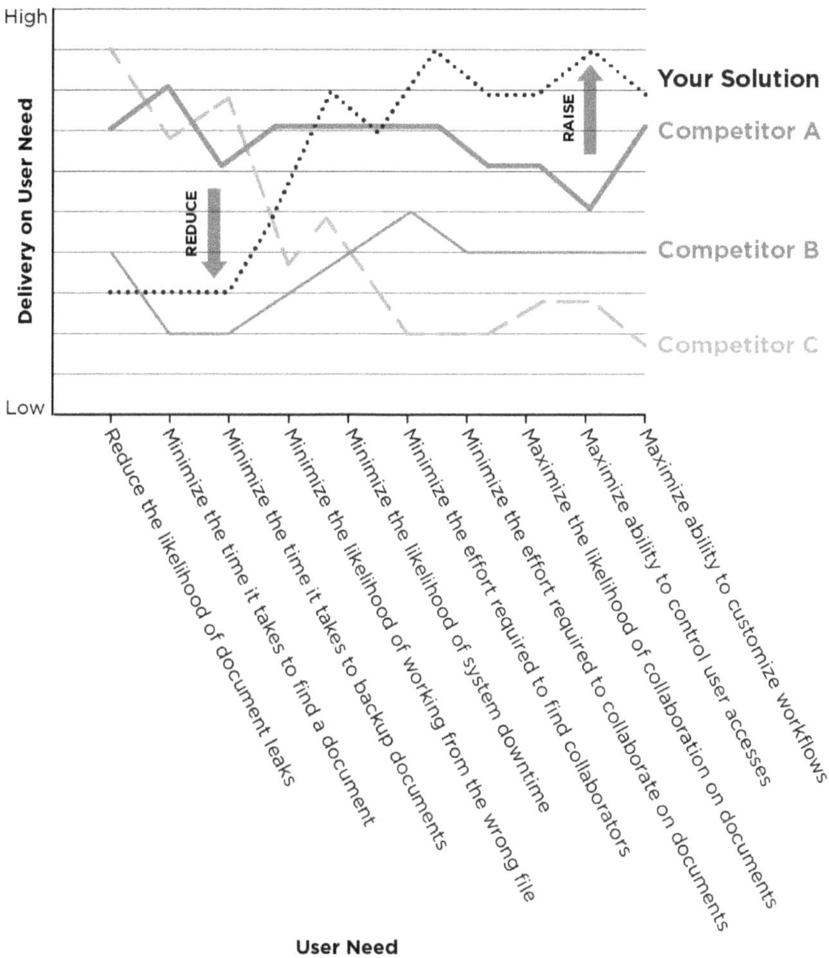

Figure 6.2 - Alternate Positionings on the Strategy Canvas

Further down the road, your product may be able to be differentiated on the basis of how well it addresses particular emotional or social attributes, but to begin with it's generally safer to create differentiation based on the functional requirements of the product[36].

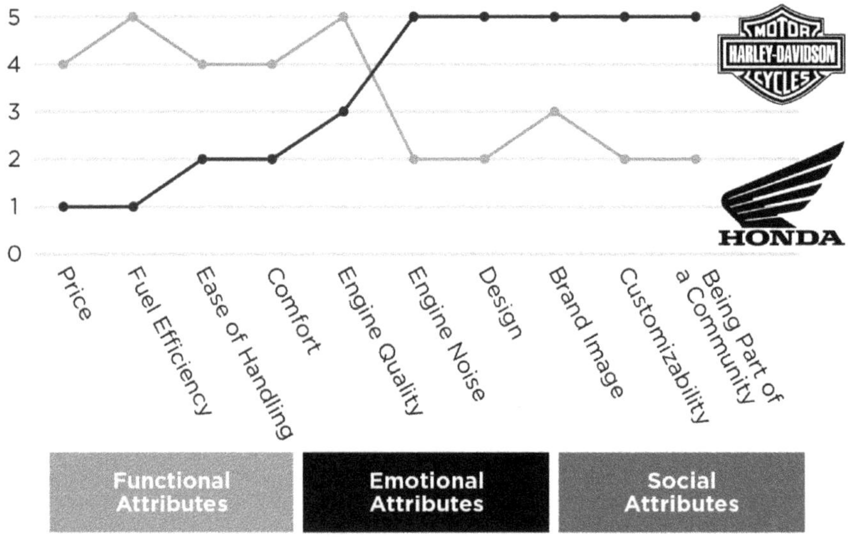

Figure 6.3 - Harley-Davidson is an Example of a Company that Competes Based on Emotional and Social Attributes

You can compete with a much less mature product by being more focused on the customers or on specific outcomes.

As Dave McClure says[37]: *"Your product can be far inferior, far more expensive, far more profitable than a big competitor's product designed for a much bigger, more un-differentiated audience."*

To avoid creating too much complexity early on, focus your positioning on a single attribute. For example:

> We help dentists find new customers **10 times faster** than traditional ads.

Can the benefit be quantified?

If it can, *what would success look like? Would your product need to drive five or fifty percent more leads to satisfy customer expectations?*

The more precise your value proposition is, the easier it is for prospects to evaluate whether your product is worth considering.

Making Progress

"Complex ideas are almost always a sign of muddled thinking or a made up problem."

Sam Altman
OpenAI Co-Founder & CEO

Once you have a first value proposition, you can either jump into designing and validating a solution (Chapter #7), or you can spend time clarifying it.

Interacting directly with prospects from your target market can help you refine your value proposition.

You can do this at events or conferences: You can iterate your value proposition, testing its efficiency speaking with one person after another. After a few drinks, you'll be able to tell how memorable your value proposition is by asking people to share back what you do.

Alternatively, you can interact with prospects over the phone: You can share your value proposition with contacts. The next day, ask them to repeat it. What they can remember is the essence of your value proposition.

As CXL founder and CEO Peep Laja says[38]: *"The less known your company is, the better your value proposition needs to be."*

Make sure your value proposition is as clear and as compelling as it can be. When it is, move on to validation.

Case Study
How LinkedIn Sales Navigator Found Its Value Proposition

"In the factory we make cosmetics; in the drugstore we sell hope."

Charles Revson
Revlon Co-Founder

Sachin Rekhi went to work at LinkedIn in 2011 after *Connected*, the business he had built, was acquired by the social networking giant. A few years after joining the company, Sachin found himself in charge of building the product that would eventually become LinkedIn Sales Navigator.

At that time, LinkedIn had a general subscription for sales professionals, but it didn't have a product wholly dedicated to sales. The new product was going to be quite a departure from LinkedIn's core product. Because of this, it would have to be built mostly from scratch.

To reduce risk and make sure that the investment would be worth it, Sachin and his team decided to focus their early efforts on finding the right value proposition. They wanted to get PMF on the concept before starting to invest significant resources in engineering.

They knew their value proposition had to convince the sales leadership and sales operation leaders—the people responsible for rolling out new tools across sales organizations—if they were to find traction in organizations. It would be difficult to get anywhere without their support.

To ensure that their value proposition got better over time, Sachin and his team set an aggressive goal.

To be able to move to the next step, a majority of the sales leaders they were meeting had to agree to their ask:

> "If this product existed today, would you put it on your road map for next quarter to implement it?"

They presented their concept, explained the pain points they perceived, shared how LinkedIn data could help, asked open-ended questions, and proceeded with their ask.

All meetings followed the same structure. Discussion after discussion, the objections came out:

> "We have all these other high priority things going on. Probably not next quarter, maybe a couple quarters from now."

Once the team began hearing the same objections over and over, it became clear that the value proposition wasn't quite compelling enough.

To drive forward momentum, the team iterated, organizing interviews with five potential customers each week. After each session, the team talked about what they heard during the session, refined the pitch and the value proposition.

As the value proposition began to really connect with sales leaders, the team changed its ask to:

> "We'd love for you to sign up for a pilot."

Although the pilot program was free, sales leaders had to sign a contract, agree to onboard their full team, and commit to monthly feedback sessions.

Again, they faced resistance and more objections came out, but after several more rounds of interviews and refinements, Sachin's team found a value proposition and a concept that resonated with sales teams.

Within a few years of its launch, LinkedIn Sales Navigator reached $200 million in annual revenue. Through constant iterations, the team had laid solid foundations and created a product that the market was willing to embrace.

Taking Action

1. Create a list of the most common competitors (direct, indirect, alternative solutions, and multi-tool solutions) for the Job.
2. Rank competitors based on the most important functional outcomes or buying criteria.
3. Explore alternative positionings.
4. Flesh out a simple value proposition focused on a single benefit targeting a single market segment.
5. Test the efficiency of your value proposition with prospects face-to-face or over the phone.
6. Keep iterating until prospects regularly buy, get excited, or want to be kept in the loop of progress.
7. *Collaborating with others?* Share a PDF version of this chapter at **solvingproduct.com/chapter-6**.

7 / 26

Validating Your Product Idea

You have created a value proposition. Now you need to see if it's compelling enough to get prospects to buy. Use the technique below to **validate your product idea**.

"You can't ask people who haven't paid how much they're willing to pay. [...] The only answers that matter are dollars spent. People answer when they pay for something. That's the only answer that really matters. So put a price on it and put it up for sale. If people buy that's a yes. Change the price. If people buy, that's a yes. If people stop buying, that's a no.[39]"

Jason Fried
Basecamp Co-Founder & CEO

The biggest risk of any entrepreneurial endeavor is that you create something that customers don't want.

To avoid endless exploration and escape the Idea stage, you need to confirm that prospects will actually buy the product that you're hoping to build.

People are willing to waste an insane amount of time—thousands and thousands of dollars of their own time and energy—meeting with you and giving you feedback, but they might not be willing to part with the 40 dollars in their pockets.

Asking prospects to buy is the quickest way to know if you are onto something—or not.

As serial entrepreneur Jason M. Lemkin says[40]: *"Putting up a new, free product on its own will get you zero customers."* Launching with a free trial, or worse, a free plan will give prospects an easy way out. At this stage, *preselling*—selling the product before building it—is the safest path forward.

To make *preselling* work, it's important to focus on a single use case for a single customer profile.

As serial entrepreneur David O. Sacks says[41]: *"A bunch of weak use cases is not as good as one strong one."* This is all the more important for small, resource-strapped companies. The more things your product tries to do, the harder it becomes to get a clear Yes/No answer from prospects.

If you were a service company...

This step would be about closing your first few customers. Can you get them to prepay, or pay 25-50% upfront?

Techniques You Can Use

Although you might come across different ways of validating a product—like capturing email addresses, asking prospects to refer other prospects, or asking them to fill out long and demanding surveys—*preselling* is the only way to get clear validation for a product.

All other techniques delay the inevitable. It doesn't matter if your product is B2B or B2C. You won't be able to build a sustainable business if you can't get paid for your product.

Preselling is the best way to get to a clear "Yes" or "No" without spinning your wheels.

Using Preselling to Validate a Product

> "It's not that the customer may not have the problem, it's just, they may not want the solution you're selling."
>
> Dan Martell
> Serial Entrepreneur

Although you can use landing pages to presell smaller dollar-value products, it's highly recommended to presell face-to-face, or over the phone even in B2C. Doing so will help you capture objections and get more direct feedback.

Create a brochure, a one-pager, or a short presentation. Focus on the Job, the needs and desired outcomes, the problems, the core value, and how your product will be differentiated. Don't go too deep into the product features and specifications. The important thing is to establish compelling value, and to ask for the sale. Creating a brochure, for example, will keep you from becoming too inwardly focused.

Don't worry too much about how much you charge. At this stage, it's more about money changing hands than generating a certain amount of revenue.

With preselling, only unaffiliated revenue counts. Go see your ideal customers, explain how your product concept addresses their needs, and try to get 10 prospects to buy before you have a finished product.

If they buy, make sure you take the money. Prospects will often start asking different questions once they are committed.

If they don't buy, make sure you understand why:

- ***Was the price too high?*** The perception of value was either too low to warrant the change or the risk is viewed as too high.
- ***Were the budgets already assigned?*** *Is this a stalling technique? What's the real issue? Can budgets be reassigned?*
- ***Is it not a priority?*** *Why isn't it a priority? What is getting prioritized over this?*
- ***Is there too much risk?*** *How can you mold your solution to make it easier to adopt? Can you take on some of their responsibilities?*
- ***Will someone object?*** *What are their concerns?*
- ***Is something missing?*** *What features are missing? What outcomes are neglected? Why do those features matter?*
- ***Was the value not clear enough?*** *Was it the pitch or the value proposition?* Take a step back. Get back to the previous chapter to refine your value proposition based on the new findings.
- ***Did the proposition not sell enough value?*** *What were the expectations? What would be deemed as 'enough'?*
- ***Was it not the right time?*** *Why is it not the right time? Are they lacking resources? Are there ways to reduce the perception of risk?*

- ***Are there other solutions in the pipeline?*** *What solutions are getting prioritized? Are they external or internal solutions? Is your product sufficiently differentiated?*
- ***Are they committed with the competition?*** *How could you create more valued differentiation?*

Take note of the objections and keep pitching. Only consider changing your concept once you've pitched more than 20 qualified prospects without being able to get a sale.

As serial entrepreneur Dan Martell says: *"Most people make the mistake of changing the specs on the product for every conversation. As a result, they end up with different feature requests, and all of a sudden, they have ten new customers and ten new features to add, and it's essentially professional services."*

Don't move forward until you're able to get 5-10 pre-orders for your product concept.

Making Progress

"When blue-sky thinking meets reality, reality always wins"

Erika Hall
Author of Just Enough Research

You won't be able to build a standardized product unless you can get traction on a clear value proposition (Chapter #6) and a clear product concept.

Your early customers should be buying the product to get the same Job done and achieve similar results. If they have different needs, you'll end up creating a disjointed product experience trying to please everyone.

If the opportunity is real, there will be a lot more prospects in the market. It might be a good idea to find more prospects who want the product that you're getting positive validation on, rather than to try and meet the expectations of prospects who have different needs.

Don't try to optimize the price, and don't be fooled by early success.

Often, entrepreneurs become so ecstatic when the first sales come in that they jump to the conclusion that they have the right product, or that they somehow found PMF.

Only move forward when at least 5-10 prospects have bought on the basis of the same product hypotheses.

Case Study
How Drift Got Pre-Sales

> "As a rule of thumb, feedback from non-paying users tends to focus on additions to the product. Feedback from paying customers focuses on improvements to the product.[42]"

Des Traynor

When David Cancel and Elias Torres started working on Drift in 2014, the pair had already been building startups and working together for over six years. Through their previous ventures, notably Performable, David and Elias had learned the importance of building products with customers.

With Drift, one of the first things they set out to do was to find early customers, getting them to pay before they ever created a product. The payment could be anything. Oftentimes, it was the amount of money prospects had in their pockets.

For David and Elias, preselling was a shortcut. It was helping them understand whether or not they were on the right track.

Early customers agreed to pay based on the promise of the software Drift was building.

David says: *"It's important to get some dollar amount from them [the customers]. It doesn't matter what the number is. They have to have that skin in the game. It's super important. No matter how ridiculously small the amount is."*

Early customers like ProfitWell were given access to the product, and the functionalities were iterated based on their feedback.

To track their progress, the team kept introducing new prospects to the products they were building. When prospects didn't care enough to part with the $20 in their wallets, Drift knew they were headed in the wrong direction.

In the first year, they killed three versions of the product, but in November 2015, they had built enough confidence to release the product to the world.

Today, even though more than 50,000 businesses use Drift's conversational marketing platform, the team still uses preselling to validate features and product ideas.

Taking Action

1. Define the smallest feature set required to deliver your value proposition.
2. Create a one-pager, a short presentation, or a brochure highlighting your product concept's, core value, and benefits.
3. Go see your ideal customers and try to get 10 prospects to buy before you build the product.
4. Learn from every conversation. Only change the product concept

when you have pitched more than 20 qualified prospects without making any sales.

5. Don't move forward unless you can close at least five prospects based on the same features and value. If you're having trouble closing four or five prospects, then it's very possible that you are chasing an opportunity that simply isn't that important.
6. *Collaborating with others?* Share a PDF version of this chapter at **solvingproduct.com/chapter-7**.

Stage 2:

Startup

Will It Work?

"While you decide what's Minimum, the customer determines if it is Viable.[43]"

David J. Bland
Co-Author of Testing Business Ideas

Product launches are both fascinating and scary.

On the one hand, they provide an opportunity to see how the ideas that you've been brewing play out in the wild. On the other hand, they can also be an opportunity to discover that your assumptions were wrong—and what product you should have built.

As author Clay Shirky says: *"The first prototype isn't meant to show a solution. It's to show that you don't yet understand the problem."*

The sad truth is that, more times than not, *unknown unknowns*—risks you didn't know existed—only surface after you have put a product on the market.

For example, if you have been building a financial product, it's quite likely that people's reactions will differ greatly when they are using their own money.

Depending on what happens after the launch, the product can go a hundred different ways.

At the onset, WhatsApp, WeChat (China), and LINE (Japan) all addressed the same need: communicating with friends and family. Yet the markets they were focused on, the voices they listened to, and the vision of their leaders pulled their products in very different directions, and created widely varying experiences for their users.

Early on, when you're working at a small scale, the importance of all decisions is magnified. The people you hire, the people you fire, the features you build, the features you don't build. These all have a disproportionate impact on the progress of your venture.

At this stage, *all* decisions are strategic in nature. For this reason, they need to be weighed and considered carefully.

The Challenge

"You can't improve anything without feedback. If you put it out there, how do you know if it's any good? How do you know people like it? You need some way to figure that out. If you can't figure that out then you're going to keep making changes that don't necessarily align with what changes you should make to make it better."

Hiten Shah

The two biggest challenges at this stage are:

1. getting enough feedback to iterate and learn fast; and
2. selecting the right voices to listen to.

It might not be obvious early on, but these challenges are both intertwined.

You can increase the volume of feedback you get by loosening your standards for the profiles of users you listen to. But while in the short run this may feel like a good idea, it can lead you to build a product that lacks clear focus.

Conversely, you can be too strict in terms of the voices you listen to, and this will drastically limit the speed at which you're able to learn and iterate your product.

It's important to find the right balance. Too often, product teams learn from a very specific market, niche, or customer group—and then, when the product launches, they open the floodgates and feedback comes pouring in from folks with different needs and backgrounds.

If too much importance is placed on all this feedback, the result may be the creation of a bloated product that doesn't fully meet anyone's needs. *Averages make terrible products.*

It's easy to get sidetracked when you don't have a clear strategy for learning from early users. A launch on Product Hunt, social media posts, or shout-outs in your network will most likely bring volume, but not qualified leads.

More specifically, you need to steer clear of feedback from:

- **Friends, family, and contacts who 'owe you a favor'**: These groups won't use your product for its core benefit. Because they know you, or have a vested interest in maintaining a good relationship with you, they most likely won't give you the objective truth.
- **The *vocal minorities***: Serial entrepreneur Dan Martell calls the people who shower you with compliments without actually using your product the vocal minorities. These people can be great advocates for your product, but you should always avoid building products for them.
- **Companies looking for consulting**: In B2B especially, there's a pull early on to jump into services. You want to make prospects happy, but they have their own needs and agendas. It's very easy to lose sight of your vision. You have to learn to say "No" and commit to building a single product, not custom integrations for each customer.

The days of *shelfware*[44], products bought by IT and used by no one, are over. It's critical that your product is actually used, because if prospects don't use it, then they won't recommend it—and your business won't grow.

At this stage, you should align the value proposition and benefits you sold with the value experienced in the product. To reach PMF, your product needs to deliver *real* value.

The Opportunity

> "You should not put anyone between the founders and the users for as long as possible—that means the founders need to do sales, customer support, etc.[45]"
>
> Sam Altman

Analytics and other quantitative measurements are not the best way to learn at this stage.

The Startup phase is about hand-to-hand combat[46] and doing things that don't scale[47].

You need to build trust and proximity to learn from a small group of customers. Your decisions should be based on *directionally accurate* insights.

To get the ball rolling and establish a cadence of feedback, consider:

- turning your initial interviewees into pilot customers, or creating a customer advisory board (Chapter #10);
- leveraging an email list or niche communities you have access to;
- using targeted ads to reach the right audience; and
- building off a distribution platform like a marketplace, which will reduce the effort needed to drive new sign-ups.

At this stage, you are in a race to achieve PMF before cash runs out.

Don't optimize, and don't build a full-fledged company before you find PMF. Without PMF, investments in marketing, sales, and customer success are premature.

No amount of sales and marketing savvy can sell a product that no one needs. There's no point in building a marketing machine if you don't have a product worth selling.

Making Progress & Moving Forward

> "If you can't get adoption of your first release, you either don't understand the problem, or your execution's broken.[48]"

Des Traynor

Too often, when innovators launch their products and they don't get the results they were hoping for, they add features. But when they add features, they make it harder for new users to experience the core value of the product.

When they realize that the new features don't improve retention, they add more features.

At that point, they've entered what David J. Bland calls the Product Death Cycle[49].

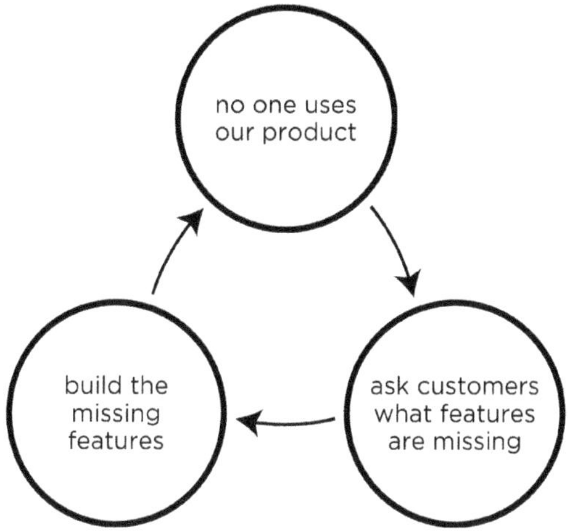

Figure III.1 - David J. Bland's Product Death Cycle Diagram

To avoid spinning your wheels, it's a good idea to set up a North Star metric, and to optimize your early product against that metric.

The metric you choose should be a close proxy of customer value. It could be a subgoal necessary to achieve PMF, such as:

- the percentage of sales operation leaders signing up and onboarding their teams for a pilot version of LinkedIn Sales Navigator (Chapter #6);
- retention for FYI's (Chapter #16) core feature; or
- the percentage of positive market reaction to a new product concept before launch for Dräger Safety.

Or it could also be a direct measurement of PMF, that is:

- a certain percentage of users stating that they would be 'Very disappointed' if the product no longer existed.

You won't get the features right the first time around. Don't add anything until your core features are getting traction.

Keep only what works, refine, and iterate.

If you were a service company...

This phase would be about validating that the work you're delivering provides solutions for customer needs, and that you are able to get customer referrals.

Creating & Sustaining Momentum

"For initial users, there isn't a hard and fast number, but you need enough users moving through so you can see whether people are sticking around and using your product or abandoning it.[50]"

Morgan Brown
Co-Author of Hacking Growth

Y Combinator, arguably the most successful startup accelerator, was started in March 2005 by Paul Graham, Jessica Livingston, Trevor Blackwell, and Robert Tappan Morris.

Over the years, learning from successes like Stripe, Dropbox, and Airbnb, their advice has evolved significantly.

One of the key ways in which the accelerator learned to drive momentum was by setting weekly goals. While *in* YC, and hopefully beyond as well, founders are expected to grow their businesses by 5-7% week-over-week[51].

Actual growth metrics vary from startup to startup, and the way teams drive growth is up to them, but similarly aggressive growth targets help drive forward momentum.

Early on, you should feel like you are making major progress every week.

There's so much to learn, and so many opportunities to improve product value and value discovery.

In the Startup phase, we focus on:

- Evaluating if our product delivers the expected value (Chapter #8);
- Refining our ideal customer profile hypotheses (Chapter #9);
- Evaluating if our product meets and exceeds customer expectations (Chapter #10);
- Evaluating whether we found PMF (Chapter #11).

Start thinking about your North Star metric and start iterating. You can learn more about North Star metrics in the Building Blocks section at the end of this book.

8 / 26 Evaluating If Your Product Delivers Value

You've shipped a product. Customers are starting to use it. Use the techniques in this chapter to **evaluate if it delivers the expected value** (or any value really).

"Simple" is good, "incomplete" is not. The customer should have a genuine desire to use the product, as-is. Not because it's version 0.1 of something complex, but because it's version 1.0

of something simple.[52]"

Jason Cohen
WP Engine Founder & CTO

Silicon Valley Group founder and product management expert Marty Cagan says that there are two inconvenient truths with products[53]:

1. At least half of your product ideas are not going to work.
2. It typically takes several iterations to get the implementation of the idea to the point where it delivers the expected business value.

In other words, despite all the customer research you do, it's almost guaranteed that the first version of your product will be at least *a little* off.

Because of these inconvenient truths, you should always keep your MVPs *minimal*. You need to discover customer requirements, not guess them.

This is why Uberflip product manager Jonathan Laba recommends building for flexibility: *"Figure out the minimum interface you can build to surface value. That interface should be easy to add to or take away from, changeable. It's really thinking about how can you get flexible instead of how can you make it look perfect."*

More often than not, a product's success will be based on one or two features. Keeping a product simple allows early users to evaluate the value of core features in isolation of the complexity brought about by a more complete product.

Do your core features provide value? Do they sustain engagement? Can they be made more impactful?

Creating Customer Proximity

"Under-scale your product so to not look to automate everything all at once but instead to be your product as much as possible."

Samuel Hulick
UserOnboard Founder

What does 'close to the customer' mean in the context of a technology product?

Watching users' every moves? Waiting by the phone? Popping up chat windows left and right?

Creating proximity with users means lowering the friction for customers to give you feedback.

This might mean:

- integrating a chat tool, and being responsive to user feedback—better yet, integrating feedback forms directly *in* the product;
- sending a manual email asking personalized questions;
- manually configuring and setting up user accounts;
- making yourself available to jump on calls;
- doing product demos with new sign-ups;
- calling users; *or*
- any mix of the above.

Figure 8.1 - Example of an Integrated Feedback Form

Don't look to automate everything all at once. Try to *be* your product as much as possible.

As Samuel Hulick says: *"The more you insert yourself into the value offering process, the more that you can just intuitively pick that up by dealing with people directly and adapting from there."*

If users think that your emails, onboarding, and chat messages are all automated, they'll be less interested in giving you feedback. You have to do the things that don't scale, first.

Spend as much time as you can offering the product more as a personal service. This will help you to learn what works, and what doesn't.

This is part of the approach Brennan Dunn and his team at RightMessage, a website personalization platform, took at launch[54].

They intentionally left off a lot of the onboarding. When people signed up, they invited them to jump on a screen share during which they helped as consultants. Users were in the driver's seat. Brennan and his team were there to lessen the load.

They wanted to do what no software onboarding could ever do: be a human being who sees this stuff day in and day out, who tells prospects, based on their unique circumstances, what they should be doing.

Although they faced resistance at first, the businesses they wanted to land—those that wanted real results and weren't tire kickers—understood that this process was better for them.

Although Brennan and his team knew that their conversion would drop once they began automating their onboarding process, this experience taught them a lot.

Look for opportunities to get close to your early customers. Focus on understanding:

1. *What they want to be different in their lives or their work?* and
2. *How you can achieve that difference for them, via your product or the services around your product.*

By focusing on delivering those outcomes, regardless of what your product is designed to do, you'll be able to learn how to make your product a better fit in people's lives, for *their* needs.

Once you understand why users feel restless before signing up, and you know what experience they hope to get after sign-up, you will be in a better position to automate customer interactions.

> *If you were a service company...*
>
> *This step would be about delivering the work, and figuring out which parts are good, and which parts aren't.*

Techniques You Can Use

Early on, you should use every opportunity possible to learn from early users and customers. There are a few approaches you can use to make sure your bases are covered:

- **Small-Scale Retention Analyses** will help you understand what users are doing inside your product, and see if they're doing what they say they're doing.
- **Learning Through Follow up Emails** will allow you to get feedback from churned and disengaged users. You can learn a lot from the people who abandoned your product.
- **Learning Through Customer Interviews and Demos** will allow you to understand customer expectations and value perception at a deeper level.

There are different ways to learn from early product engagement, or lack thereof. Establish customer proximity and use as many of the techniques in this chapter as you need to test if your product delivers the expected value.

Small-Scale Retention Analyses

"If the key behavior in your product does not occur within the frequency of a week's time or less, it will be very difficult to change your user's habit."

Nir Eyal
Author of Hooked and Indistractable

It's easy to get carried away when you start instrumenting the analytics of your MVP. You don't know for sure where insights will come from, and as you have time available, it feels easy to add.

But, since you won't have a lot of volume, and any analytics that you put in place will most likely be wrong, you're better off focusing your efforts elsewhere.

At this early stage, you'll learn more quickly from activity streams or user activity logs.

Analyzing behaviors user by user will help you get a feel for the flows, key actions, and break points in your product.

At this point, since it won't be clear what *meaningful* retention is, overall retention numbers (e.g. how many people came back within the first seven days) will be too general to learn from.

To dig deeper, look at profiles one by one, focusing on feature usage and retention:

- *Are users experiencing the core value of your product?*
- *Is this value what you had expected?*
- *How many steps are there between sign-up and first value? How long does it take?*

- *Are they completing their tasks?*
- *How often do they come back?*
- *Do they come back on their own?*
- *What are they doing when they come back?*
- *How well does the frequency of engagement map to the natural cadence of the Job users are performing?*

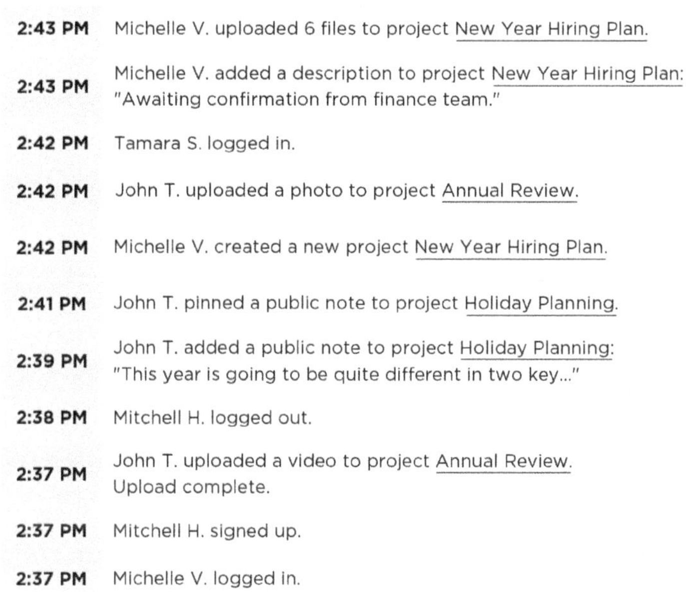

Figure 8.2 - Example of a User Activity Log Screen

Your goal is to get users to experience the product's core value as quickly as possible. It will be very difficult to get good retention if your product's "Aha moments"—the moments when users realize that the product is valuable—take a while to get to.

Establish a weekly cadence looking at the past week's sign-ups, their activities, and the evolution of behaviors amongst cohorts from previous weeks.

Look at the sequence of events: *How far do they get inside your product? Are they performing the core actions? Are they getting blocked? Are they coming back? Are there things that they do that you don't understand?*

You can't buy engagement. Resist the urge to look at aggregate data until you have a clear understanding of the small-scale patterns. In fact, it's a good idea to keep doing this until it's really no longer scalable.

Iterate. Eventually, the retention curve should flatten.

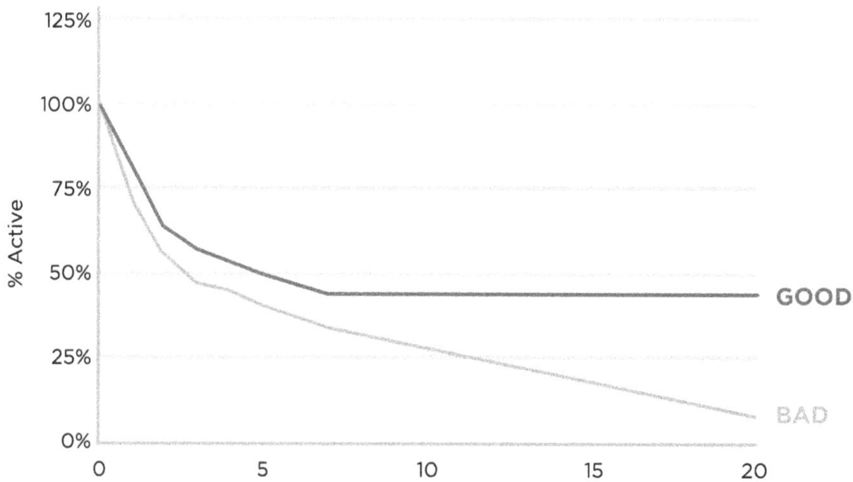

Figure 8.3 - Retention Curve Flattening

Learning Through Follow up Emails

"Always seek negative feedback, even though it can be mentally painful."

Elon Musk
Serial Entrepreneur

There's a lot that you can learn from churned and disengaged users.

The people who abandon your product may be difficult to get ahold off, but they can be instrumental in helping improve your product.

Chances are, these users gave up on your product because something was missing, something was broken, they got confused, or they felt your product wasn't right for them. Understanding why users drop off is key in understanding what to focus on.

These users probably don't know you, and they have already made the decision that your product isn't for them. If they value their time, they won't be jumping at the opportunity to get on a call with you.

To get them to open up, cut friction and send them a follow up email.

You can find these users by querying your database, pointing them out from your activity logs, or getting a list of them from analytics or customer communication tools like Drift or Intercom.

The people who abandoned in the last seven days will be the most responsive. The response rate will be much lower if you reach out beyond that time.

You can use a template like the one Hiten Shah sent in the early days of *FYI*:

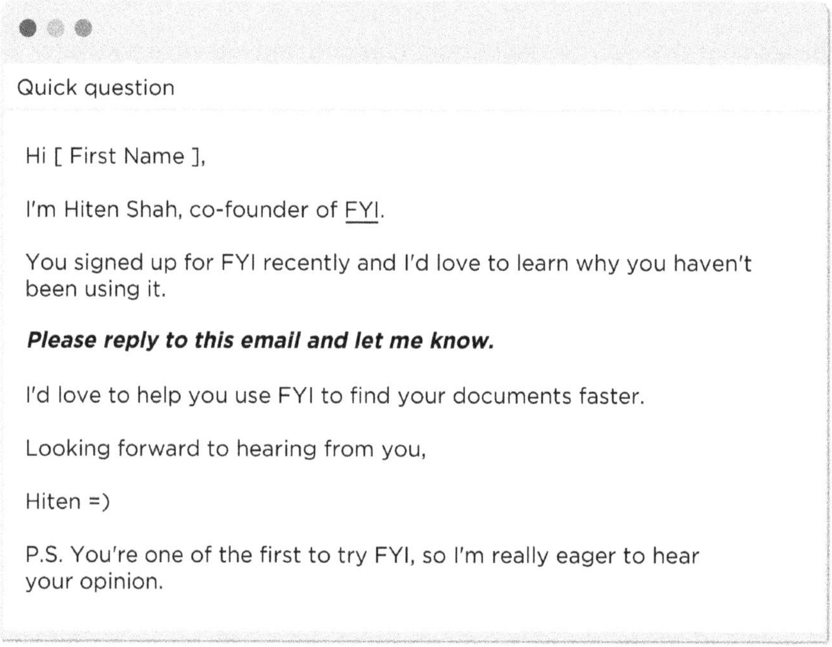

Quick question

Hi [First Name],

I'm Hiten Shah, co-founder of FYI.

You signed up for FYI recently and I'd love to learn why you haven't been using it.

Please reply to this email and let me know.

I'd love to help you use FYI to find your documents faster.

Looking forward to hearing from you,

Hiten =)

P.S. You're one of the first to try FYI, so I'm really eager to hear your opinion.

Figure 8.4 - Hiten Shah's Follow up Email Script for FYI

The email script was crafted to get as many responses as possible. Hiten explains[55]:

> *"This subject [line] has the highest open rates and response rates. The reason is that it's perfectly aligned with exactly what you're asking of people. [...] It implies that it won't take much time or effort. [...] The first sentence should set the context of who you are. If the customer knows that the email is coming from a person who cares and will listen to them, they are that much more likely to respond. Sending the email from a co-founder or executive helps demonstrate to the customer how important their response and opinion is. Adding a link to your product [...] reminds people what your product is in case they forgot. The second sentence should tell the customer what they did. [...] It's key to tie the request to an action the user took, so they are more likely to remember and give you specific feedback. [...] You should remind the user about your product's value proposition - the reason your product exists and what you're there to do for them. This solidi-*

fies the positive intent you have to solve the customer's problem in increasingly more effective ways. [...] Remind the customer you're excited to hear from them."

The last sentence and the P.S. are about making the users feel special, and reiterating your ask.

Create your own script or consider adapting FYI's email. Use the responses to identify friction points, reveal gaps and misunderstandings, and learn more about your users and customers.

Learning Through Customer Interviews and Demos

> "Be wary of feedback that contradicts reaction. Lean in close and watch how people use it—before they think.[56]"

Jake Knapp
Author of Sprint

It can be a good idea to launch your product without a self-serve mode, as Brennan and the team at RightMessage did.

Not only will it cut development time, if you can drive traffic to the product, the added friction will help weed out the tire kickers.

As we saw in the LinkedIn Sales Navigator case study, prospects who are willing to invest time to use a product are showing signs of interest. If a prospect isn't willing to go through a demo or a setup process to access a product, they may not be that interested.

The idea then is to use this first session to:

1. capture expectations before first run;

2. evaluate how well the product matches their expectations; *and*
3. unearth constraints, issues, and objections.

You can conduct these sessions face-to-face or via video using conferencing software. It's better to do one-on-one sessions so you can make sure you're learning about the specific person's needs and challenges, not a mix of his or her team's take on the topic.

It's also a good idea to create an account for them beforehand, sharing the login credentials by email at the time of the meeting. This will help simplify logistics.

Before diving into the product, it's important to understand why they 'hired'—or were hoping to 'hire'—your product. *What Job are they trying to get Done?*

Switch interviews, developed by Bob Moesta and Chris Spiek, are the ideal tool for this type of research. These interviews can be used to improve a product, or to create more demand for it.

Switch interviews focus on a single story—in this case, the story of how they realized that they had an unmet need and discovered your product.

You're trying to recreate the timeline leading up to using the product:

1. **First thought**: The initial moment when a change is needed.
2. **Passively looking**: The prospect notices options, but isn't actively seeking change.
3. **Actively looking**: The prospect starts investing time and energy into finding a solution. The second event transitions the prospect into making a purchase decision.
4. **Deciding**: The prospect weighs alternatives. This stage ends with a purchase decision, or the act of signing up.
5. **Consuming**: After signing up or making a purchase, the user uses, and ideally gets value from the product.

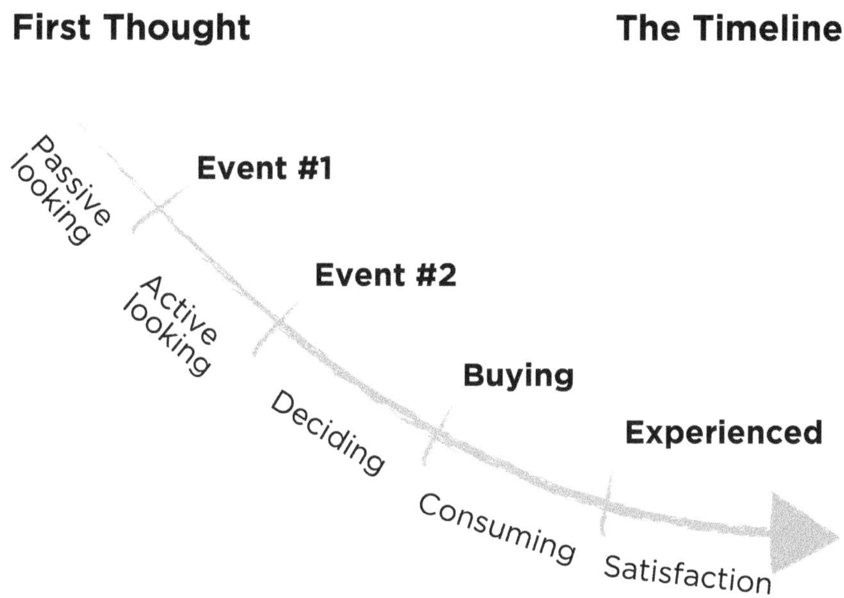

Figure 8.5 - The Switch Timeline

A sample script could look something like this:

1. *When did you first realize you needed something for [Job to be Done]?*
2. *Tell me about how you looked for a product to solve your problem.*
3. *What kind of solutions did you try? Or not try? Why or why not?*
4. *Before you [Signed up / Purchased] did you imagine what using the product would be like?*
5. *Did you have any anxiety about our product? Did you hear something about the product that made you nervous? What was it? Why did it make you nervous?*

You can download a Switch interview template at **solvingproduct.com/switch**.

These questions will help you understand the gap that users are trying to address (first thought), the options that they considered, whether they are seriously looking, what their evaluation criteria are, and if there was anything that prevented them from asking for a demo.

You can then let the users log in, configure their account, and explore the product for a few minutes.

As they're using the product, try to understand whether the product matches their expectations:

- *Was that what you were expecting?*
- *What problem do you feel [Product] addresses?*
- *How does it compare to [Competing Solution]?*

Ask open-ended questions. Learn from both what they say and what they do.

Don't ask them to 'think aloud' or explain what they're thinking. If you do, you won't get natural behaviors.

If they haven't purchased the product yet, consider trying to close the sale (Chapter #7).

There's a lot you can learn from similar discussions. After the demo, track their use of the product and evaluate the match between their expectations and their actions. Follow up after a few days if they're not using the product to address the needs identified in the interviews.

Making Progress

> "Introduce one feature at a time to be able to evaluate and roll back if necessary."

Lance Loveday and Sandra Niehaus
Authors of Web Design for ROI

Every product starts out as a feature or a small group of features. You can grow your product's usage and usefulness by focusing on its core differentiated value.

The general idea is to figure out what's the number one thing that people do in your product, why they are (or aren't) doing it, and from there, discover what the next logical step should be.

Hiten Shah says: *"What a lot of people fail at is figuring out the next logical thing to do. Because the next logical thing to do has everything to do with the thing they're already doing and it has everything to do with the thing that people are doing the most."*

Are early users and customers seeing the value of your product? What value do they experience? What value were they expecting?

Understand and address the value gap—the discrepancy between what customers expect and the value they're receiving—before considering introducing new value.

Clarify product value and remove friction, iteration after iteration, in order to get more early users or to get customers to perceive the product as valuable.

As serial entrepreneur Jeff Atwood says[57]: *"The iteration machine is the most powerful thing you can harness as an entrepreneur."*

Case Study
How Gym Fuel Created Customer Proximity

"If I owned a retail store that sold jeans and people walked in and left without buying, and three or four people did that in a row. I would run out after them to ask what was missing or what they were expecting because if I don't solve that that day, it doesn't get better on day two, three, or four."

Dan Martell

Mostafa Elhefnawy is senior product manager at SnapTravel in Toronto, Canada. Before joining the company, and before his time at HomeStars and Influitive, Mostafa was, like many product leaders, an entrepreneur.

In 2014, he started Gym Fuel to address a need he had—getting high quality meals that matched his workout regimen. He quickly put together an MVP by hiring a chef and a driver by the hour and renting out a kitchen by the hour. Once the "product" was available, it didn't take long for Mostafa to realize that he needed to go well beyond his intuition to understand the product's true potential.

To learn about the market, Mostafa began calling and emailing customers—asking specific questions about their experience, how they discovered Gym Fuel, and what their motivations were for using the service.

He soon realized that two distinct customer groups were using Gym Fuel:

1. People who cared about fitness. These people wanted to see the levels of calories and macros in foods, which is something Gym Fuel provided.
2. People who didn't feel like cooking, but still wanted to eat healthily. These people wanted to have meals ready to eat at their convenience.

Mostafa added a question during the ordering process to segment buyers into these two groups. He wanted to understand how they had discovered Gym Fuel, and whether they would use the service long term.

To further learn from customers, Mostafa often took on the role of the delivery driver (or tagged along). Although interactions were short, they helped Mostafa improve the service. They also helped drive sales to more than $10,000 per month.

At this stage, much like Mostafa did, it's important to look for any excuses or opportunities to learn from early users.

The more proximity and momentum you can create, the faster you will learn about what works and what doesn't.

Taking Action

1. Make it as easy as possible to give you feedback. Get creative. Find ways to get early users to share their thoughts and ideas.
2. Establish processes to learn from sign-ups, early usage, and disengagement using the techniques described in this chapter.
3. Try and assess how much value users are getting from your product.
4. Iterate, focusing on removing friction and improving product value.
5. *Collaborating with others?* Share a PDF version of this chapter at **solvingproduct.com/chapter-8**.

9 / 26

Refining Your Ideal Customer Profile

Users are getting value from your product. Now you want to **assess the value fit**. Use the techniques below to **refine your ideal customer profile**.

> "Your best fit customers hold the key to understanding what your product is."
>
> April Dunford
> Author of Obviously Awesome

One mistake commonly made by entrepreneurs at this stage is to try to learn from their whole user base.

Sure, anyone can access your product, but that doesn't mean everyone's feedback matters equally.

If a need emerged while interacting with a certain segment of customers, then it's important to maintain—even refine—your focus on those customers to iterate your way to PMF.

In early discussions, you're looking to understand how well the product aligns with the customers' original expectations: *Does this thing that we built actually address the need?*

Until your product *actually* solves the need of a precise group of people, you have to rely on good will and the promise of a great product to learn from users.

To move your product forward, it's important to learn from the users who match your ideal customer profile. You will learn faster by being laser-focused on that segment. This will also reduce the risk of having conflicting discussions that pull your team in different directions.

From your target segment, you're trying to understand:

- *Which profiles are most and least likely to use your product?*
- *Why do some people use the product, and why don't others?*

You need these two perspectives to find your true *best fit* customers and get more people to use your product.

Your *best fit* customers want your solution to succeed. They'll ask you to iterate until it gives them the benefit they seek. Make sure you're listening.

> *If you were a service company...*
>
> *This step would be about assessing the work delivered to your first few customers, and figuring out who benefited the most.*

Techniques You Can Use

Will you be *WhatsApp*, *WeChat*, *LINE*, or *Facebook*?

Your business can really go sideways if you decide to listen to the wrong voices. You might not even realize that you're listening to the wrong people, but if you do, you'll likely start building the wrong product.

It's understandable. Listening to fewer voices can feel like limiting the size of your market. By narrowing down your market, you might be excluding desirable customers that your product could help.

But the reality is as Sam Altman says, *"It's better to build something that a small number of users love, than a large number of users like."*

At this stage, one of the best things you can do is to narrow down the definition of your ideal customer profile even further.

In this chapter, we look at a technique to help define and **Find your High-Expectation Customer (HXC)**.

Finding the High-Expectation Customer (HXC)

> "Progress is directly proportional to motivation.[58]"
>
> Prachi Nain
> Bayzil Co-Founder

Julie Supan is a positioning expert. Over the years, she has honed and refined her unique method, working with companies like YouTube, Dropbox, and Airbnb.

She helps companies to define their brand and positioning by, first, identifying their High-Expectation Customers (HXCs)—the people who will benefit most from the product.

You can think of HXCs as a subset of your early adopters.

As Julie says[59], *"[The HXC] is the most discerning person within your target demographic. It's someone who will acknowledge—and enjoy—your product or service* ***for its greatest benefit****."*

In other words, HXCs want the core benefit of your product. They are highly motivated to solve their pain, they have high expectations, and others view them as clever and insightful.

At this stage, you can probably point to a few users or customers that 'get it', or who are finding real success with your product.

To make sure you're not building the product for outliers, or a market of one, you need to find as many of your HXCs as possible.

You can use the PMF survey developed by entrepreneur and marketer Sean Ellis to segment your early users and customers.

Use the guide on Creating Effective Surveys at the end of this book as a reference.

Let customers know that your goal is to understand their perception of the product, and that their thoughts will go into the product's strategy.

The survey's core questions are:

1. *How would you feel if you could no longer use [Product]?*
    - Very disappointed
    - Somewhat disappointed
    - Not disappointed
    - N/A – I no longer use [Product]
2. *What is the primary benefit that you have received from [Product]?*
3. *What type of person do you think would benefit most from [Product]?*

4. *How can we improve [Product] to better meet your needs?*

Collect responses from as many users as possible. One of the beauties of this kind of research is that many of your least motivated users simply won't complete the survey.

The customers who respond 'Very disappointed' to the first question are those that perceive great value in your product.

By analyzing their answers to question two, you'll be able to identify themes that relate to the core benefits of your product: *Is there a benefit that stands out above the rest? How well does that align with the reason why you're building the product?*

Once you've homed in on a strong benefit, look at the profiles of the users seeking this benefit: *Are these people that others would want to emulate? Could your product exceed their expectations?*

Clarify your product's core benefit:

Our product allows [HXC Profile] to [Benefit].

You're looking for a homogeneous group of HXCs. If you have found more than five, refine your segmentation some more. If you have found less than five, then use the Recruiting Prospects for Interviews guide at the end of this book to find more.

Make sure your team buys into the concept. As Brian Chesky, Co-founder and CEO of Airbnb says: *"The entire team needs to agree that this person is worthy of their time. In many ways, they need to aspire to be the HXC, too."*

Your product *is not* for everyone. Refine the user group that you are listening to, and move forward.

Making Progress

"A niche market is the key to the mass market.[60]"

Andy Rachleff
Wealthfront Co-Founder & CEO

In research published in *Predictably Irrational*[61], Dan Ariely found that when people are given many paths to potential success, they often try to keep all options open as long as possible. They do this even when selecting a specific option would lead to greater success.

Focusing on the right HXCs can make or break your startup, but as you'll see in the Superhuman case study below, PMF is often best found by zooming in and keeping fewer doors open.

To make progress at this stage, clarify the core benefit sought by your HXCs, rank their feedback, and improve your product so that it better meets their needs.

In the next chapter we will explore techniques for iterating value around that core benefit.

Case Study
How Superhuman Focused on the HXC

"Power users are the biggest sign of product-user fit. Making the leap from product-user fit to PMF is about listening to these users to evolve your product to attract more users.[62]"

Peter Lauten and David Ulevitch
Andreesen-Horowitz Partners

Rahul Vohra has been working on email products since 2010. Before creating the email client Superhuman, he found success with Rapportive, an email add-on that displayed social media information about contacts inside a users' inbox.

He subsequently worked at LinkedIn after they acquired his company. There, working on integrations, Rahul was able to observe the gradual decline of the Gmail user experience. Not only was it becoming slow, it didn't work well offline, and was becoming cluttered with plugins.

When Rahul, Conrad Irwin, and Vivek Sodera launched Superhuman in 2014, they knew they had their work cut out for them.

Gmail was free, it was a mature product, and millions of users had already been using it for 5-10 years. They would have to create a product so good that users would want to switch over.

It was a massive challenge. Two years in, they had few customers and Rahul was struggling to explain the issue to his team. Although, at a high level, they knew what PMF was, they didn't have a clear way to evaluate the progress they were making towards it. It was difficult to iterate without a clear metric.

> "The PMF definitions I had found were vivid and compelling, but they were lagging indicators."

This all changed when Rahul discovered Sean Ellis's PMF survey.

His team could ask users *"How would you feel if you could no longer use the product?"* and measure the percentage who answered 'Very disappointed.' As per Sean's benchmarks, they would know that they had found PMF when 40% of the respondents answered that they would be very disappointed[63].

To get started, Rahul and his team sent the four-question survey to their entire user base. Only 22% of respondents indicated that they would be very disappointed.

Instead of letting that score stop them, they began segmenting the data.

Focusing only on the roles of the people who had indicated that they would be very disappointed (founders, managers, executives, and business development), they realized that the responses of these professionals actually brought their score closer to 33%.

Digging through the answers to the survey's second question: *"What type of people do you think would most benefit from Superhuman?"*, they were able to clarify and define their HXC:

> *Nicole is a hard-working professional who deals with many people. For example, she may be an executive, founder, manager, or in business development. Nicole works long hours, and often into the weekend. She considers herself very busy, and wishes she had more time. Nicole feels as though she's productive, but she's self-aware enough to realize she could be better and will occasionally investigate ways to improve. She spends much of her work day in her inbox, reading 100–200 emails and sending 15–40 on a typically day (and as many as 80 on a very busy one).*
>
> *Nicole considers it part of her job to be responsive, and she prides herself on being so. She knows that being unresponsive could block her team, damage her reputation, or cause missed opportunities. She aims to get to Inbox Zero, but gets there at most two or three times a week. Very occasionally — perhaps once a year — she'll declare email bankruptcy. She generally has a growth mindset. While she's open-minded about new products and keeps up to date with technology, she may have a fixed mindset about email. Whilst open to new clients, she's skeptical that one could make her faster.*

Since the score for that segment was still under 40%, they wanted to understand why 'Nicoles' loved Superhuman.

By digging through the segment's answers to the third question: *"What is the main benefit you receive from Superhuman?"* they realized that the core benefits HXCs got from Superhuman were speed, focus and keyboard shortcuts. From then on, these benefits helped to guide product development.

Knowing that happy Superhuman users enjoyed speed as their main benefit, Rahul and his team went on looking for dissatisfied users (the 'Somewhat disappointed' group) who were also looking for a faster email experience—maybe they could find ways to win them over by addressing their concerns and hesitations.

Moving forward, the team focused its development effort 50% on improving the experience for the HXC, and 50% on filling gaps expressed by the 'Somewhat disappointed' group. Doing so allowed them to both improve the product experience and expand their market fit.

The PMF scores they got quickly improved. Within three quarters, they had nearly doubled the score for their HXCs (58%).

Although they have since expanded their targeting with over 300,000 people on their waiting list, the team still uses the PMF survey to guide their progress.

As Superhuman did, you can focus your product improvements on meeting the needs of your best customers.

Taking Action

1. Create a PMF survey. Send it to all your users and customers.
2. Focus on the respondents who answered 'Very disappointed' to the first question. *What do these users feel is the key benefit of your product?*
3. Looking at the profiles of the respondents looking for the same benefit, find the users that others would want to emulate and who have the potential to recommend your product to others.
4. Refine or adjust your targeting until you've identified a list of five HXCs for your product.
5. Consider turning the profile of your HXCs into customer segmentation or a persona.
6. *Collaborating with others?* Share a PDF version of this chapter at **solvingproduct.com/chapter-9**.

10 / 26

Iterating Customer Value

You have refined the targeting of your product. Use the techniques in this chapter to **evaluate whether your product meets (and exceeds) customer expectations**.

> "It's better to build something that a small number of users love, than a large number of users like. [...] It's much easier to expand from something that a small number of people love, to something that a lot of people love.[64]"
>
> Sam Altman

By this point, you should have a clear idea of the users or customers you are trying to please, and the value your product needs to deliver.

Your goal now becomes ensuring that your product meets—and exceeds—customer expectations.

To do this, first you should clarify the value sought: *Is it time-saving? Revenue? Lead quality?*

What criteria do your core customers use to evaluate the value of your product?

Once you have clarity around value, your work becomes about:

1. removing friction to make sure more HXCs or *best fit* customers experience the value quickly; and
2. improving the ROI or value until it meets customer expectations.

Since you won't have statistically significant data at this stage, you will have to rely on small-scale evaluations and subjective assessments of performance.

You can use data to quantify the value-add later on, but for now, focus on iterating the perception of product value.

> *If you were a service company...*
>
> *This step would be about figuring out your customers' core evaluation criteria, and iterating to deliver more value.*

Techniques You Can Use

The techniques in this chapter will help you to identify any friction points that could be limiting product use, and to iterate product value:

- **Analyzing Visitor Recordings** will help you to see the friction points and create hypotheses for product improvements.
- **Learning by *Dogfooding* the Product** can be a great way both to identify the bottlenecks and to iterate product value. Dogfooding can be particularly useful when your company could realistically be users of your product.

- **Customer Advisory Boards** can help you create more proximity with core customers to accelerate learning.

Use a combination of the techniques in this chapter to flesh out and iterate product value. Don't jump ahead too quickly. It's critical that your product delivers actual value.

Analyzing Visitor Recordings

> "When a user has intent, their experience is actually a little bit different versus when you tell them, 'Hey use this thing, and tell me if it's usable or not.'"
>
> Mostafa Elhefnawy

Visitor recordings, also known as session replays, are renderings of real actions taken by users or visitors as they use a site or product.

Although visitor recordings might look like qualitative research (e.g. user tests), they're more like quantitative research (e.g. analytics). Recordings help you see *what* is happening, not *why* it's happening.

Recordings can help reveal stumbling blocks, technical issues, and opportunities for improvements. They'll also help you to come up with hypotheses for further research and improvements, and get a feel for what real usage is like.

Unlike user tests, recordings help you see how users with real intent use your product.

To get started tracking visitor recordings, you need to install a third-party tool like Hotjar or FullStory. These tools allow you to record user actions on your website or in your product by targeting specific pages, or full sessions.

Initially, it's a good idea to record all sessions, even quick bounces—visitors leaving almost instantly. Don't be too restrictive. Leave room for discoveries.

Watch all recordings in their entirety. Focus on the sequences of events, how users navigate, where they hesitate or get stuck, the core tasks they try to get done, bugs, clicks in the wrong places, and drop off points.

Compare the lengthiest sessions to the quickest, and the most successful to the least. *Are there any patterns that emerge?*

Take note of the issues. Once you're starting to get a sense of what normal usage looks like, start evaluating alternate flows and digging deeper into core actions.

At this stage, it's more about understanding the value, the desire to use the product, and the friction points than trying to improve the product's usability.

Most session replay tools will allow you to search, tag, and share sessions based on select actions. This can be a useful way to track and compare reactions as you move forward.

It can be tempting, when looking at the feature sets of these tools, to start using heatmaps, funnels, or form analytics. However, these functionalities won't be very useful at this stage.

Watching people with real intent use your product should help you to reveal opportunities for improving product value and discovery.

Learning by Dogfooding the Product

> "The best software is created and consumed in parallel. Its makers are its users, its users are its makers.[65]"

Des Traynor

According to Esteban Kolsky, Head of CX Strategy at SAP, for every customer that complains, there are 26 other unhappy customers who have remained silent[66].

For new products—especially in the early stages when users aren't completely convinced of the product value—this ratio is likely much higher.

Users will churn and move on (sometimes perhaps in frustration) instead of taking the time to write and explain the issues they had with the product.

For this reason, it's a good idea to set up at least one extra way to learn from early product engagement.

Dogfooding is the practice of using your own product. It's also a great way to learn from repeated use of the product.

Being able to dogfood your product can give you a real advantage. When the product can be *dogfooded*, employees can more easily understand the product they're building, and why they're building it.

This means that the sales team has a better understanding of the product they're selling; the product team knows what bugs need to get fixed; and the customer success team can better empathize with the customers.

To *dogfood* your own product, consider:

- having your entire team use the product;
- using it in a real-world context the same way—and for the reasons—that your users would;
- getting into the habit of creating new accounts (e.g. john+1@companyname.com, john+2@companyname.com, etc.);
- systematically tracking confusing copy, usability concerns, and feedback based on repeat use; *and*
- reproducing issues and concerns flagged by users and customers when they happen.

Unless the product was built for people like you or your team members, you should disregard your team's feedback on desirability and product value.

If the product *was* built for organizations like yours, make sure you use the product the same way that your users would, and for the same purpose.

Track your teammates' retention (Chapter #8). It's always a major red flag when the people who *should* be using the product aren't using it.

It's too easy to create a chasm between your team and your end users (*"Oh, we're not the target audience."*). Stay close to your users. If no one on the team fits the target profile, then make sure you at least set up a customer advisory board to learn from your best customers.

Learning from a Customer Advisory Board

"The highest ROI I've ever had on user research is not a focus group or interview session: it's developing a close relationship with a handful of representative customers where I feel comfortable asking 5-minute questions over informal channels (text, email, phone, even Facebook Messenger). It is incalculably valuable to be able to get a quick gut check on your ideas in the moment to help short-circuit paths that are totally unworkable as well as encourage you to pursue ones that do have signal."

Alex Schiff

The more proximity you have with your customers, the faster you'll learn.

If, every time you have a question, you need to define segments, write emails, create an interview script, contact users, conduct interviews, and then analyze the data—then it's quite likely that you're not getting in front of customers as often as you should.

While you were interviewing prospects (Chapter #4), validating your product (Chapter #7), and building relationships with users and customers, chances are that you met people that match the profile of your HXC (Chapter #6), or people you would eventually like to sell to.

To increase your learning velocity, consider creating a Customer Advisory Board (CAB)—an advisory board composed of users who represent a sample of the people that your product is being built for.

Through a CAB, you can:

- get feedback on ideas;
- understand the context of use of your product;
- ask more open-ended questions;

- do quick user tests; and
- test and validate feature ideas.

To set up your CAB, look for people who are vocal, passionate, and visionary. Early on, most participants should match the profile of your HXC.

Although you want people who share the same needs, they can have radically different visions and ideas.

As the business grows, you'll want to recruit other members based on the new challenges that you are facing. Serial entrepreneur Peter Kazanjy says[67]: *"Make sure the composition of your CAB matches the challenges in front of you."*

You should have 25 people at most in your CAB. The important thing is not to let customers opt in or to feel coerced into adding users from the wrong organizations.

Focus the feedback on your product, your road map, and your strategy. Since the members of your CAB will be very familiar with your product, their feedback on onboarding flows or landing pages won't be very valuable.

To reward your advisors, you can give them privileged access to new features, mention them in releases, suggest they advertise their advisor role, or offer product discounts.

As Kazanjy says: *"You'd be surprised how many people will be interested when you mention the idea of promoting their work as an advisor."*

The members of your CAB will appreciate being part of the process of making and building a product.

With a CAB, you'll learn faster, and participants will get a better product they want to use.

Making Progress

> "Find the wow. People need to be able to talk about it."
>
> Fred Lalonde
> Hopper Co-Founder & CEO

At this stage, you will learn a lot, but if what you are learning doesn't bring you closer to PMF, you'll eventually realize that you're spinning your wheels.

Defining a North Star metric, and evaluating each release in relation to that metric, will help drive your business forward. At this stage, your metric will be more qualitative—but if it's indicative of customer value, it will tell you whether you're headed in the right direction.

It's really important to validate that what you are learning through qualitative research is meaningful. As CXL founder Peep Laja says[68]: *"Data, by itself, doesn't tell you shit."* If what you're learning doesn't bring you closer to your goal, then reevaluate the way that you are learning from your users.

Stick to your core users and the need that you're addressing. This step is about increasing precision, so keep iterating until you have clear indications that your product is useful and exceeds customer expectations.

Case Study How Flowtown Reduced Early Friction

> "The ONLY data source that's going to tell you what your value is, is your customer.[69]"

Patrick Campbell
ProfitWell Founder & CEO

When Dan Martell, Ethan Bloch, and David John started working on Flowtown, they had already been through the ups and downs of startups. Their product, Timely, was a precursor to Buffer—a simple tool letting users auto-schedule Tweets at the best time to amplify impact based on their Twitter following.

Dan and his co-founders were able to get people to sign up, but initially, only 10% of the people that signed up actually started using the product. To get more users to see the value of Timely, they dove into user activity logs and retention data.

When it became clear that users weren't coming back to the tool, Dan picked up the phone and emailed users, hoping to get on calls with them.

> "Hey John, you just signed up for Timely, do you have five minutes to jump on a call? Here's my cell, text me."

These discussions didn't turn out the way Dan expected. Users kept telling him that Timely was amazing, that they loved the idea, and that they were going to look at it the next week, or later during the day. Users had signed up with the intent to use Timely, but they were delaying usage.

Through discussions, the team realized that a major reason why users were delaying was that they had nothing to tweet.

Once the team came to that realization, they began looking for the most universal type of Tweets that they could preload to get users started, prompting them to schedule a Tweet right after sign-up.

It was clear that if users didn't publish a Tweet through Timely, then they wouldn't experience the core value of the product—the Aha moment—and they wouldn't come back to use it.

Through careful evaluation, the team settled on motivational quotes. While the quotes weren't for everyone, they were straightforward enough to get users to engage.

People could add them to their queue with a single click. Once shared, users would receive emails when their Tweets got retweeted.

More often than not, when users experienced the value of the product and saw its benefit, they realized that they were better off using it. A small change unlocked early growth for Flowtown.

What's preventing users from discovering the core value of your product?

Taking Action

1. Clarify the criteria that your *best fit* users and customers use to evaluate the value of your product.
2. Analyze usage to identify friction points that prevent early users from discovering the product value.
3. Work with your CAB to iterate the product value making sure customers get a lot of value from the product.
4. Don't move forward until you have tangible proof that five or more of your *best fit* customers are getting real value from your product.

5. *Collaborating with others?* Share a PDF version of this chapter at **solvingproduct.com/chapter-10**.

11 / 26

Evaluating Product/ Market Fit

Your product delivers value. Users are sticking around. Use the following techniques to **evaluate whether you have found PMF**.

"Founding a startup is deciding to take on the burden of Sisyphus: pushing a boulder up a hill. [...] Pushing a boulder: don't have PMF. Chasing a boulder: have PMF. Both are very demanding, but feel totally different. If you're still pushing the boulder, you don't have it yet.[70]"

Emmett Shear
Twitch Co-Founder & CEO

A lot of effort has been put into defining PMF over the years.

The reason is clear: it's a critical step in the life of any startup, and helps set up everything that comes after.

The reality is that if you aren't growing, if you have high churn, if your product is difficult to sell, or if customers just don't seem to care all that much—then you don't have it.

Post-product, you can tell you have PMF when:

- **Users stick around**: Long-term retention is the best metric for determining PMF[71].
- **Users and customers have built habits**: When you have PMF, at least some of your users come to rely on your product.
- **You're growing organically**: Users are getting enough value from your product that they're inclined to tell others.
- **The unit economics start to make sense**: You can repeatedly acquire customers for less money than they're worth to you (e.g. CAC < CLV[72]).
- **People are using your product even if it's broken**: You can screw a lot of things up and still succeed. Product value and usefulness significantly exceed friction[73].

Although there are many definitions for PMF, most product leaders and entrepreneurs would agree that PMF tends to be a combination of 1) retention, 2) revenue, and 3) organic growth.

Are customers sticking around? Are they telling others about your product? Are they satisfied with their purchase?

> *If you were a service company...*
>
> *This step would be about figuring out if the work you delivered drives referrals and positive reviews, and whether customers come to rely on you as a vendor.*

Techniques You Can Use

Since trying to scale a company without PMF is one of the most consistent predictors of startup failure[74], it's important to be clear about where your product stands.

- **Customer Retention Analyses** can be done manually when you don't have a lot of data, or with analytics tools when you're starting to get more data.
- **The PMF Survey** is the most common tool used to assess PMF. The survey will give you *directionally accurate* results.

It's a good idea to conduct different analyses, trying to triangulate the data before moving on to the next stage.

Analyzing Customer Retention

> "Plot the % active over time (for various cohorts) to create your retention curve. IF it flattens off at some point, you have probably found PMF for some market or audience.[75]"
>
> Brian Balfour
> Reforge Founder & CEO

Several years ago, Facebook almost reached a 70% retention rate[76]. At the time, and probably still to this day, this level of product stickiness had never been seen before.

Facebook, as a company that generates the bulk of its revenue from advertisements, has long understood the game it's playing. Over the years, they have acquired two of the most engaging apps on the market (WhatsApp and Instagram), and have made several failed bids to buy another

(Snapchat)[77].

As Facebook (and Google[78]) realized long ago, retention is key.

This goes well beyond ad-driven businesses. No matter what your product's revenue model, becoming the go-to solution for a need in a market will help to ensure business success.

For retention, the important thing is that a percentage of users are making a habit of using your product.

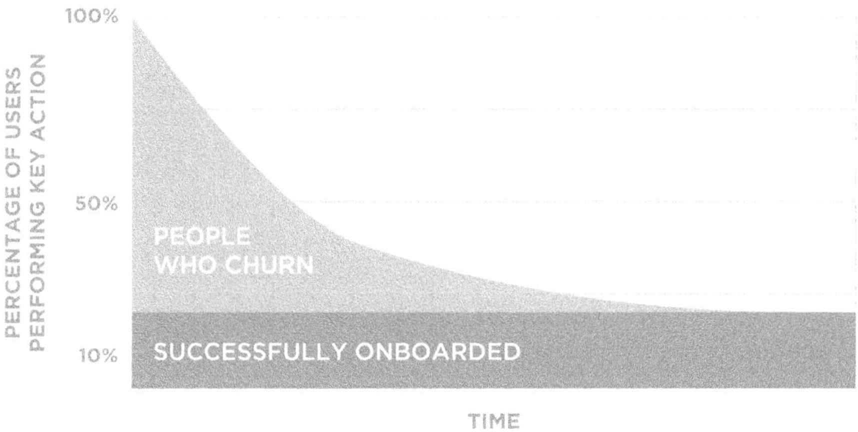

Figure 11.1 - Successful Retention

The key parts of retention are:

1. **The core action**: The main action that signifies that users are getting value from your product.
2. **The frequency of use**: How often should users receive value from the product. The frequency of use should align with the frequency of the Job that your product helps facilitate.

Nir Eyal, the author of *Hooked*, defines retained users as *habituated users*.

The specific definition of a habituated user will be based on the type of product you have built.

- If your product is a social network, a habituated user might be someone who checks in every day.
- If you're building enterprise software, a habituated user might be someone who performs a certain task every morning.
- If it's tax preparation software, a habituated user might only use the product once a year.

The important thing is that there is a regular cadence of use.

To assess your product's retention, check the percentage of users whose usage matches the expected frequency of use for your product.

As Nir mentioned during our interview, you probably don't have PMF if less than five percent of your users are habituated.

Once you start seeing five, 10 or 15 percent of sign-ups stick around and become habituated, this generally means that you're starting to have some level of PMF.

Look at your HXCs (Chapter #11): *Are at least 10% of them habituated? Is your product driving ongoing usage?*

The PMF Survey

> "People have this PMF score, "How disappointed would you be if this product no longer existed?" A lot of people try to shoot down the framework. I don't even argue with it. Yeah, you're right, but you're missing the point. The point isn't the score. The point is all the valuable information you can get when you ask open-ended questions."

In Chapter #9, we looked at ways to use Sean Ellis' PMF survey to refine our product targeting.

In its essence, *The Sean Ellis Test* is the only true, standardized way to evaluate PMF.

The full survey has seven questions:

1. *How would you feel if you could no longer use [Product]?*
2. *Have you recommended [Product] to anyone?*
3. *How did you discover [Product]?*
4. *What would you likely use as an alternative if [Product] were no longer available?*
5. *What is the primary benefit that you have received from [Product]?*
6. *What type of person do you think would benefit most from [Product]?*
7. *How can we improve [Product] to better meet your needs?*

The core question on which the PMF score is based is *'How would you feel if you could no longer use [Product]?'*. The multiple choice options are:

- Very disappointed
- Somewhat disappointed
- Not disappointed
- N/A – I no longer use [Product]

In Sean Ellis' model—based on research surveying hundreds of startups—a product that would leave more than 40% of its users disappointed if it disappeared has PMF.

Although there are questions about how valid the PMF score is[79]—because the core question asks respondents to project themselves into the future, and Sean himself has admitted that the 40% threshold is a bit arbitrary[80]—the survey can still point you in the right direction.

You need at least 40 respondents to get valid data. I recommend asking respondents to clarify their answers to the PMF score question:

> *"What is the main reason for your answer?"*

By using the first question to segment the rest of the responses, you'll be able to find ways to improve your product if you haven't found PMF.

You can use the survey guide in the Building Blocks at the end of this book to help with setting up your survey.

Use the PMF survey with caution. Make sure you're using at least one more technique to confirm that you have PMF.

Making Progress

> "My number one predictor of whether or not a company will find PMF: High shipping cadence.[81]"

Naval Ravikant
AngelList Co-Founder

This stage is about iterating until you reach PMF. You need to keep at it until you have clear signs that you have PMF and that your product delivers the expected value[82].

Startups are about survival—surviving long enough to achieve PMF and get distribution before the competition does.

Moving to the next stage without PMF means that if your business stagnates, it will be hard to figure out if it's because of the growth strategies you have chosen, or because your product wasn't ready for prime time.

As entrepreneur and marketer Andrus Purde says: *"You should only market things that don't need marketing. The product needs to be good enough to not need marketing."*

Case Study
When PayPal Found PMF

> "PMF isn't a one-time, discrete point in time that announces itself with trumpet fanfares. Competitors arrive, markets segment and evolve, and stuff happens—all of which often make it hard to know you're headed in the right direction before jamming down on the accelerator.[83]"

Ben Horowitz
Andreessen Horowitz Partner

PayPal is arguably one of the biggest startup successes in history. Not only is the business still going strong after 20+ years on the market, its founding team, nicknamed the PayPal Mafia[84], has gone on to create several of the products we use and love today (LinkedIn, YouTube, Yelp, Yammer, etc).

David O. Sacks, PayPal's original COO recalls the moment PayPal found PMF[85].

In November 1999, David was forwarded an email from an eBay *PowerSeller*. The seller had turned the PayPal logo into a button she was hoping to use for an auction. She had written to the PayPal support team asking for permission to use the logo. David was reviewing the email from a legal standpoint.

At the time, the team was vaguely aware of eBay auctions. It was one of the many use cases they were considering along with splitting dinner tabs and student allowances. The team had a vision for the product (emailing money), but they didn't know who would really get value from that solution.

To David and his colleagues, it was crazy to think that a seller had taken the time to create her own PayPal button. They had to figure out if there were other people who cared this much.

Going through eBay, they searched for 'paypal'. Soon, they realized that hundreds of auctions were already mentioning PayPal as a method of payment. This blew their minds.

It turned out that the alternative for eBay sellers was waiting weeks for a check to arrive in the mail, and then waiting for the money to clear. There were real benefits to using PayPal on eBay.

The team knew they had found *signs* of initial PMF.

To speed up the process, they had their web designer, Chad Hurley, future founder of YouTube, create a Pay with PayPal button that sellers could embed in their auctions. All they had to do was copy and paste the HTML code.

Right away, PayPal spread like wildfire in the tight-knit eBay community. Enough so that the team dropped other plans and went all in on eBay auctions. Within a few months they hit 100,000 users, then a million, then 5 million the next summer.

The team identified the most desperate customer segment, went all in on their use case, and found ways to speed up adoption and distribution.

It all started by listening to the right signals.

Taking Action

1. Make a general assessment of your product looking at retention, revenue, and organic growth: *Do you think you have PMF?*

2. Focus on your *best fit* customers: *What percentage of these users are habituated?*
3. Run a PMF survey and analyze the data: *Do you have PMF?*
4. Don't move to the next stage until you've confirmed that you have a strong PMF through different analyses.
5. *Collaborating with others?* Share a PDF version of this chapter at **solvingproduct.com/chapter-11**.

Stage 3:

Growth

Can It Scale?

"Growth is connecting people to the value that you're creating. Reducing friction in understanding the value of the product.[86]"

Casey Winters
Eventbrite Chief Product Officer

Famed entrepreneur and investor Marc Andreessen once wrote[87] that the life of any startup can be divided into two parts: before PMF and after PMF.

Whether you see this transition as a discrete event or not, the reality is that, once you have found PMF, things change:

- Your business has growth momentum.
- You start to see demand that you did not directly generate.
- There's a certain level of requests, customer feedback, and discussions that get generated whether you like it or not.
- Investors, consultants, and bankers start calling.
- A lot of things need to be put in place just to be able to scale and keep the product running.
- If you're hiring or raising capital, you start spending a lot of time in meetings thinking about your vision and business strategy.

With all this comes new goals, new responsibilities, and tremendous amounts of pressure put on the organization.

Like it or not, at this stage, your team needs to manage several "versions" of the product:

1. the product that got you to PMF;

2. the product you need to build to scale;
3. the analytics *product* you need to put in place to start getting more clarity around the business model;
4. the product story that you tell investors and the people you hire;
5. the product vision that you share with your team and executives; and
6. the key performance indicators (KPIs) you use to drive focus and momentum.

Somehow, all these "products" have to be kept in sync and iterated on while the business is undergoing significant change.

The Growth phase is a big challenge for the team, but an even greater challenge for the leadership group responsible for setting the course and keeping the ship moving.

The Challenge

> "Typically, the larger the company you work for, the smaller the parts of the product that fall into your teams' responsibility.[88]"

Alexander Hipp
N26 Senior Product Manager

When companies reach the Growth stage and start scaling, product teams usually come under pressure to deliver at a certain speed. Sales start banging at the door because they need features to sell. Big missing features need to be added to the product. Marketing needs to start ramping up.

Teams focus on delivery. Exploration becomes a luxury few get to have. Getting the product out the door quickly often takes precedence over getting the right product out the door.

To accelerate, teams get split up and managers get hired. As a result, product and customer-facing teams often become *siloed* from one another:

- Support is viewed as a necessary cost center that needs to be reduced.
- Sales focuses on landing new customers, and is not incentivized to speak to product.
- Product is too busy churning out features to meet with other teams.

It's not uncommon for teams to set up their own processes for learning from users, customers, and competitors.

Product teams, for one, may only pay attention to feedback that is directly related to their current product.

But the problem is, as Bob Moesta mentioned in our interview: *"A lot of people who run product are stuck making strategic decisions. They might feel like they're making product decisions, but they're actually making strategic decisions."*

At this stage, strategic decisions need to be front and center. There needs to be a clear plan to learn your way to the next stage.

What Got You Here Won't Get You There

> "If talking to customers is the best way to build momentum, then not talking to customers is the easiest way to lose it.[89]"

Mat Vogels
Zestful Co-Founder & CEO

Organizations need to have a very different mindset once they reach PMF.

It's no longer about *trying* to survive. Before PMF, you were *searching* for a market opportunity. Now, the opportunity has been set, and you have to see how far you can take it. Your focus switches to engagement, distribution, and monetization.

The leadership style and systems that worked in early phases often fail to scale.

There are different challenges, and different opportunities—and the way that you learn from users and customers will need to change.

What got you to this stage won't get you to the next one.

The good thing is that you can build a team to help out. As Sam Altman says: *"In general, hiring before you get PMF slows you down, and hiring after you get PMF speeds you up."*

Case Study
Why Statflo Changed Customer Research Strategy

"You're starting to get more data-driven. You went from being completely manual to now starting that initial stage of data-driven, and as you get more and more customers, even that's hard to do. Now you have to start adding more tools like Segment. So, then you start adding Segment and Mixpanel, and you tighten it. You want to get more of those raw metrics, because now you're starting to get into millions of actions, and when you start getting into millions of these happening and every couple days you're going, 'There's no way to keep up with this if I have to look at it!'. At that point, the tools become super useful because now you can graph everything, you can see what features are done. But initially when you do it, you kind of throw everything into Segment, and you get too much data. You got so excited about this data that now it's too hard to make a decision, so then you're learning what data is actually important."

Ian Gervais

We first met Ian Gervais, Statflo's VP of Products, in Chapter #4.

As Statflo grew, Ian's team kept spending a lot of time in each store they signed.

While visiting customers on-site had been a key to their early success, and customers valued the proximity they had with the team, the interactions were becoming more of a burden than clear success drivers.

Not only were these meetings creating a constant flow of feature requests, they were also putting pressure on Ian's team to provide added services. While some of the requests made by users felt meaningful, many of the features that Ian's team eventually implemented—calendar integrations, appointment bookings, etc—got used *instead* of Statflo's core product features.

The flow of constant discussions was diverting Statflo from its goals. The product team was losing focus and efficiency. As a result, their customers' workflows and productivity were negatively affected.

Ian says: *"There's always a push when you're an early startup to jump into services. Your customer has lots of asks and you jump in and you want to make them happy. It's very easy to lose sight of your vision, what you want to do with the product."*

Ian's team had wanted to learn how to create a great product experience. It was no longer sustainable for them to visit all customers on-site.

To scale, they had to make significant changes to the way that they learned from their customers.

The Opportunity

> "If you have PMF, improving your marketing/market fit might be the highest ROI investment you can make.[90]"
>
> Rand Fishkin
> Serial Entrepreneur

In technology, PMF often gets mythicized. It's this bigger than reality concept, with a still somewhat fuzzy definition, that has the potential to make or break a product business.

In reality, however, PMF is not a permanent state. It's a per market, per feature, per segment thing.

To grow predictably, you need to strengthen your PMF and provide a valuable, and consistent, experience to customers across the entire journey.

This means:

1. **Learning from your best customers**: figuring out who they are, how they use your product, and why they feel the it's a "must-have".
2. **Democratizing understanding and optimizing the way you deliver value**: aligning value delivery and optimizing the "must-have experience" from acquisition all the way to retention.

At this stage, it's better to introduce more users to the value your product delivers than to create new value.

As serial entrepreneur Dan Martell says, there's a mental movie that customers create in their minds. You want to influence that movie.

> "You're trying to figure out the way people describe the product, figure out what problem they're trying to solve. So, if there's a disconnect between what they expected and what you did, it's worth understanding that gap, but to me it's refining the mental movie and knowing that everything from who first introduces them to the solution, to the homepage, to the signup flow, to the first-time user experience, to your retention re-engagement emails, are all going to be a thoughtful consistent clear mental movie of the problem you're solving."

It's easy to get caught up in individual actions and send conflicting messages. At this stage, **everything you do should communicate to your customers that you care about their success**.

You need to find the reliable and predictable parts of your model and double down on them.

Once you know that there's a clear correlation between efforts and results, it becomes a lot easier to focus on actual drivers and make progress.

During the Growth stage, we focus on:

- Finding the leaks in our funnels (Chapter #12);

- Understanding why customers buy our product (Chapter #13);
- Aligning what we sell with the way we sell it (Chapter #14); and
- Finding the best acquisition channels to scale the business (Chapter #15).

Customers have to go through a journey to use your product—it's important to help them along.

Time to get deliberate about growth.

> *If you were a service company...*
>
> *This phase would be about figuring out the kinks in your service offering, improving the way you sell, and figuring out how to land more customers.*

Clear Actions

> "Success is driven by a million incremental improvements to your business model.[91]"

Gail Goodman
Constant Contact Ex-CEO

Because of all the different "versions" of products that you have to maintain, and the need to have an overarching strategy that ties everything together, it's natural to start making big plans.

The problem with big plans, however, is that, as David Cancel says[92]: *"They often satiate company curiosity more than they solve customer problems."*

Planning too far ahead often reduces your ability to react to market changes, which can limit your ability to iterate and grow fast.

To make progress, it's important to have 1) clear goals and metrics that are both transparent and close proxies for customer success, and 2) an experimental and outcome-driven mindset.

To make it out of this phase:

1. Embrace an experimentation mindset.
2. Have a clear strategy and set North Star metrics aligned with your customers' success.
3. Set weekly goals, planning no further than 90 days ahead.
4. Share learnings across the business.
5. Experiment, focusing on outcomes, not tasks.

It's surprising how much *strategically evaluating opportunities* can lead to better, and more predictable growth.

Let's get to it!

12 / 26

Finding the Leaks in Your Funnel

You've found PMF. Reduce friction before attempting to scale user acquisition. Use the techniques below to **find (and address) the leaks in your funnel**.

> "The much bigger share of the total addressable market comes from getting people to change what they are doing today, overcoming natural human and organizational inertia."

Bill Aulet
Disciplined Entrepreneurship Author

You've found PMF. Your business is growing.

That's amazing—but unless you invested significant time in optimizing messaging and workflows before PMF (which you shouldn't have), only customers with a degree of imagination are going to adopt your product.

Until now, early adopters have been compensating for suboptimal messaging, less than ideal usability, and gaps in your feature set, because their need for your product outweighs the friction that they experience when using it.

The problem is not only that early adopters are notoriously fickle[93], they also represent only a small fraction of the market.

Diffusion of Innovations author, Everett Rogers, estimates that early adopters—innovators included—represent, at most, 16% of the market[94]. If your business doesn't evolve at this stage, your entire customer base will be limited to 16% of the market.

To keep growing and take things to the next level, you need to overcome the friction points across the customer journey.

With enough funding, you could try to power through, but this approach is highly ineffective and costly.

Adopting a new product generally means replacing a previous solution—be it a habit, a workflow, a manual process, or another technology product. The smoother the transition to your solution, the easier it is to bring in and onboard new users and customers.

To highlight this tension, JTBD thought leaders Chris Spiek and Bob Moesta created the Four Forces, also known as the Progress Making Forces diagram[95]:

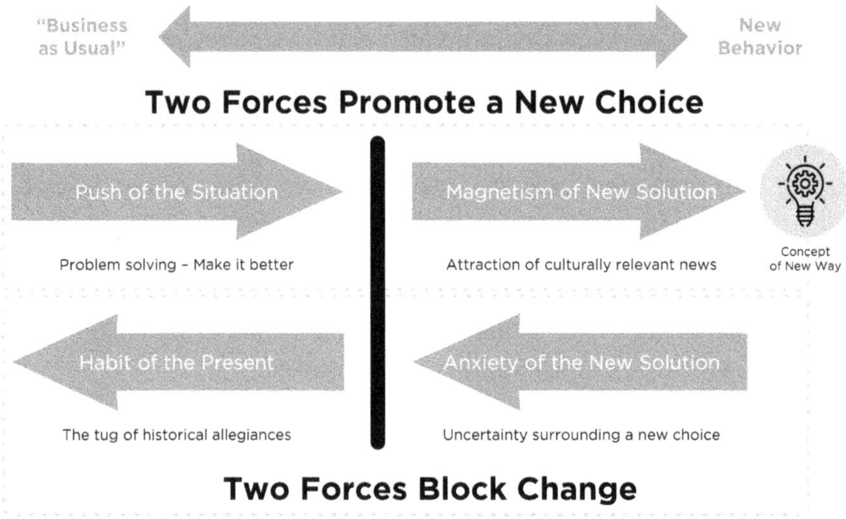

Figure 12.1 - Chris Spiek and Bob Moesta's Progress Making Forces Diagram

Jim Kalbach sums it up well: *"A problem with the current product leads a consumer to consider a new solution (Push). The attraction of a new product pulls them away from their existing ways of working (Pull). Uncertainty about change provides a reason to stay (Anxiety). Habits keep consumers from switching (Allegiances)."*

And as serial entrepreneur Marc-Antoine Ross says, *"Until users understand how to use their solution, it adds yet another problem."* Whether it's time, money, reputation, training, or lost opportunity, switching from one solution to another *always* has a cost.

Convincing people to adopt a new product means smoothing out the stages on the following journey:

- Users determine they have a need;
- They discover your product;
- They evaluate the product;
- They acquire the product;
- They start using the product;
- They use the product;

- They measure the value gained (or ROI) from the product;
- They pay, and pay again;
- They get support from your team;
- They spread awareness about the product.

The greater the friction, the leakier the funnel.

When a qualified prospect rejects your product, it's generally because the full cost of adoption—considering risks, training, etc—outweighs the perceived value.

To increase growth velocity, reduce friction across all touch points and the customer journey.

> *If you were a service company...*
>
> *This step would be about figuring out what's preventing prospects from working with you, implementing your recommendations, or referring your work.*

Techniques You Can Use

There are many ways to identify friction points. To get a complete picture, you'll want to analyze the way you acquire customers, why they decide to leave (or stay), what keeps them from buying, and whether product usage drives new growth.

Acquisition

- **Analyzing Your Traffic** will help you to understand if your current website and acquisition strategy are attracting the right leads.
- **Testing for Language/Market Fit** will help make sure that prospects understand the right message when they interact with your brand.

Revenue

- **Learning from the Sales Process** will help improve your pitch based on the learnings of your sales staff.

- **Analyzing Objections** will help you to discover what makes prospects hesitate before they agree to buy from you.

Retention

- **Learning from Customer Success** will help you understand product setup, onboarding, and feedback post-sale.
- **Analyzing Key Behaviors** will help you to understand why users do/don't do certain actions in your product.
- **Analyzing Feature Engagement** will help you dig deeper into retention, to understand which features are perceived as valuable.
- **Analyzing Switching Behaviors** will help you find the gaps in your feature set, to increase retention and land more customers.
- **Analyzing *"Delightion"*** will help you to figure out whether your product meets or exceeds customer expectations.
- **Analyzing Support Communications** will help you establish processes for learning from every customer interaction.

Referral

- **Analyzing Virality** will help you understand if product usage drives new acquisition for your business.

It's a lot to get through. Start by analyzing traffic, feature engagement, and objections. Expand your analysis based on your business priorities.

ACQUISITION

Analyzing Your Traffic

"To increase retention, don't sell to the wrong customers."

Jason M. Lemkin
Serial Entrepreneur

At this stage, it's a good idea to start to view your sign-up process as a funnel. It can help with benchmarking, and with evaluating progress against those benchmarks.

Tracking each step of the funnel (e.g. landing page visit > sign up > first use) will help you to reveal the friction points.

Some general rules of thumb are:

- > 1% of qualified traffic should be signing up to use your product;
- > 5-10% of blog visitors should be visiting your landing pages; and
- > 20-40% of landing page visitors should be signing up.

Ratios will vary depending on your market, the type of product you have, and how tight your market fit is.

If your site doesn't attract the right prospects, it's unlikely that the traffic will convert. Even worse, if they *do* convert, they'll probably churn and be a drag on your business.

Before attempting to scale, it's a good idea to try and understand the profiles that your product funnels naturally attract.

You should already have a good idea of who your *best fit* customers are (Chapter #9). *Is your product for dentists in Germany, or US-based Software-as-a-Service companies?*

The moment you can start getting signals from users—be it a site visit, an email, or a sign-up—you can start figuring out what profiles your site attracts.

When you get a site visit, you can:

- Infer the profile based on the pages they visited. *Was the content aimed at engineers, marketers, executives?*
- Look at traffic demographics to start building a profile. *Where are visitors from? What's the dominant age group? Is it business or consumer?*
- If they came in through ads, *what ad did they click? What was the message? Who was the target? What can you infer from the ad click?*

- If they came in through organic search, *what keywords did they use? Can you infer something from those?* You can use the Google Search Console in combination with Google Analytics to see search keywords.
- If you're selling to businesses, you can use products like Clearbit Reveal or Leadfeeder to detect visiting companies. *Are they in the right market? Can the visits reveal something else?*

When you get an email address, you can:

- Look at the landing page or email capture flow messaging to infer profile. *What pitch convinced them? Did they sign up from a content or landing page catered to a certain type of users?*
- Enrich the email to get social and company data. You can use tools like Clearbit Enrichment or TowerData to get more data points like role, location, or even income brackets.

Once you get a full sign-up, you will get all these data points and more—but as you can see, you can begin to learn about traffic quality before users even sign up.

Not all traffic is created equal. You should be aiming for at least 30% qualified traffic—traffic from your target market. If you're not currently getting at least 30%, then use the techniques in Chapter #15 to improve your acquisition strategy.

You will have a hard time learning from and iterating your funnel if you can't get enough qualified traffic.

Testing for Language/Market Fit

> "The people coming to your website start with a base belief. For example, they believe that messaging is good on a website, or they believe that they should do A/B testing, or they be-

lieve that they should email their customers. Most people don't have enough belief and motivation to convert immediately. Your goal is to increase belief and motivation to make them convert.[96]"

Guillaume Cabane
Growth Advisor

Expectations for a product are set the moment someone mentions its name.

If your product is listed in app marketplaces, you're running ads, or you have copy describing what your product does, you need to understand that touch points all contribute to setting user expectations, and that those expectations are used to evaluate your product.

If you're selling Customer Relationship Management software (CRM), but everything about your copy tells visitors that you are a consulting company, visitors will be very disappointed to discover that you can't help them set up their database. Chances are, they won't use your product—and you'll never know why.

For this reason, it's often a good idea to start this phase with a comprehension test to figure out if prospects actually understand your messaging in the way that you intended it. This will help to reduce problems when conducting the other analyses outlined in this chapter, and can also provide benchmarks to optimize against.

One of the most popular forms of comprehension test is the Five Second Test. In a Five Second Test, people are shown a value proposition, messaging, a screenshot, or a full-fledged website for 5-15 seconds before they're asked to sum up their understanding:

> *"What is this [Page / Site / Product] about?"*

Comprehension tests need 20-40 participants and can take as little as one hour to run.

You're not looking for significant or representative results. Directionally accurate results will be enough.

Look for a positive response of 80% or more. The responses should help point out gaps in comprehension for your messaging. Cognitive load limits conversion rates, so it's a good idea to make your messaging as simple as possible.

Although participants don't need to be part of your target market, they should have the same level of language and vocabulary as your intended audience.

UsabilityHub has the best—also the original—Five Second Test. But you could organize your own comprehension tests during customer interviews or user tests.

As your market expands and your messaging evolves, it's a good idea to run new comprehension tests regularly, with both prospects and existing customers.

For customers, you should optimize for word of mouth, while for prospects you'll want to make sure that the messaging remains clear and effective.

REVENUE

Learning from the Sales Process

> "Remove the fear, and people will be more willing to pay you. People don't like uncertainty—especially when they have to pay for it.[97]"

Jason Fried

A lot can be learned by speaking with the people in the trenches, those that work with customers day in and day out.

In a sales-driven organization—or any organization with a sales function—salespeople are constantly learning about needs, expectations, and objections.

For this reason, many business stakeholders view the insights that sales staff gather as the voice of the customer. Unfortunately, it's often not so simple. Sales teams have their own agenda.

As *Lean Enterprise* co-authors Trevor Owens and Obie Fernandez say: *"Salespeople are masters of confirmation bias; their work often depends on finding encouragement in signals that others would deem negative"*.

It's not uncommon for product leaders working in sales-driven organizations to feel like they're taking orders, building feature after feature to close deals.

Salespeople are incentivized through commissions. When large deals are about to close, they stand to profit. Their mind isn't always on the product experience. Often, sales staff will overcommit, and will request features that don't fully solve the customer problems.

Over time, the product can end up becoming bloated, with more features than necessary.

Learning from the sales process is critical. To make sure you're learning the right things, you can:

- join in on demo or sales calls;
- record and analyze sales calls using tools like Gong or Chorus.ai;
- train sales staff teaching them to ask the right questions; and
- collect information after the fact through interviews.

The fewer ears there are between what the customer says and you, the more reliable the information will be.

Before agreeing to jump on a call, it's a good idea to review call participants. This will help make sure that you're learning the right things from the right people.

Sales staff can help you uncover and map:

- customer pain points;
- triggers;
- motivators;
- benefits that connect with prospects;
- initiating stakeholders;
- emotional drivers (e.g. I'm going to lose my job);
- desired outcomes;
- budgets and budget owners;
- objections;
- fears and anxieties;
- internal decision-making processes;
- the organizational context;
- roles of the decision-makers; and
- the mandatory requirements.

That's a lot of valuable information that can be used to improve your positioning and sales process.

You can use the following questions to get the ball rolling:

- *Who generally initiates the purchase? What are their roles?*
- *What are the typical triggers? Why now?*
- *What are the main [Problems / Jobs] that they're trying to address?*
- *What factors tend to positively or negatively influence the sales process?*
- *What [Benefits / Arguments] work best?*

- *What are the most common objections?*
- *Who also gets involved in decision-making?*
- *Who are the four or six people who make the decision?*
- *Do prospects need to ask for approval before purchasing new tools or technology?*
- *All things considered, what is the "typical" length of the approval process?*
- *Before buying, how much are they spending to do what the product does?*
- *How much value does the product add for them?*
- *When do you know that the sale is guaranteed to close?*

You can learn more systematically (and effectively) if you can get the sales team to help out. Cindy Alvarez, principal group product manager at Microsoft, recommends training sales staff to help them better define customer needs[98].

This can be as simple as following up any feature requests with two questions:

- *How would it make your life better?*
- *What would it allow you to do?*

The right process can make this a win-win, making customers feel more involved in decision-making. Customers tend to view sales conversations that end with "we'll let the product team know" as being a bit dismissive.

The best way to go beyond surface-level answers is to use Toyota's *Five Whys* interrogative questioning, asking "why" after each answer until you get to the root cause. This technique can be used whenever a prospect or customer expresses new needs or asks for new functionalities.

Here's an example of *Five Why* questioning:

"We need a system that will manage and deliver information on time."

1. *Why?* Because information is incomplete and disorganized.

2. *Why?* Because there are different ways to manage information in the organization.
3. *Why?* Because the rules for organizing content aren't always enforced.
4. *Why?* Because there's no clear way to communicate the guidelines.
5. *Why?* Because there's no central place to share this information.

By systematically capturing core Jobs, prospect reasoning, and the language used by prospects and customers, the insights gained are useful in helping to guide product development. There's a good chance that your team will be able to solve customer issues one way or another. Getting to the root cause will help you get clarity, and will reduce the risk of building the wrong functionalities.

Analyzing Objections

"I get it, it's hard. It's like lining up to get kicked in the stomach. But if you know that the opportunities on the other side of that activity [are worth it], you gotta have the faith and push forward."

Dan Martell

This may sound harsh, but rejection is often the best teacher in innovation.

If you power through rejection and iterate on value, you'll learn extremely quickly. This is one of the key reasons why serial entrepreneur Dan Martell prefers month-to-month subscription models.

He says: *"Every month, I need to earn the investment. Every time I pay*

$89 for Trello or $250 for my email marketing tool, I'm asking myself "Did I get that kind of value out of the product?". I just love the honesty and purity of that exchange. Sometimes enterprise products don't get that. If you're three or four years in two to three million ARR, it's actually really bad for you because you're not getting the data set that you should be getting."

There's something to be said for opening the door to rejection and welcoming complaints.

Even if you're selling an app or a consumer product, it's a good idea, at first, to spend time selling it face-to-face. You'll be able to uncover objections faster this way.

As ConvertKit co-founder Nathan Barry says[99]: *"When you ask someone to buy, they're socially obligated to give you a reason."*

This means that unsuccessful pitches should generate at least one objection. If you go through the process enough times, eventually you will have heard all possible objections.

If you don't make efforts to hear all objections, you'll limit your ability to grow your product.

Be proactive. Beyond trying to close deals, you can start collecting objections by asking prospects:

- *What's your biggest fear or concern about [Product]?*
- *What's preventing you from [Buying / Upgrading]?*
- *Why do you buy from [Competitor] and not from us?*

Or new clients:

- *What's the one thing that nearly stopped you from becoming a client?*
- *Why did you hesitate to buy [Product]?*

Questions like these will help you learn what objections customers have. Then you can find ways to overcome them.

Objections can help fuel your marketing copy, develop your Frequently

Asked Questions (FAQ), and improve your product.

Although objections will sometimes be clear and direct, you need to learn to read between the lines when dealing with more indirect objections. For example, pricing objections tend to be more about value than price. These generally mean that you haven't properly communicated the product's value.

When dealing with price objections, ask prospects to rationalize *why* the product is too expensive. Try to get to the root cause.

If you are proactive with your search, eventually there won't be any objections that you haven't heard. The information you gain will help you improve your messaging and better meet customer expectations.

RETENTION
Learning from Customer Success

> "A dissatisfied customer does not complain; he just switches."
>
> Dr. W. Edwards Deming
> Engineer & Author

The customer success (CS) team plays a big role in helping prospects and customers to find success with your product.

They spend a lot of time interacting with customers, helping them experience the value of your product. They are constantly learning about gaps, customer needs, and issues that prevent users from maximizing their use of the product.

Like the sales team, however, they have their own agenda. Often times, customer success will be made accountable for onboarding, retention, and renewals or repurchases.

In B2B, customer success specialists may be assigned to as many as 30-40 customers each. Chances are, they'll want to get any issues that are plaguing their customers resolved first.

When working with CS staff, it's a good idea to keep your focus on the larger themes of problems and friction points.

To learn, you can jump on onboarding or follow up calls, or listen to call recordings. What you're looking for are friction points, the words customers use, and issues with long-term retention.

CS staff will also be great at pointing out specific use cases that could be turned into case studies.

Eventually, your best source of growth will be your existing customers. It's a good idea to understand what challenges customers face after they buy.

To learn from individual CS specialists, ask questions like:

- *What's our best source of customer acquisition?*
- *What pitch and benefits help attract our best customers?*
- *What profile of organizations tend to make the best customers? Why?*
- *Who gets involved during the sales process? During the onboarding process?*
- *What are the factors that most influence onboarding success?*
- *What are the factors that most influence upgrades and renewals?*
- *Who are our most successful customers? Why them?*
- *Who are our least successful customers? Why them?*

To overcome groupthink, speak to CS staff one-on-one and then merge their insights yourself afterwards.

Chances are that the CS team will create its own reports. You can compare your insights with theirs. Ask questions, but never forget that the CS team has its own agenda.

Analyzing Key Behaviors

> "We've been trained to look at patterns, look at a line that fits the data points, but when it comes to qualitative research, those anomalies make a lot of difference because that may be a node to understanding a completely different market, a completely different customer. Anomalies need to be understood and need to be unpacked."

Ashwin Gupta
VWO Head of Growth

When you start really digging through your data, you will start to notice patterns and behaviors that you don't instinctively understand. These are likely to include:

- users who sign up without ever using your product;
- users that max out their free trial without upgrading;
- users who drop out at critical points of product flows;
- users consistently using secondary product features; and
- users with atypical usage patterns.

To continue finding friction points, look at the entirety of the customer journey and your funnels.

Are there areas of hyper engagement? Big drop offs? Behaviors you're not sure you understand?

Identify the biggest friction point. Your goal is to understand the differences in profiles, goals, and behaviors that make some users convert and others drop off.

Are you able to reach users right after they drop off or perform the task you're hoping to explore? Timely surveys can help you break down the behavior that you are trying to understand.

Set up a single question survey probing:

- **Users who completed the action**: *"What made you decide to do [Action]?"*
- **Users who decided to drop off**: *"What made you decide not to do [Action]?*

The less friction involved in answering the question, the more likely it is that users will respond. For example, a survey delivered through an In-App message or a popup in your product will get more—and better—responses than a survey sent via email.

With good analytics and segmentation, you will be able to target the exact activities that users are doing inside your product. This will help ensure that your survey is both timely and relevant which, in turn, will help increase your survey response rate (benchmark of 2 to 4%[100]) and the quality of the answers you're getting.

A customer who just bought will give better feedback because they're only recently removed from the buying process. They will also be more likely to give useful information about why they bought, what emotional event caused them to look for your product, and which parts of the product they find valuable.

Once you start to get responses to your surveys, compare the answers of the users who dropped off with the answers of those that completed the action. *Are there noticeable differences? Does looking at the data through different lenses (personas, profiles, CLV, etc) reveal new patterns?* Answers should help you to understand the success drivers, and identify friction points.

If the answers don't lead to a conclusive theory about behavior, consider using the exact same targeting to recruit users for interviews. You can use the Recruiting Users or Customers for Interviews guide under Building Blocks to help with your recruitment efforts.

Survey fatigue happens when surveys aren't relevant to user activities. To keep your response rate high, make sure you get the timing right, and keep your surveys short.

Conversely, research shows that if you can get someone to answer a survey question, the likelihood that they'll answer following questions is higher than 90%[101]. So, if the targeting makes sense, consider asking more questions.

As you capture insights, keep in mind that the responses you get will most likely be skewed towards dissatisfied users and customers, because these people are more likely to respond. For this reason, it's often a good idea to triangulate your findings by also getting insights from customer interviews or analytics.

Once you have begun to understand a certain behavior, move on to the next biggest drop off.

Analyzing Feature Engagement

> "Feature engagement is more important than feature retention in my mind because if users come back, what are they coming back for? So it's kind of that next layer and what are they doing when they come back? It's just deeper into retention."

Hiten Shah

User experience thought leader, Jared Spool, breaks down time spent using a product into two categories[102]:

1. **Goal time**: time spent achieving core objectives, perceived as high value by users; and
2. **Tool time**: time spent using the product itself, perceived as low value (e.g. logging in, managing the app, waiting, etc).

The thinking behind this breakdown—and Brian Balfour's notion of *meaningful usage*[103]—is that in the eyes of users, not every moment spent using a product adds value.

If users come back every week to unsubscribe from emails or to remove notifications, their usage can't be compared to that of a user who performs core actions daily.

To dig deeper into retention, list all your product's features excluding administrative features like account creation, password reset, etc.

What percentage of your user base uses each feature? How often do your users use the features? For each feature, is usage trending up, or trending down?

Set thresholds based on your product's engagement. You can visualize feature usage using a chart like the following:

Figure 12.2 - Feature Usage Overview

On the x-axis, plot out the proportion of users using each feature. On the y-axis, plot out the frequency of use.

Does this more granular breakdown match your understanding?

Now, slice-and-dice feature usage, looking at key dimensions:

- users vs. customers
- engaged vs. disengaged users
- roles within organizations for business products
- languages
- billing cycles for subscription products
- lifetime revenue
- payment plans
- profiles or personas, etc

Are there any outliers?

A feature engagement analysis will help you identify features that are not being used (or confirm which features are being used as anticipated). It can also help you to gain a better understanding of the gap between what people *say* and what they actually *do*.

Senior product manager Nick Mauro recommends taking this even a step further. At SevenFifty, they assigned various weighting factors to the features and behaviors they perceived as most valuable. They were then able to measure the impacts of specific changes by looking at how scoring changed when features got updated, or when the feature set changed.

Go beyond retention cohorts. Dive deeper and evaluate whether real feature usage matches your expectations.

Analyzing Switching Behaviors

"Customers leaving without saying anything are moments of truth. As a leader, you can learn from those moments."

Ari Weinzweig

As growth expert Alan Klement says: *"Comparing the habits of your best customers with the habits of those who recently quit is a great way to figure out how to turn switchers into loyal customers."*

When users sign up to use your product, they show intent. When they churn, they communicate unmet expectations, or at least, expectations that can be better met by another solution.

You can learn how to improve your product's retention by exploring the decision-making processes of churners.

Since decisions to cancel usually happen weeks, months, or even years before the actual cancellation, you have to go back in time to understand the sequence of events that led up to their cancellation.

Switch interviews (Chapter #8) are the ideal tool for this job.

To conduct Switch interviews, recruit 10-15 users who have recently cancelled their accounts. If your product is freemium, consider also interviewing freemium users who recently stopped using your product. You can focus on users whose usage falls just outside the regular usage window.

You will generally need to compensate these users for their time. They've most likely moved on, and have already shown a lack of interest in your product. You can use the recruiting guide under Building Blocks to help with recruitment.

Through these interviews, you should build the timeline of events leading to their cancellation. You can ask questions like:

- *Why did you initially sign up for [Product]?*
- *What was your previous experience with [Solution Space]?*
- *Did you evaluate other products?*
- *What were you using [Product] for? How often were you using it?*

- *When was the first time you had the thought that maybe [Product] wasn't going to work for you?*
- *What happened the last time that you used [Product] for [Job to be Done]?*
- *What happened the first time you had [Job to be Done] that you didn't use [Product] for?*
- *Why did you cancel the day that you cancelled? Why that day, and not the day before or after?*
- *What are you using now? How do you feel it compares to [Product]?*
- *What happened the day you started to move to the new [Product]? Why did you start that day and not after?*
- *How much do you feel [Product] improves [Job to be Done]?*
- *What is the biggest benefit of [Product]?*
- *What would it take for you to reconsider subscribing to [Product]?*

Your goal isn't to try to win back customers one by one. Your goal is to understand how to increase the habit-forming aspects of your product, and to find ways to solve the issues that drove these customers away.

You can summarize your findings using the Four Forces diagram presented earlier in this chapter.

First, identify the push and pull motivations. *What brought them to your product and what made them leave?*

Next, map their existing habits and anxieties.

Position your findings in the appropriate categories (push, pull, anxiety, and habit). Keep interviewing switchers until patterns begin to emerge.

Once you start to get a grip on why customers churn, consider systematizing the way that you capture cancellation reasons by, for example, prompting users before you let them cancel.

Keep whatever survey you create short. Ask open-ended questions like:

- *What is the primary reason why you decided to cancel your account?*
- *How has [Product] benefited you?*
- *What did you like about the product?*
- *What didn't you like about the product?*
- *What would have prevented you from leaving?*
- *How can we improve?*

You can use the answers to improve your product.

Learn from these answers and make the necessary adjustments to keep users and customers around. After all, as entrepreneur Jason Langella says: *"If you don't appreciate your customers, someone else will."*

Analyzing Delightion

"Absence of cancellation is not proof of the presence of delightion.[104]"

Dharmesh Shah
HubSpot Co-Founder & CTO

With the increase in global competition for markets, satisfying customer expectations is no longer enough.

As W. Edwards Deming says: *"It will not suffice to have customers that are merely satisfied. An unhappy customer will switch. Unfortunately, a satisfied customer may also switch, on the theory that he could not lose much, and might gain."*

Every customer interaction is an opportunity to delight and to create word of mouth from your product. Stewart Butterfield, Slack co-founder and CEO says: *"Every customer interaction is a marketing opportunity. If you go above and beyond on the customer service side, people are much more likely to recommend you."*

So, *is your product delightful?*

The best way to evaluate delight is to use a disconfirmation scale (based on expectation confirmation theory[105]).

A disconfirmation scale asks respondents to rate whether an experience was better, the same, or worse than expected.

The input, a multi-point scale, can be captured by email, via an In-App message, or via a survey:

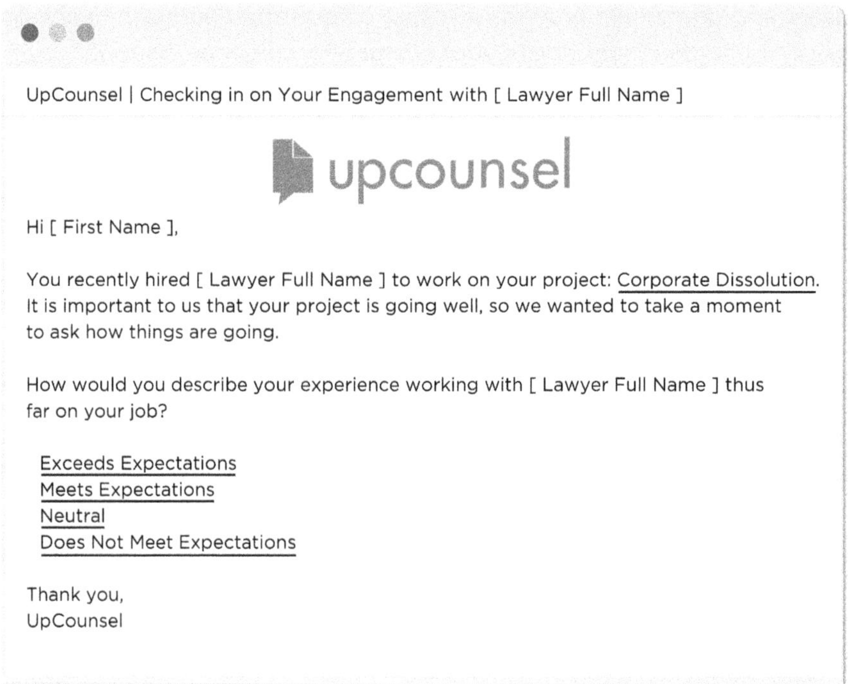
UpCounsel | Checking in on Your Engagement with [Lawyer Full Name]

upcounsel

Hi [First Name],

You recently hired [Lawyer Full Name] to work on your project: Corporate Dissolution. It is important to us that your project is going well, so we wanted to take a moment to ask how things are going.

How would you describe your experience working with [Lawyer Full Name] thus far on your job?

Exceeds Expectations
Meets Expectations
Neutral
Does Not Meet Expectations

Thank you,
UpCounsel

Figure 12.3 - Example of a Disconfirmation Scale Survey

Because, in some ways, delight is an extreme form of satisfaction, it makes sense to look at data in relation to customer satisfaction.

Expectation confirmation theory surveys compare expectations against the experience. They look at three different states:

1. **Confirmation**: *Did the experience meet the expectations?*
2. **Positive disconfirmation**: *Did it exceed the expectations?*
3. **Negative disconfirmation**: *Did it fall below the expectations?*

Answers will obviously be subjective—we all have our own standards and expectations.

With this survey, an unexpected positive experience can be viewed as delight. Responses can be used on their own, or calculated as a score using values -1 (negative), 0 (confirmation), and 1 (positive disconfirmation).

It can be interesting to dig further and understand which part(s) of the experience most influenced delight or dissatisfaction by asking a series of follow up questions:

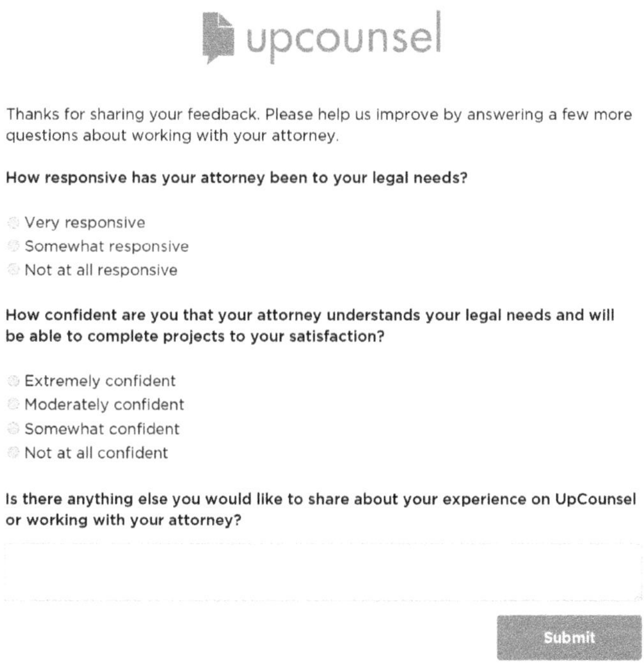
upcounsel

Thanks for sharing your feedback. Please help us improve by answering a few more questions about working with your attorney.

How responsive has your attorney been to your legal needs?

- Very responsive
- Somewhat responsive
- Not at all responsive

How confident are you that your attorney understands your legal needs and will be able to complete projects to your satisfaction?

- Extremely confident
- Moderately confident
- Somewhat confident
- Not at all confident

Is there anything else you would like to share about your experience on UpCounsel or working with your attorney?

Submit

Figure 12.4 - Example of Follow up Questions

Venture capitalist Tomasz Tunguz points to two key drivers of customer delightion[106]:

1. making the product evolve quickly; and
2. great customer support.

In Chapter #16 we will look at deeper analyses to help define improvements that can delight our customers.

Analyzing Support Communications

> "I'm (almost) always encouraged when I hear people complain about the service, because it means that people care."

Daniel Ek
Spotify Co-founder & CEO

What if you had access to not one, not two, but an army of researchers?

In too many organizations, support is perceived as a cost center—something organizations need to have, but would prefer to do without. Too often, this function gets siloed off. The insights that support specialists come across every day never make it to the product team.

As a result, 80-90% of the customers who complain end up more unhappy after their complaints has been handled than before they ever spoke to support[107].

This can hardly be blamed on support. The feedback received was never made to have an impact on what customers care most about: the product. Insights got lost on the way.

Done well, support can be a strong predictor of future sales. It can also help generate an almost endless stream of customer insights and referrals.

Some of the highest-performing organizations on the market have trained their support staff on JTBD theory. To get to the heart of the matter, they ask customers about their reasonings and struggles. Then they structure the insights obtained in a way that makes them usable by other teams within the organization.

At his fifth startup, Drift, David Cancel, decided to take *learning from support* to the next level. This led him to create The Spotlight Framework[108] to help make customer feedback actionable.

He says: *"People tend to focus on the wrong part of the feedback [they're getting]. Instead of focusing on the root cause or underlying issue behind the feedback, they focus on the subject of that feedback."*

The part of customer feedback that teams should be focusing on is the type of questions that users are asking.

David recommends categorizing feedback into the following three buckets:

1. user experience issues;
2. product marketing issues; and
3. positioning issues.

User experience issues tend to start with:

- *How do I...?*
- *What happens when...?*
- *I tried to...*

For example, *"How do I create a new spreadsheet?"*.

When customers ask similar questions, they are already aware that the product can create spreadsheets. They just don't know *how* to go about doing it.

Product marketing feedback tends to start with:

- *Can you/I...?*
- *How do you compare to...?*
- *How are you different than...?*
- *Why should I use you for/to...?*

For example, *"Can you guys integrate with Salesforce?"*. When users or customers are asking these types of questions, they are trying to understand what the product can and cannot do.

If the product actually has a particular feature, and questions about this feature come up often, it can be a good idea to improve the discoverability of this feature, or to promote it to certain user types.

Lastly, David says that positioning feedback often starts with:

- *I'm probably not your target customer, but...*
- *I'm sure I'm wrong, but I thought...*

Positioning feedback almost reads like apologies. An example of similar feedback might be *"I'm probably not your target customer, but could I actually embed your tool on my website?"*

If the customer asking the question matches your *best fit* customer profile, there may be something wrong with your positioning, which is leading qualified prospects to think that your product isn't for them.

Spotlight Framework Cheat Sheet

User Experience	Product Marketing	Positioning
How do I...	Can you/I...	I'm probably not your target customer...
What happens when...	How do you compare to...	I'm sure I'm wrong but I thought...
I tried to...	How are you different than...	
	Why should I use you for/to...	

Figure 12.5 - The Spotlight Framework's Cheat Sheet

Understand the type of questions users are asking. Categorize the feedback in these three buckets. Make it available across the organization.

Track the evolution of feedback categories over time: *Are issues getting fixed? Are there issues that are getting worse? Any new issues bubbling up?*

If you have a help, FAQ, or support section on your site, track search queries. Keywords will tend to be very precise: *What are your users searching for? What struggles do they face?*

Sachin Rekhi recommends running every search query again to make sure that users are getting good results. You can then improve the results to reduce the support work downstream.

Customers are not product thinkers. Focus on problems, not solutions when evaluating support feedback.

REFERRAL

Analyzing Product Virality

> "Refine your messaging until it spreads for free, *then* start to put money behind it.[109]"
>
> Austen Allred
> Lambda School Co-Founder & CEO

Acquiring customers is becoming difficult and expensive.

Content marketing is getting saturated. Facebook and Google ads—60.9% of all ad spend[110]—are increasingly competitive. Marketers are becoming smarter, and there are now fewer channels to grow from.

As a result, customer acquisition costs (CACs) increased by nearly 50%

over the past five years[111].

To counter this, more and more businesses have turned to their product to drive new acquisition— through word of mouth, viral loops, or other product-led growth mechanics.

The reality is that it's more important than ever to understand how a cohort of new users can lead to the acquisition of new users.

This measure is sometimes called a viral coefficient—where a coefficient (or K-factor) above one means that each user brings in more users, while a coefficient above 1.6 means that the product has 'gone viral'—and it can be a good metric to track

In theory, this is exactly where the NPS survey *should* help by giving product teams data on which users are most likely to recommend the product. But, as mentioned in Chapter #5, the NPS has many issues, including a lack of predictive value.

It's one of the reasons why Netflix changed its NPS survey question[112] to:

> "In the last six weeks, have you referred us to a friend or colleague?"

Instead of asking users to predict their future behavior, the question collects facts. The more users answered "Yes", the faster Netflix grew. Conversely, when more customers answered "No", cancellations increased and growth slowed down. The new question was better correlated to the company's growth.

You can use a similar question. As a follow up, consider asking:

- *Why did you decide to recommend [Product]?*
- *How have you explained [Product] to friends or colleagues?*
- *What is the primary benefit that you have received from [Product]?*

Analyzing the responses to these open-ended questions—looking at the profiles of the people who did recommend your product—will help you find better messaging to amplify sharing on the market.

The impact gets magnified when the same message gets amplified via word of mouth, reviews, and social media.

If your product requires many users within the same organization to start using your product, you need to give them the tools to sell and promote it internally. The more visibility your product has with stakeholders, the more likely it is that team members will start using it.

As you start to make the process more systematic, you can use the "Aha moments" to ask people to share, tell a friend about the product, or refer new customers.

Find the Aha moments (Chapter #14), productize the sharing loops, and reduce sign-up friction to improve product virality.

Where the Net Promoter Score Fails

> "NPS is the Ecstasy of business metrics. People use it because everyone else is. You think it's helping you. (It's not.) It's easy to get addicted to it. It's really hard to quit using it. It distorts your perception of reality. "Consultants" are happy to keep selling it to you.[113]"

Jared Spool
UX Influencer

The NPS is a metric that was developed and trademarked by Fred Reichheld, Bain & Company, and Satmetrix Systems in 2003.

Its original aim was to help gauge the loyalty of a company's customer relationships.

The score is calculated based on responses to a single question: *"How likely is it that you would recommend our [Company / Product / Service] to a friend or colleague?"*, expressed on a 11-point scale (0 to 10).

The resulting scores range from -100 to +100, with scores from -100 to 0 indicating issues, scores of 0 to 30 indicating that there's still room for progress, and scores above 30 indicating that your company's doing great.

An NPS above 70—like Apple's—means that your company is generating a lot of positive word of mouth on the market.

There are lots of reasons why more than two thirds of the Fortune 1000 companies are tracking their NPS[114]:

- It's a simple question, which makes it easy for customers to respond to.
- It *feels* actionable. After all, everyone's work can impact customer satisfaction.
- It creates a score that a company can benchmark against.
- It seems like a helpful proxy for creating organic word of mouth customer acquisition.
- It's easy to understand, and was originally supported by Harvard[115].

In spite of all this, criticism of the NPS survey has been mounting. Many companies misuse the data. They use it interchangeably as a means to express customer happiness, or love of a product.

It's also a lagging metric. It's hard to know exactly how to drive up or down the score. *Did my work improve the NPS?* Teams can make a lot of progress without seeing their work reflected in the overarching score.

It is also a projection. People are terrible at predicting their future behaviors. Asking "how likely" someone is to do something is misleading at best.

You may also be selling in a market in which your customers don't know anyone else like them. Their friends or family might not need your product. They may be getting a lot of value from your product, but still, in the end, give you a low NPS.

Last, but not least, organizations often ask the question for the wrong reasons. They want the benchmark, the positive ranking, but not the insights that come with it.

The NPS is easy to game. During our interview, customer experience expert Karl Gilis shared a story about a visit to a Volvo dealership. Upon receiving his vehicle, he was told: *"Oh, you'll receive a survey from Volvo. Please give us a 10."* The staff was hoping to win an award, not create a positive customer experience.

With all that said, NPS surveys can be useful. To get the greatest value from them, I recommend asking follow up questions based on the scores. For example:

- **Detractors** (Scores 0 to 6): *Can you tell us how we can do better in the future?*
- **Passives** (Scores 7 and 8): *What would persuade you to use us more often?*
- **Promoters** (Scores 9 and 10): *What did you love about the experience?*

You will get a lot of value from these open-ended questions.

Making Progress

"No amount of clever marketing tricks, product design patterns or user interface (UI) trends will ever outperform leveraging the basic knowledge of how your audience perceives their current situation, and how they would like it improved."

Samuel Hulick

A lot of different analyses can help reveal leaks in your funnel.

Surely a business has to address all these challenges at once if it's going to grow fast? That's the reason why businesses raise capital and hire people, *right?*

Looking at the trend of businesses post-PMF burning capital, hiring too fast, this would seem like the thing to do, but the reality is actually quite different.

It has been proven that goals are best achieved sequentially[116]. As a business, it pays to focus on a North Star metric, or on one or two key goals at a time. This way, it becomes easier to evaluate performance and to understand which actions drive results. Teams get to focus more energy on fewer goals, which makes it easier for them to understand what really matters.

Entrepreneur and investor Dave McClure created the AARRR framework[117], also known as Pirate Metrics, to make this idea clear.

In McClure's model, innovators measure how users go through five key steps of the customer life cycle:

1. **Acquisition**: visitors entering the funnel through various channels
2. **Activation**: visitors enjoying a first experience with the product
3. **Revenue**: users purchasing the product, becoming customers
4. **Retention**: users coming back, becoming loyal customers
5. **Referral**: users or customers referring the product to friends or colleagues

A prospect gets **A**cquired, he/she is then **A**ctivated, converted for **R**evenue, **R**etained, and if the experience is positive, he/she can **R**efer the product[118].

By tracking the full life cycle as a funnel and evaluating cohorts of users, it becomes easier to identify break points.

A funnel for a product might look a bit like this:

	Week 1
Users in Cohort	1000
Acquisition	
Visits the blog	100.0%
Clicks a link to the homepage	15.0%
Clicks the signup button	2.5%
Begins signup process	2.0%
Completes signup	1.7%
Visitor is considered Signed Up	17
Activation	
Views 1st step of onboarding process	1.7%
Completes 1st step	1.6%
Completes 2nd step	1.3%
Completes 3rd step (optional)	1.2%
Accesses the main interface	1.2%
User is considered Activated	12
Retention	
User comes back to the product	0.6%
User uses the product 3 times	0.3%
User is considered Retained	3
Revenue	
User upgrades his subscription	0.2%
User pays for a second month	0.2%
User pays for a third month	0.2%

Figure 12.6 - Example of a Funnel Using the AARRR Framework

The questions this funnel help answer are, for example: *Of the people that visited the blog (1,000), how many also visited the homepage (150)? Clicked the sign-up button (25)? Actually completed the sign-up process (17)?*

By looking at the drop from one step to the next and comparing data with both internal and external benchmarks, you should be able to find the bottlenecks—opportunities to both learn and improve performance. You can get started analyzing your funnel using the template at **solvingproduct.com/funnel**.

Once you have identified a drop off, you should analyze the step through various lenses, for example:

- *Do users acquired through different channels behave differently?*
- *Are there regions, countries, or cities that perform better than others?*
- *Can users on mobile, tablet, or desktop complete the same tasks?*
- *Are there considerations in terms of site performance?*

This will help you create hypotheses for improvements and experiments.

To make progress, focus on one or two main goals, make improvements, and iterate. Once you begin to get results, move on to the next break point.

By following this process, you'll be able to continuously grow performance across the entire customer journey.

Case Study
How Grubhub Built Product Habits

"One excellent way to find insights that can increase conversion is to stop focusing on why people say "yes", and zoom in on what makes them say "no"."

Gregory Ciotti
Shopify Content Marketer

In 2008, Casey Winters joined Grubhub, the online food-ordering marketplace, as the 15th employee. At the time, the startup had 40,000 users, it had found PMF, and it was growing.

As the company's first marketing hire, Casey was responsible for accelerating the company's growth. To start improving the service, and to set the right expectations for product usage, Casey wanted to understand how loyal users were.

Based on research that the team had done—calling restaurants asking about delivery orders—they had figured out that the average person ordered delivery food once or twice a month. Casey wanted to understand if Grubhub was generally the preferred food ordering option for its users.

Since they didn't have a research team, or a full product team for that matter[119], Casey and the product designer took on the roles of researchers.

They started their research by sending a survey. The questions they wanted answered were how often users ordered delivery, and how often they ordered delivery through Grubhub. What they wanted to figure out was how many people used Grubhub regularly for delivery, but not for every order. And conversely, how many users relied exclusively on Grubhub for delivery.

To their surprise, 40% of respondents were ordering more delivery outside the platform than on Grubhub.

To understand why these users weren't always using Grubhub, Casey began calling them. From discussion after discussion, the reasons began to emerge.

To quantify the importance of the reasons he had collected, he then sent a survey to a larger part of their user base. The survey listed the answers he had collected and asked: *"When you order delivery and don't use Grubhub, what's the most common reason why?"*

Very quickly, they learned that the main reason why users were ordering delivery outside of the marketplace was that they had been ordering from those restaurants before Grubhub came around.

These surveys and interviews helped Casey and his team understand what was holding users back. It helped them improve their onboarding and their segmentation strategy.

Casey's ability to combine both customer research and marketing strategy helped him lead Grubhub's user and revenue growth to 3M users and beyond. In April 2014, the company went public.

Taking Action

1. Create your product's funnel using the AARRR framework.
2. Identify the biggest break points in your funnel. Analyze data from different angles to understand the composition at each break point.
3. Focus on the biggest break points. Select the best analyses to understand causality and move your product forward.
4. Over time, conduct all the analyses in this chapter.
5. *Collaborating with others?* Share a PDF version of this chapter at **solvingproduct.com/chapter-12**.

13 / 26

Understand-ing Why Customers Buy

Time to act on your findings. Use the techniques in this chapter to **understand why customers are buying your product**.

> "Purchase frequency has to do with the nature of the problem, degree of urgency, and user satisfaction with the product.[120]"

Ish Baid
Virtually Founder & CEO

Earlier on, we mentioned that maximizing deal size and conversions wasn't a priority. Learning was. Well, things change.

At this stage, it pays to start understanding the real economic drivers of your business.

What are customers buying? Why do they buy? Why do they buy again? At what price is your product too expensive?

The first sections of this book were about making sure that the product you were building was valuable, and that you could get paid for it. This stage is about building and growing a sustainable business.

Whether you have already raised capital, intend to raise capital, or plan to fund growth through sales and revenue, you stand to benefit from improving your sales funnel.

If you have already raised capital, you'll extend your runway and get to postpone your next fundraise (fundraising is time-consuming!). If you intend to raise capital, you'll get more data points, and solidify your fundraising position. And if you plan to fund growth through revenue, there you go. Your business will simply go faster.

This step is about refining your pitch and improving your sales process.

What benefits should you promote? How do you talk about them? How do you overcome objections and reduce sales friction?

> *If you were a service company...*
>
> *This step would be about figuring out why customers choose to work with you, and why some of your customers end up more satisfied than others.*

Techniques You Can Use

Figuring out *why* customers buy your product involves getting closer to the customers that are getting the most value from your product, and trying to understand why they feel your product is valuable.

- **Learning Through Behavior Segmentation** will help you identify the segments within your user base that are getting the most value from your product.

- **Understanding Your Product's True Value** will help you flesh out the real reasons why these customers agree to buy and rebuy your product.

It's a good idea to conduct both analyses and learn before attempting to scale your business.

Learning Through Behavior Segmentation

"Just because someone walks in and buys a high-margin good doesn't necessarily mean you should prioritize that person as a customer."

Jason Stanley
Element AI Design Research Lead

In spite of your best efforts to acquire users who match your *best fit* customer profile, you'll probably notice that:

- Some customers are engaging much more than others.
- Different goals and use cases have started to emerge.
- Some customers are spending more than others.
- Users from other segments with different needs are getting value from your product.
- Your homogenous group of customers will start to appear less homogeneous.

As your business grows, it's normal to start noticing a wide range of usage and consumption patterns.

You might have built your product with the aim of attracting a certain type of users, but if over time you notice that other profiles are getting more value from your product, you would be foolish not to adjust your targeting.

Amplified, today's edge cases can become tomorrow's best opportunities.

Researchers at EPFL University in Lausanne, Switzerland have concluded that 73% of startups ultimately pivoted to other markets once they realized that their initial market wouldn't be able to support their growth[121].

Are you sure you're focused on the right users and customers?

At this point, it makes sense to start looking at the composition of your customer base. You may already be leaving money on the table.

To start discovering the segments in your user base, you should define success along three key dimensions:

1. **Revenue**: Customer lifetime value (CLV)—how much revenue is generated over the entire duration of the customer relationship—is often a good way to find your highest-spending customers.
2. **Engagement/Retention**: A good way to evaluate engagement might be how often core product actions are performed, *habituated* users (Chapter #12), or 7-, 14-, or 28-day retention rates.
3. **Referral/Word of Mouth**: For word of mouth, it can be the number of referrals sent or completed.

Looking at the breakdown of those results, create three buckets:

1. **Your best customers**: the top one percent in terms of engagement, revenue, and referrals;
2. **The next best**: customers ranked within the 2nd to 10th percents;
3. **Your worst customers**: the bottom 10%.

Depending on how technical you are, you might be able to find these users with SQL, a CRM, database exports, or by looking at people analytics in tools like Mixpanel, Amplitude or Intercom.

You should focus on these three groups because the top one percent represents your product's "fans", your advocates.

The next 10% gives you a good comparison point. It can help reveal low-hanging fruits.

The last 10% helps you define who you probably *shouldn't* be targeting.

Randomly recruit 15-20 candidates in each of these buckets. Schedule 20-minute interviews.

You'll want to understand who they are, what need(s) the product solves for them, and what value they perceive.

You can get started with the following questions:

- *How would you describe your role as [Role]?*
- *What does success look like for you?*
- *Why did you initially sign up for [Product]?*
- *Did you evaluate other tools?*
- *What was your previous experience with [Solution Space]?*
- *What made you decide to [Buy / Use] the product?*
- *Can you walk me through how you use [Product]?*
- *What is the main value you feel you've received from the product?*
- *Why do you keep using the product?*
- *What is the main [Problem] you feel the product solves for you?*
- *If we took away [Product] from you, what would be the things you miss most? What would you use as alternative?*

Through these interviews, you are trying to evaluate different positionings.

What are the commonalities in the stories of your best customers? What use cases tend to lead to sustained product usage? What needs do your best customers have? What value do they seek? How do they explain your product's core value?

It's not uncommon for similar analyses to reveal that your best customers are actually quite different from who you thought they were.

Once patterns are starting to emerge, consider expanding your research by sending a survey to a larger group of customers. You can ask open-ended questions like those asked during the interviews. If you feel like the patterns are clear, consider providing multiple choice answers, always making sure respondents have a way to input free-form answers.

You can use the guide on Creating Effective Surveys in Building Blocks at the end of this book to guide your work.

At LANDR, through a similar analysis, we noticed that occupations seemed to have a big impact on the CLV.

We used the basic occupation groupings that we had uncovered through interviews, and surveyed a large part of our user base to understand what kind of work they did.

Since we weren't sure about the groupings, we made sure respondents had the option to add other occupations.

Although we weren't able to get answers from all users, the much larger sample of respondents helped refine our segmentation.

Kieran Flanagan, VP of marketing at HubSpot, recommends using regression analyses—a statistical process for estimating the relationship between variables—to see what users in your best-performing segments did in their first week after sign-up, how they got onboarded, and how they ultimately became customers. The insights gained from these analyses will help you improve overall performance.

If you intend to use the segments you uncovered to create personas—fictional profiles based on interview data used to summarize information about customers—you should definitely validate them by surveying larger populations.

Once you know which segments perform best, you can make prioritization decisions. The fewer segments you target, the clearer your messaging will be, and the more certainty you'll have that your pitch will connect.

Understanding Your Product's True Value

> "People's reasons for buying things often don't match up with the company's reason for selling them.[122]"
>
> Jason Fried

There's a reason why hiring a bunch of salespeople or scaling sales often fails at this stage. The Growth Stage is about learning, but it can easily be mistaken for a process problem.

Many businesses set up processes, hire sales staff, and expect sales to start rolling in. Salespeople, used to selling well-defined products with clear benefits, then fail to meet expectations.

The reality is that there are big differences between the people who first figure out the sales strategy, and those who execute it.

As Jason M. Lemkin says[123]: *"You can't hire some magic salesperson to "get you more sales". You have to figure it out first yourself."*

Unless you know *why* customers buy, and then buy again from you, you're not ready to scale.

There are countless examples of businesses that misunderstood the real reasons why customers were buying their products. As a result, they sold to the wrong customers, and eventually, growth stalled.

In our interview[124], demand generation expert Rene Bastijans shared the story of an e-Learning business he was working with. This company had marketed its product as a platform to help share knowledge internally.

Through interviews, Rene realized that buyers were struggling so much with finding time to do their work that they were using the software to onboard new employees, so that they could have more time to do their work. Employees were leaving all the time, and buyers were looking for a platform to onboard employees, so that they could focus on getting things done.

Very different, *right?*

April Dunford explains: *"Often, the product we end up with is not what we started out to build. Our email system seems more like group chat, our database seems more like an analytics platform and our cake has become muffins. This transformation happens so gradually that we, the product creators, often don't notice it. We still see the product as the thing we set out to build. What else could it possibly be?"*

To be able to operationalize your sales process, you have to understand *why* prospects buy. The best way to do this is through Switch interviews, which evaluate purchase decisions.

Recruit a random sample of 15-20 customers from your best-performing segment. Ask questions like:

- *How did you first hear about [Product] ? What did you know about it at the time?*
- *What was going on in your life at that time?*
- *Did you imagine what life would be like with the product? And what were you expecting?*
- *What made you decide to sign up and try the product?*
- *Did anyone else weigh in on the decision?*
- *Did you evaluate other products?*
- *Once you signed up, how did the product compare to your expectations?*
- *Did you feel you had all the information you needed to get started?*
- *What made you decide to buy the product in the first place?*
- *What was the main thing that convinced you?*
- *Did anything make you hesitate in buying [Product]?*

- *Now that you have [Product] what can you do that you couldn't do before?*
- *What is the main value you feel you've received from the product?*

What were they hoping to get done? How do customers want to feel or avoid feeling? How do they want to be perceived by others?

By asking about the Job they were hiring your product for, and asking what specific value they got from the product, you can compare expectations with reality. You'll also be able to get a feel for the real value drivers.

It can be a good idea to compare their answers to those of re-purchasers—customers who have been subscribed for several months (monthly plan), several years (annual plan), or who have bought several times (one-off purchases).

Repeat purchases are a great sign that your product keeps delivering value to customers.

For interviews with re-purchasers, you can ask questions like:

- *What made you decide to buy the product in the first place?*
- *What was the main thing that convinced you?*
- *Why did you decide to buy again?*
- *What were your criteria for this decision?*
- *What is the main value you feel you've received from the product?*
- *Did that change over time?*
- *Now that you've used [Product] for [X] months, do you feel that the product's value has increased or decreased? Why?*
- *Have you recommended the product to anyone else? Why?*
- *Have you evaluated going on the annual plan?*
- *Why did you decide for/against that?*

By contrasting expectations with the reasons to buy and rebuy, you can start understanding how the perception of value evolves over time.

Do these reasons align with the reasons why you built the product? Are there patterns you weren't aware of? Are you discovering new reasons why customers use your product?

Founder of OpenView Venture Partners Scott Maxwell, says that[125] *"50% of startups have an inaccurate understanding of why customers buy".*

Dig through product usage: *Do the users you interviewed use your product in the way they say they do? Can you notice anything else from the data?*

Once you begin to figure out what customers buy, then you can start thinking about ways to drive more revenue per customer through expansion revenue.

As Pardot co-founder and ex-CEO David Cummings says[126]: *"The Holy Grail of Software-as-a-Service (SaaS)[is] a business that grows year-over-year without signing any new customers."*

Making Progress

> "Your target market is the customers who buy quickly, rarely ask for discounts and tell their friends about your offerings."
>
> April Dunford

At this step, your business should be getting a steady stream of customers. Some of these customers find value—and some don't.

This step is all about finding the customers who are getting a disproportionate amount of value from your product, contrasting their beliefs with those of other customers, and understanding the true reasons why they buy. You're trying to find the gold in your customer base.

To make progress at this step, you need to uncover:

- the Customer Job your best customers are trying to address with your product;
- their desired outcomes and how they evaluate your product;
- how they categorize your product and what they might replace it with;
- how they evaluate the ROI of your product, and how they justify continuing to pay for it;
- comparisons they make when assessing the ROI; and
- budgets that purchases come from, and whether there is competition for the same budgets.

The more precise your answers are, the better.

Contrasting the answers of your best customers with those of customers who feel like they're getting little value from your product will be revealing.

Once you have figured out *why* your top customers buy, much like the team at Clarity did below, you should be able to find ways to get more of them.

Case Study
How Clarity Learned Why Its Best Customers Buy

"Find out who you are and do it on purpose."

Dolly Parton
Singer-Songwriter

Dan Martell and Mike Wu created Clarity, a marketplace to help experts monetize their expertise, in 2012. When they started, there was no marketplace. Users could search a list of experts, sort by expertise, and schedule calls. That's all Clarity did.

This made it all the more surprising when Dan noticed that one very early adopter named Omar had spent seven thousand dollars connecting and speaking with experts in a single week.

It was so far from the norm that Dan knew he had to speak with that customer. He says: *"I needed to figure out what he believed that made him do that ROI calculation, and made him decide to pull the trigger."*

Omar had discovered the product, understood its value, and paid for half a dozen calls all on his own. Better yet, he had no relationship with the business or any of its co-founders. Over the course of their call, Dan learned that Omar used to spend a lot of money traveling to events, standing in line, waiting to ask questions to speakers and experts. Most times, his questions would only get answered at a high level because the discussion had to be relevant to everyone—it was *hit or miss*.

Now, with Clarity, Omar had access to the same quality of speakers at a fraction of the cost that he used to spend going to conferences and events. Omar couldn't believe that others didn't get that.

Dan had both found his *best fit* customer, and a core reason why people bought through the marketplace.

It turned out that Clarity was for growth-minded entrepreneurs who valued counsel, advice, and expertise. They believed that investing in themselves or their teams was worth it.

Taking a step back, looking at Omar in the context of who he was, his values and his business, Dan found that most *Omars* used Evernote. In 2012, Evernote was an advanced tool. It could be seen as a signal that entrepreneurs were collecting information, and that they were investing in tools to better themselves or their business.

Dan and his team used this new-found knowledge to find other *best fit* customers like Omar.

This discovery helped propel Clarity forward. At the time of its acquisition in 2015, more than 17,000 entrepreneurs were using Clarity to learn from other experts and promote their expertise.

Taking Action

1. Dig into the composition of your user base, and analyze the customer segments that extract the most value from your product.
2. Recruit engaged customers for interviews. Understand why they buy, and how they rationalize their purchase decision.
3. Clarify the value *best fit* customers are getting from your product.
4. Refine your targeting and try to understand at a deeper level the characteristics of your best customers.
5. Don't attempt to scale unless you know *why* customers buy, and buy again.
6. *Collaborating with others?* Share a PDF version of this chapter at **solvingproduct.com/chapter-13**.

14 / 26

Aligning What You Sell with How You Sell It

Now that you know *what* customers buy, make sure your funnel sets the right expectations. Use these techniques to **align what you sell with how you sell it**.

"Concentrate positioning on "consid-eration" rather than "retention" attributes. Customers who don't see enough value to consider buying the product will never stick around long enough to experience retention attributes such as your excellent customer service."

April Dunford

Knowing why customers buy is one thing. Communicating it is another.

If you can't communicate the core value of your product effectively, then you'll have a hard time attracting your *best fit* customers.

Your communications need to focus on the true value of your product. This means:

- Your ads, product descriptions, and product reviews
- Your landing pages, testimonials, and product demos
- Your emails, onboarding, and product messaging
- The way your team talks about your product
- Everything

It's common to think that a broader value proposition will appeal to a broader audience, but in fact, as Tony Ulwick reminds us: *"Precision, not vagueness, is the key to communicating a product's true value."*

The clearer your product is to prospects, the easier it is for them to make a clear "Yes" or "No" decision, and to recommend it to others.

To speed up growth, align *what* you sell with *how* you sell it.

> *If you were a service company...*
>
> *This step would be about improving the way prospects discover your work, and how they make sense of your service offering.*

Techniques You Can Use

Aligning what you sell with how you sell it means evaluating how your product is perceived and understood at different stages of the customer journey, and making sure the right story comes across.

Analyzing Sign-up Reasons will help you iterate the messaging of your funnel to attract *best fit* customers, while **Analyzing Time to Value (TTV)** will help you to optimize value discovery after prospects sign up.

Use both techniques to make sure that your user acquisition strategy attracts the right folks, and that your product quickly guides users to its core value.

Analyzing Sign-up Reasons

> "No matter how great your product is, it is very likely that 40-60% of your free trial users never see the product a second time."
>
> Samuel Hulick

People perceive and understand value differently.

Two perfectly qualified prospects can look at the same ads, landing pages, messaging, and feature sets, and come to completely different conclusions.

One might become hyper-engaged recommending your product to all his/her friends, while the other might misunderstand the product completely, posting on social media how he/she is looking for the exact product you built.

This explains Omar's frustration from the previous chapter: *Why don't they get how cool this product is?!*

But the responsibility of figuring out your product, shouldn't fall entirely on your users' shoulders.

To understand value perception, Dan Martell recommends surveying new sign-ups, asking them how they would explain the product to others:

> "How would you explain [Product] to friends or colleagues?"

Dan says that 80% of the time when he first begins working with clients, the answers to this question differ from the messaging on the company's homepage.

To get started learning about sign-up reasons, set up a single-question survey prompting users with an open-ended question.

By targeting users during their first session with a survey as an In-App message or a popup, you'll be able to capture spontaneous reactions—your users' original reason for signing up will still be fresh in their minds.

You can ask Dan's question, or you could perhaps ask:

- *When you signed up, what expectations did you have for our product?*
- *What is your main goal for using [Product]?*
- *What were the three main things that persuaded you to sign up today?*

Eventually, you could also ask about alternatives:

- *Which other options did you consider before choosing [Product]?*

This will help you to understand what product category prospects perceive your product to be in.

Look through the profiles of new sign-ups (Chapter #8)—*do they match the profile you're targeting?* If less than 30% of new sign-ups resemble your target profile, then improve your messaging and acquisition strategy.

Focus on the responses of users that *do* match your target profile—*do at least 30% of them 'get it'?*

Iterate until more than 60% of the users from your target profile sign up for your product's core value.

As advertising expert Dave Trott says[127]: *"Once you know the niche your market's in, you can spend a lot of time publicly turning off everyone else."*

Quickly disqualifying wrong-fit prospects will help free up resources, and will allow you to spend more time acquiring the right users, and getting them to experience the product value.

Refine your messaging until sign-up reasons match your product's core value. This begins with setting the right expectations.

Analyzing Time to Value (TTV)

> "The sooner you help people experience a meaningful quick win in the product, the sooner your users will come back to your product and eventually turn into customers.[128]"

Wes Bush
Product-Led Growth Author

Once the right users are signing up for the right reasons, you've won, *right?*

Not quite.

As we saw in Stage #2, there's a difference between buying into a value proposition, and experiencing the actual value of a product.

Once users sign up, your goal is to establish your product's value quickly, by getting users to their desired outcomes.

The faster you can convince them that your product addresses their needs, the faster you'll create engaged and happy subscribers.

To do that, you need to:

1. identify the must-have experience in your product; and
2. look for ways to front-load that experience.

This means getting users to the *Aha moment* as quickly as possible.

Activation, or activation rate, is the metric that is most often associated with a user's Aha moment. It's also the metric that has the most influence over conversion and long-term retention.

The better users understand the value of your product, the more likely they are to use it, come to depend on it, and be happy to pay and keep paying for it.

The problem with activation and activation metrics is that, unlike most of the other Pirate Metrics like acquisition, revenue, or referral, your activation metric will be unique to your product. You need to find what drives the Aha moment for your product.

To do this analysis, you have to understand which actions or behaviors are most closely correlated with long-term retention.

This can be done by calculating the correlation coefficient—the strength of the relationship between two variables—between specific actions and retention.

For example:

- Users who stayed engaged more than 6 months AND customized their profile information;
- Users who stayed engaged more than 6 months AND used the product daily; or
- Users who stayed engaged more than 6 months AND live in the United States, etc.

By going through all scenarios, you can identify the behaviors that are most closely correlated with long-term retention.

Analytics tools like Amplitude have built-in functionalities to help get this data quickly:

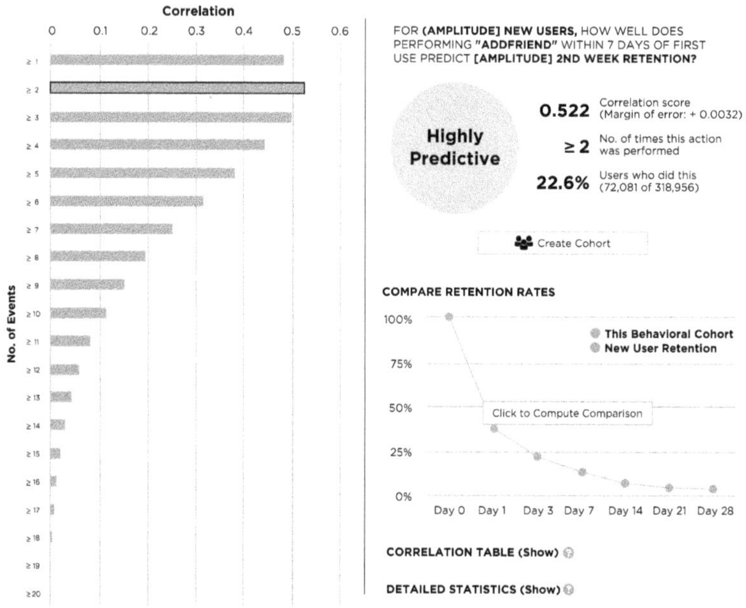

Figure 14.1 - Compass by Amplitude

The same analysis can allow you to uncover which actions are most closely correlated with conversion, referrals, or any other goal.

It can help you map and sequence your Aha moments, to get the right users to the value in your product as quickly as possible.

For example, if your product was a smartphone, your Aha moments might be:

1. quick setup;
2. calendar and email sync;
3. camera quality;
4. video content suggestions; and
5. easy app management.

Helping new users discover these features in this sequence would help them realize how valuable and essential the smartphone could be for their work, or for their personal life.

This concept is also sometimes called the Minimum Path to Awesome (MPA)—the optimal path to value discovery in your product.

If your product is complicated to use, or if it takes a long time to experience a first win, then you will have a hard time scaling the product in a self-serve mode.

So, what action is most correlated with long-term retention? What are the absolute minimum steps required for a user to experience that value? How long is your TTV?

Create a visual diagram where you map out chronologically and sequentially what users need to do in order to get to that value. Cut anything that's unnecessary.

Users should experience the product value during the first session. Your product, emails, and onboarding flow should help guide users to the product value.

As product onboarding expert Samuel Hulick says, *"In a lot of ways, a website is really just a conversation, with one side of it pre-recorded."*

Make sure the conversation speaks to the right problems and value drivers, and has the right prompts in the right sequence.

Keep iterating until at least 35-45% of your sign-ups "activate", and become active users of your product.

Making Progress

> "If you are not advancing the sale, you are diminishing the sale. "Does it advance the sale?" It's a tough test."

Dan Kennedy
Direct Response Marketing Strategist

Improving alignment from acquisition to sign-up and to value discovery is an iterative process.

It starts by bringing in enough qualified traffic. *Does your site attract at least a few hundred visitors a day?* If it doesn't, consider using ads to attract more qualified leads.

You should set up a testing cadence of one to four weeks to evaluate your funnel from acquisition, to sign-up, to activation and retention.

Focus on one goal at a time. Start by analyzing the quality of your traffic (Chapter #12). Iterate until at least 30% of your traffic is qualified.

Once that's the case, move on to sign-ups. Iterate your value proposition, pitch, and benefits until the right users sign up for the right reasons.

Once 60% of your target users are signing up for your product's core value, move on to improving value discovery. Keep iterating until at least 35-45% of sign-ups "activate".

Experiment. This phase is never really over. Your pitch, messaging, and sales processes can always be improved. Slack, for example, tested more than 40 versions of their homepage messaging[129], and they're still testing today.

Your funnel should always reflect your latest understanding of what makes your *best fit* customers come to consider your product.

Case Study
How PandaDoc Found Its 'Best' Messaging

"[Intercom] uses Jobs as an onboarding tool. They're doing interviews all the time. Partly it's to get language. If you look at it, one of the things that they kind of morphed from is this notion of 'help me onboard' to 'help me message'. Messaging was what people were asking for in the language they used though, when we first found it before they had the messaging language, it was 'people are coming but they're stuck and they can't actually use my product'. And so they've now changed it to onboarding and messaging. They're constantly monitoring how that language is evolving as the technology is changing."

Bob Moesta

I first met PandaDoc's founding CTO, Sergey Barysiuk, in Minsk, Belarus where the company got its start. Sergey and his co-founder, Mikita Mikado, founded the sales proposal software company as a side project for their consulting business in 2011.

A few years in, after going in full time and landing thousands of customers, it felt like their brand promises (Look professional and Close deals faster) no longer aligned with the value customers were getting from the product. Sergey set out on a project to update PandaDoc's messaging.

What they wanted to get at was the true Job their customers were hiring PandaDoc for.

Sergey wanted to start with what customers were saying about their product. To get customer data, he used Python and Scrapy to *scrape* 365 product reviews from G2, and 657 from Capterra.

The data had been well structured by the review sites. Each review had pros, cons, demographic data, and a rating along many dimensions:

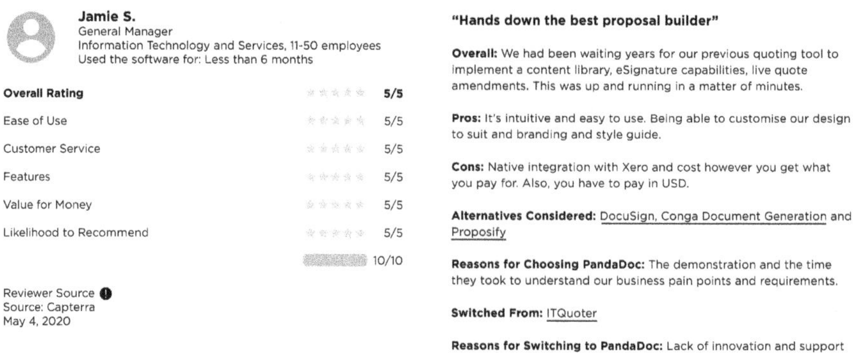

Figure 14.2 - Example of a Review of PandaDoc's Product

To make sense of the reviews, Sergey created word clouds using Voyant Tools' concordance tools[130].

To identify the functional Job, Sergey had to get to different elements:

- **Verb**: what customers were trying to achieve;
- **Object**: what work customers want to get done; and
- **Context**: what triggers lead to product usage.

Since the object was the most obvious of the three, Sergey decided to start there.

He looked for the action words used in conjunction with 'Proposal', 'Quote', 'Contract', 'Agreement', and 'Document', the words most commonly used by customers.

Across each analysis, the action words that kept coming up were 'Create', 'Send', 'Sign', and 'Track'. And of all the object words he evaluated, 'document' was the one that appeared the most frequently.

To get to the benefits, Sergey looked at the keywords most frequently associated with 'process'.

When looking at the benefits that came out (Streamline, Speed up, and Simplifies), he realized that there were other words that he had overlooked. It turned out that 'easy' and 'time' came up more often than any other value words.

But, *what did 'easy' really mean?*

To figure this out, Sergey dug further into the context of the benefits:

Easy (338)

... to customize documents	... to manipulate (1)	**... to build (10)**
... to maintain (3)	... to understand (1)	... to navigate (4)
... to track (5)	... to set up (5)	... for the team (2)
... to use (110)	... to complete (1)	... to edit (4)
... to share (3)	**... to get signatures (8)**	... to manage (6)
... to send (13)	... to make a template (2)	... to learn (2)
... to customize (3)	... to style (2)	... to organize (3)
... to adopt	... to train (1)	... to generate (2)
... to produce proposals	... to find (4)	... to adjust
... to work (3)	... to fill out	... to collaborate (1)
... for the customer (6)	... to get started (2)	... to generate (1)
... to create (22)	... to configure (1)	... to modify (1)
... to update (1)	... to put together (2)	... to execute (1)

Figure 14.3 - Added Context for 'Easy'

The data confirmed his assumptions—PandaDoc was about streamlining processes.

The functional Jobs were: 1) Create and send proposals, 2) Create, send and sign contracts, and 3) Create, send and sign documents. Tracking documents came up more as a wow factor than a consistent Job.

Customers were hiring PandaDoc to create, send, track and sign proposals and contracts.

In his mind, proposals and contracts could be summed up as 'Sales Documents' while create, send, track and sign could be summed up through a 'Streamlined process'.

The resulting value proposition became:

Streamlined Process for Sales Documents

Before going all in on the new messaging, Sergey and his team decided to do an A/B test (Chapter #20) to determine which messaging worked best.

Lo and behold, the new messaging, reflecting the words of satisfied customers, increased PandaDoc's sign-up, onboarding and retention rates.

Taking Action

1. Look at the profiles of your new sign-ups: *are at least 30% of them from the segment you're targeting?*
2. If not, refine your ads, landing pages, and sign-up flow messaging, iterating until more qualified leads sign up.
3. Survey new sign-ups asking how they would explain your product to others.
4. Iterate the communication funnel until the majority of sign-ups are both qualified, and understand your product's true value.
5. Align *what* you sell with *how* you sell it before pressing on the gas pedal.

6. *Collaborating with others?* Share a PDF version of this chapter at **solvingproduct.com/chapter-14**.

15 / 26

Finding the Best Acquisition Channels for Scale

Your product is ready to scale. Use the techniques in this chapter to **accelerate your growth rate**, and **find the best acquisition channels**.

"There are two types of companies: 1) Tugboats, where growth feels like you have to put a ton of fuel in to get only a little speed out, and 2) Smooth sailors, where growth feels like wind is at your back. The difference between these two are not the common mantras of build a great product, PMF is the only thing that matters, or growth hacking.[131]"

Brian Balfour

Throughout this section, we have talked about the importance of holding off on scaling customer acquisition until most friction has been overcome.

Doing so helps us to:

1. **Get a feel for the real unit economics of the business**: Starting to establish your own benchmarks for acquisition costs, conversion rates, churn rates, and sales cycle duration will help narrow the list of channels you can use to grow your business. As Bill Aulet says: *"The length of the sales cycle is a crucial determinant in how expensive it will be for you to acquire new customers."*.

2. **Identify possible issues when attempting to scale**: Earlier, we mentioned that businesses are like Rubik's Cubes. The more parts of the Cube your team figures out, the easier it is to spot the issues. When you try to scale a business without PMF, issues compound. This makes finding the root cause of problems challenging.

Once you've reduced friction in your funnel (Chapter #12), clarified why customers buy (Chapter #13), aligned what you sell to how you sell it (Chapter #14), and got a feel for the unit economics, then you are ready to start scaling.

Congrats. Let's begin.

If you were a service company...

This step would be about finding more best fit customers, and establishing processes to get more customers.

Techniques You Can Use

On the surface, it can seem as though there are a thousand ways to acquire users and customers. In reality, however, once you factor in the specific mechanics of your organization, the list gets much shorter.

- **Analyzing Acquisition Channels** will help you create the shortlist of channels worth testing to run acquisition experiments; and
- **Analyzing Freemium Potential** will help you see if freemium should be part of your acquisition strategy.

Run through both analyses and find the best way to scale your business.

Analyzing Acquisition Channels

> "Focus on marketing strategies that are repeatable and predictable."
>
> Noah Kagan
> Sumo CEO & Co-Founder

In their seminal book, *Traction*, authors Gabriel Weinberg and Justin Mares examine the 19 channels businesses can use to acquire customers[132]:

1. Affiliate Programs
2. Business Development (BD)
3. Community Building
4. Content Marketing
5. Email Marketing
6. Engineering as Marketing
7. Existing Platforms
8. Offline Ads

9. Offline Events
10. Public Relations (PR)
11. Sales
12. Search Engine Marketing (e.g. ads on Google or Bing)
13. Search Engine Optimization (SEO)
14. Social and Display Ads (e.g. prospecting ads)
15. Speaking Engagements
16. Target Market Blogs
17. Trade Shows
18. Unconventional Public Relations (PR)
19. Viral Marketing

Although many of these channels won't grow endlessly, they can still be a part of your strategy building the top of your funnel (TOFU).

Acquisition channel hypotheses should already have begun to emerge when you were interacting with early users in the earlier parts of this book. You should explore those hypotheses one by one.

Chances are that you'll be able to find channel opportunities by looking for nascent behaviors. For example, when looking at your analytics:

- *Are there sites or platforms that have started sending traffic your way? Could any of those be scaled?*
- *Looking at campaign parameters (UTMs), are there emails or other platforms that are sending traffic to your site?*
- *Have some pieces of content grown virally? Did some of your content start to attract a lot of organic search traffic?*
- *Looking at your site's internal search, could some tangentially related searches be turned into side products or long-form pieces of content?*
- *Could some behaviors within the product be amplified?* Nomad List founder Pieter Levels recommends taking big features that could stand on their own and spinning them off to drive acquisition[133]: *Could that be an option?*

It's important to cast a wide net. Consciously or not, we tend to focus on the tactics and strategies that have made us successful in the past. At this stage, ruling out channels too quickly can hurt your ability to grow your business.

Some channels will work best at different stages in the life cycle of your business. Content marketing, for example, can take more than six months to actually start generating results[134], so it's important to plan ahead.

You need to run experiments in order to find the right acquisition channels for your business. In Chapter #20 we cover the testing process at length, but for now, you should make sure that your tests are as cheap and as fast as possible—don't spend a huge amount of time or money on your first experiments.

What you are looking for is a channel that:

- will allow you to acquire users with a *reasonable* amount of effort;
- can yield a positive ROI when you consider the time, costs, and resources involved;
- can last, at least, for the next six months;
- can attract your *best fit* customers; and
- can work for the unit economics of your business.

For each channel you evaluate, ask yourself:

1. *Can this channel allow me to directly reach prospects from our target market?* and
2. *If it works, can we scale it?*

In a famous series of posts[135], growth expert Brian Balfour explains how some businesses—based on their Costs of Acquisition (CAC) and their Customer's Lifetime Value (CLV)—won't be able to make certain channels work.

The unit economics of your business will limit the number of channels that can sustain your business.

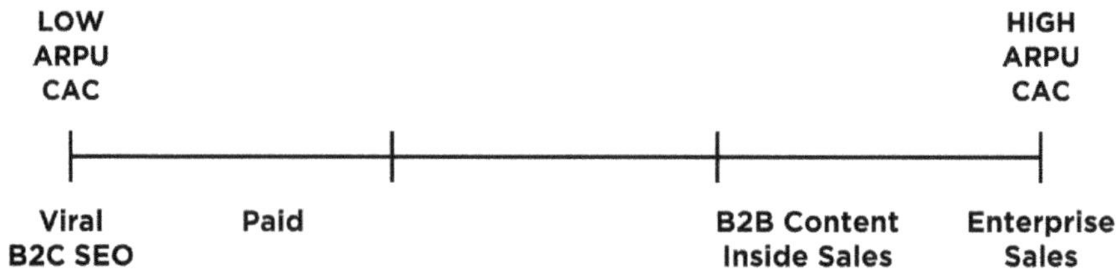

Figure 15.1 - Brian Balfour's ARPU <-> CAC Spectrum

The CLV should always be higher (much higher) than the CAC. As you will see in the case study below, you also need to avoid situations when the CLV is too low, in order to use the most appropriate acquisition strategies.

Figure 15.2 - Example of Wrong Model Market Fit

Determine your own criteria for evaluating channels.

Go through the list of 19 and any other channel hypotheses that you've come up with. Gabriel Weinberg and Justin Mares recommend doing a first assessment of the channels in a spreadsheet before prioritizing them, and then focusing on the top three channels for experiments.

Channels can be tested one at a time afterwards.

Analyzing Freemium Potential

> "Freemium is like a Samurai sword: unless you're a master at using it, you can cut your arm off.[136]"

Rob Walling
Serial Entrepreneur

This quote from Rob Walling captures the danger of freemium.

When freemium works, it really works. Spotify, for one, acquires millions of users through the free tier of their music service, and then manages to convert over 26% of them to paid plans[137]. For most product businesses, however, freemium can be downright dangerous.

Freemium is not a magic solution—it's also not a business model. Freemium is an acquisition strategy that, much like the other strategies covered in this chapter, doesn't always work.

Freemium, by itself, won't generate any revenue. For this reason, it's generally best to *add* a free tier than to start with a free plan right away. First you first need to make sure you have a working business model before you attempt to widen the top of the funnel.

The reason why users love freemium is that it lets them control the evaluation, engagement, and purchase process. They get to try the product and see for themselves if it can work for them. And since there's less risk and friction in trying a free product, freemium products are easier to recommend to others.

To test if freemium can work for your business, ask yourself:

- ***Who's buying the product?*** If the person using your product isn't the buyer, it will be difficult to reach the right audience through freemium.
- ***Who are the people in your users' networks?*** Freemium works

best for viral or networked products. Your free tier will be more effective if your users have other people like them in their networks and your product can leverage sharing mechanics.

- ***Is the product simple enough to stand on its own?*** For virality, a product needs a quick TTV (Chapter #14), a broad value proposition, and the product needs to be self-explanatory.
- ***Would usage be sustained month-over-month?*** It will be difficult for users to experience enough value to want to upgrade to a paid plan if they don't come back to use the product every month. There needs to be value in using the product every month, ideally every week.
- ***Could a free tier create disruption on the market?*** Freemium makes sense when you're trying to disrupt the market. As entrepreneur Andrew Nadeau says[138]: *"Freemium's place in the world of business is for products that people don't know they need, until they start using it."* In that way, freemium can help create new behaviors.
- ***Would a 4% conversion rate help sustain your business?*** A good freemium funnel will convert roughly 4% of users into paying customers[139]. *Could that be sustainable?* Products with free trials convert better than freemium products[140]. The Total Addressable Market (TAM) needs to be large enough to compensate for the lower conversion rate.
- ***Can you afford it?*** The marginal cost of adding new users should be negligible. You may need to carry these users for a long time, so make sure that the cost of maintaining these accounts won't hurt your business.

There are typically two kinds of freemium products:

1. **On-demand models**: In this model, the number of core product actions (leads, conversions, uploads, etc) is limited. Each month, credits get topped up. For this model to work, the core action needs to happen often enough to eventually trigger the need to upgrade.
2. **Premium feature models**: In this model, the user has access to a basic feature set and can upgrade to unlock extra functionalities. For this model to work, upgrades must flow naturally from the free use of the product with little to no friction.

Adding a freemium model to your business often means managing a second product. The free plan needs to create enough value to be able to stand on its own, but not enough for it to cannibalize your paid plans.

To sum it up, you need:

- an attractive basic offer;
- the right fencing to convert first-time buyers; and
- enough stickiness to turn first-time buyers into repeat customers.

As pricing expert Hermann Simon says: *"The usage difference between "free" and "paid" must be large enough to get customers across the penny gap."*

To find the right fencing, look at retention for your product's core action: *What percentage of customers perform this action each month?*

If most customers use the product every month and perform a certain number of core actions, then maybe you can offer 50, 60, or 70% of that value for free.

If there are both primary and secondary reasons why customers buy your product, maybe you can provide one of these benefits for free. *Would this be enough to get users to sign up and use a free tier?*

Evaluating opportunities to create a freemium offering is a segmentation challenge. You need to find features or product usage thresholds that are valuable enough to get users to sign up and use the product, but are not so valuable that users want to stay on the free plan.

Dig in your data. Explore different variations. Only ever consider adding a free tier when you have done the work of validating its potential.

Making Progress

> "The kitchen sink approach doesn't work. Most companies get zero distribution channels to work. If you get

just one channel to work you have a great business. If you try for several but don't nail one, you're finished. Distribution follows the power law."

Peter Thiel
Serial Entrepreneur

To make progress at this stage, focus on one acquisition channel at a time. Run rapid experiments to look for signs that you're heading in the right direction. *Are you attracting the right users?*

Iterate and test a few concepts, but hold off on optimization. You'll be able to improve effectiveness later on once a channel starts performing.

Depending on the size of your TAM, you should give a few hundred to a few thousand prospects the chance to check your product.

Keep experimenting until you find a channel that works. Once you find one, put all your efforts into acquiring as many users as possible from that channel.

As investor and entrepreneur Peter Thiel says in his book *Zero to One*: *"Distribution follows the power law."* You need to find a few channels that work, but recognize that one channel will most likely drive the vast majority of your growth.

As Brian Balfour says: *"We always build our businesses off the back of someone else's platform."* We don't control the channels, but we can control our product. When a channel shows real potential, consider molding your product to that channel.

Tripadvisor did this when they optimized the search engine indexing of the user-generated content (posts, reviews, guides, etc) on their platform, Airbnb did this by creating a double-sided referral program[141], and Unito did this by optimizing their presence in their partners' app directories.

Keep in mind the power law. Make experimenting with new platforms and channels a part of your processes. Set time aside for finding and testing new channels.

Most channels eventually dry up. You need to make sure that you're balancing your investments in short-term acquisition and future growth opportunities. Keep testing new acquisition strategies, even when your business is growing.

Case Study
How Brandisty Got the Wrong Model Market Fit

> "The product that wins is the one that bridges customers to the future, not the one that requires a giant leap.[142]"

Aaron Levie

Before Dribbble and before the Rocketship podcast, Michael Sacca was the co-founder of Tiny Factory, a web development firm based in San Diego. As designers and developers working with dozens of clients, they often had to use digital asset management tools.

At the time, most of the tools on the market were geared towards enterprises with long-term contracts, and had monthly licenses north of $500. Because there weren't any products serving the low end of the market, Michael and his team had the idea of creating Brandisty. The strategy for Brandisty was to go for volume, helping teams store and access brand assets at a lower cost (~$25 per month).

Right from the start, Michael began doing interviews trying to understand customer struggles and find use cases. Over the course of a few months, he had done well over 150 interviews. Through these discussions, Michael and his team were able to identify key pains: internal sharing, exporting files, dealing with varying requirements, etc. These were clear pain points that Brandisty could address.

What Michael and his team didn't validate at that stage was how much people would be willing to pay for their product.

It turned out that smaller businesses were okay with designers manually exporting the assets.

In Michael's words, *"The pain point wasn't enough to get mass adoption"*. Because it was priced low and they were bootstrapping the product, they weren't able to build fast enough to compete. They tried changing the target, targeting agencies (those managing and creating the brands), startups, and mid-sized organizations.

Over time, they ended up working with Groupon, a large Danish TV station, and several other organizations, but as their customers grew in size, their expectations also increased significantly. Customers now wanted integrations, multiple hierarchy tier management, quarterly billing, etc—a lot of features they hadn't planned on building.

Eventually, Michael and his team realized that the reason why digital asset management tools existed at enterprise level was that it was only at enterprise level that there were there enough people who felt the pain and were willing to pay money to fix it.

One after the other, competitors came to the same realization.

In the end, Michael and his team failed to generate enough revenue to compete and sustain the business.

Taking Action

1. Analyze your current acquisition channels. Understand how your best users are discovering your product.

2. Narrow down the list of ‘traction’ channels based on your business model and unit economics.
3. Rank acquisition channels and run experiments testing the top three channels on your list.
4. Only start optimizing acquisition when a channel shows real potential.
5. Only ever consider adding a free tier or going freemium when you have validated its potential.
6. *Collaborating with others?* Share a PDF version of this chapter at **solvingproduct.com/chapter-15**.

Stage 4:

Expansion

Can It Get Bigger?

"It is sometimes difficult in a big successful organization to have the sense of urgency and hunger. No company can defend only. If you have a high market share and you are a market leader, if you start defending you cannot sustain."

Olli-Pekka Kallasvuo
Nokia Ex-CEO & Chairman

You've grown your team to meet market demand. Managers have been given objectives and made accountable for delivering on key results. A human resources (HR) team has been created. Standards have been set for conduct and hiring. The profiles and accomplishments of the executives you hire are increasingly impressive. The people you're hiring look nothing like the people that first built the company. The business is growing—but it's also changing.

Individually, all of these were perhaps the right decisions. But even the best decisions have consequences.

A few rules can help explain what tends to happen in organizations:

1. *"People behave the way they are paid.*[143]*"* – Dr. Dean R. Spitzer, Author of Transforming Performance Management

2. *"Anything that you measure automatically creates a set of employee behaviors."* – Ben Horowitz, Andreessen Horowitz Partner

3. *"You do not rise to the level of your goals. You fall to the level of your systems."* – James Clear, Author of Atomic Habits

In other words, **the rules, the systems, and the rewards your team puts in place dictate business outcomes**. As Naval Ravikant wrote[144]: *"Almost all human behavior can be explained by incentives."*

And since large and growing organizations are complex systems with various points of failure, it can be difficult to anticipate the outcomes of any system that the company puts in place.

This is why many organizations tend to emphasize the importance of values and corporate culture at this point. Culture and values help guide behaviors and decision-making when the answers aren't obvious.

Growing a business at this stage requires processes, systems, and incentives, as much as it does talent, insights, and creativity.

The Challenge

> "There will always be a healthy tension between *what you are* (the current state of your product) and *what you want to be* (some new reality you want to enable with your product)."

John Cutler
Amplitude Product Evangelist

If you work in product or in innovation, chances are that you've heard the story of Kodak.

The founder of Kodak, George Eastman, invented roll films. For a long time, Kodak was a leader in its market, creating some of the best cameras and film products available. In 1975, the company's R&D department invented the digital camera (15 years before first commercialization)[145]. Kodak executives felt that the invention would hurt their core film business, so they chose not to commercialize it.

On January 19, 2012, after the digital camera market had mostly destroyed roll film profitability, Kodak filed for bankruptcy[146].

Or maybe you have heard the story of video rental giant Blockbuster. At their peak, the company had more than 9,000 stores around the globe. In 2000, Blockbuster had the opportunity to buy Netflix for $50 million[147], but passed on the opportunity. In 2013, Blockbuster ceased operations.

Or maybe you've read the late Clay Christensen's book *The Innovator's Dilemma*, which explains how large organizations tend to get disrupted by new entrants that are better suited to exploiting new technology or opportunities. New entrants start with a beachhead, solidify their businesses, and then expand. Eventually, they're able to take on the market leaders.

No matter which stories you have heard, they all tend to point to organizational complacency, and a lack of innovation.

Maybe in previous eras businesses were able to rely solely on operational excellence for growth. But operational efficiency, while important, isn't enough.

Nowadays, *all* businesses need to innovate to survive.

As Tony Ulwick says: *"A company that always plays to its strengths is likely to end up addressing outcomes that are already overserved."*

Reinventing your products and organization means stepping out of your comfort zone.

Maintaining the operational excellence that got you there, while still growing your core business and innovating, is a real challenge.

At this stage, there's often legacy to drag along, revenue to preserve, and a reputation to safeguard. It's easy to get trapped in the daily routine, focusing on your territory with your current total addressable market—and neglecting the other opportunities that are out there.

To keep growing, you have to keep pushing the boundaries—even if that means altering the way you do business.

Where New Growth Comes From

"Value delivery drives sustainable growth.[148]"

Sean Ellis

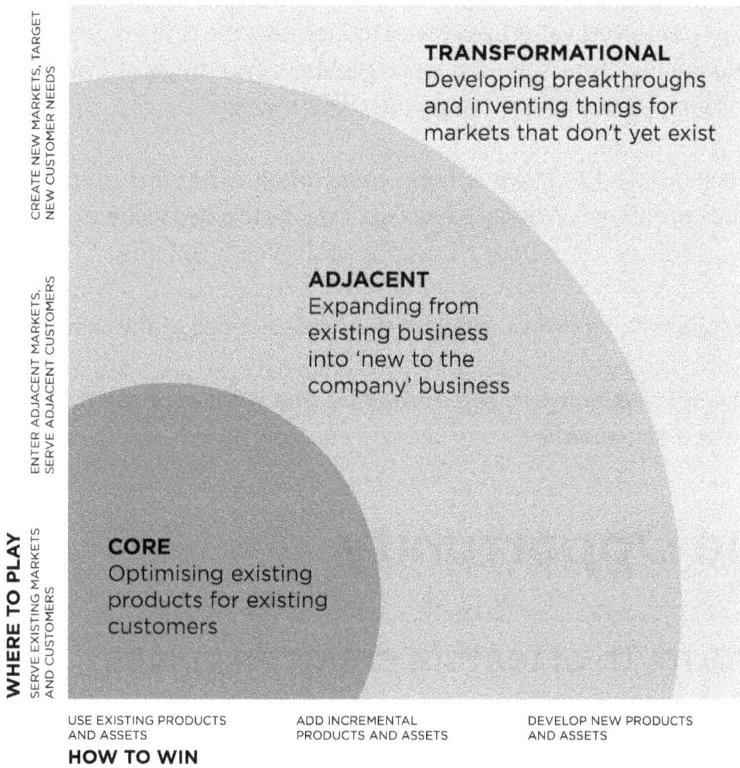

Figure V.1 - Bansi Nagji and Geoff Tuff's Innovation Ambition Matrix[149]

Quite simply, growing at this stage means increasing the value of your product.

This might mean:

- improving your product's core functionalities (better, faster, easier, greater ROI, etc);
- introducing your product's unique value to new markets;
- expanding functionalities (new features, new tools, new desired outcomes, etc);
- improving the experience (more usable, better support, better ecosystem support, etc); or
- creating new products for current (or future) customers.

Greater perceived value allows you to increase the price of your product, to get new customers, to convert a greater percentage of trial users into customers, and to keep existing customers longer.

As QuickSprout CEO Lars Lofgren says: *"Most marketing problems are a product problem."* When you increase the perceived value of your product, you solve a lot of your marketing and sales problems.

But as great as value is, it may be the fuzziest word in the dictionary.

What is it? And how can you make sure that what your team works on is perceived as valuable?

The Opportunity

> "The myth of feature creep disguises the real problem: the inability to execute on the core value of your product.[150]"

Hiten Shah

World-class organizations like Amazon, Google, and Microsoft strike out about 50% of the time[151]. These organizations have some of the best engineers in the world, their research and data teams do product discovery, and their development processes are the envy of the competition—yet half of the products and features that they build fail to deliver on their original intent.

Defining value from a user or customer's perspective is one of the most challenging parts of product development. It's a skill that can be learned and improved on, but even the best product leaders find it challenging.

As Marty Cagan says: *"It doesn't matter how good your engineering team is if they are not given something worthwhile to build."*

The promise is real though. If your team was able to define and deliver value more often than the competition, you would eventually become the market leader (if you aren't already).

The problem with defining 'value' is that it's highly subjective and contextual[152]. Different users or segments of users will perceive different things as valuable at different times.

To define value the way customers perceive it, you need to keep your ears to the ground and be a student of the landscape you operate in.

At the Expansion stage, we focus on:

- Uncovering *valued* product improvements to increase customer engagement and monetization (Chapter #16);
- Finding other segments that could benefit from the product *as-is* (Chapter #17);
- Improving our product to attract new users and customers (Chapter #18); and
- Finding opportunities to create new products for our users (Chapter #19).

If you were a service company...

This phase would be about exploring the market to get more repeat business, introducing your services to new markets, and solving new problems for your customers.

Moving the Business Forward

> "Good prioritization is based on cold, hard facts. When you have data and you have a clear strategy, prioritization becomes easy.[153]"
>
> Melissa Perri
> Author of Escaping the Build Trap

To make progress at this stage, it's important to have a product strategy that sets out a logical and deliberate sequence of markets and opportunities to take on.

There always needs to be a strategic filter on top of what you learn from the market. This filter should help separate what falls in and out of your product's scope.

To move forward, you should:

1. uncover all opportunities;
2. define the options (what can be delivered);
3. evaluate the value of each option through experiments or product discovery;
4. refine the option set as you learn;
5. ship the highest value items based on your product strategy; and
6. re-start from the top, re-prioritizing the option set.

Because you'll need to balance improvements for your users and strategic expansion into new markets, it's a good idea to lock certain capacities to balance core product enhancements and expansion.

This will ensure that your team makes progress on both fronts and carefully considers what goes into each box

- Rahul Vohra recommends spending 50% of development capacity improving the core, and 50% on expansion opportunities.
- Jason M. Lemkin recommends assigning 25% to expansion.
- AgentAssistant co-founder Matthew Norton recommends spending 95% of your capacity iterating on things you've already built, and 5% on new ideas[154].

No matter what ratio you choose, ensuring balance between expansion and improvement opportunities will help to ensure that you make progress.

The better your team is at defining and delivering new value to the market, the faster you'll grow.

Let's keep growing!

16
/
26

Finding Valued Product Improvements

Your business is growing. Use the following techniques to **identify *valued* product improvements** to **increase customer engagement and monetization**.

> "Doing product configuration right means you design a product with the right features for a segment—that is, just the features customers are willing to pay for."
>
> Madhavan Ramanujam and Georg Tacke

Product features don't all hold the same value in the eyes of customers.

Some features create higher levels of customer loyalty and have a greater potential for impacting customer satisfaction than others.

The best way to explain this is through the work of Dr. Noriaki Kano, the Japanese professor who created the Kano model. In his research, Dr. Kano concluded that features fall into one of five categories:

1. **Mandatory (Must-be)**: These features are the *must-haves* of a new product like a login or a user profile. They aren't perceived as adding any value to the product, but they are expected to be there. These are features that your product needs, but that users take for granted.
2. **Performance (One-dimensional)**: These features represent the core of your product—they're the two or three features that your customers pay for. These features are the main value you provide, what you write your marketing collateral around, and what businesses typically compete on.
3. **Exciter (Attractive)**: These features are not expected by customers, but are perceived as adding value. For example, an accounting solution might have automatic tax calculation or local tax rules and exemptions. These features help delight customers, but they don't cause dissatisfaction when they're absent.
4. **Indifferent**: These features don't make a difference in whether people want to use your product. They tend to be perceived as bloat, or non-monetizable and non-value-adding features.
5. **Reverse**: The presence of these features has a negative effect on customer satisfaction.

According to the Kano model, a winning product *meets* all mandatory requirements, *outperforms* competitors along the performance dimension, contains a few exciters, and avoids bloat, reverse, or indifferent features.

Simple enough?

The problem is twofold:

1. Performance features don't excite and don't tend to get requested, while customer requests and *exciters* don't tend to impact perfor-

mance. You have to find a way to balance these different types of needs.

2. The features that fall into each of these categories will change as customer and market expectations change. This process is sometimes called the natural decay of delight[155].

Over time, exciters no longer excite (e.g. Wi-Fi in hotels or coffee shops), performance expectations increase, and the list of mandatory requirements grows and grows.

This is one of the reasons why a product that doesn't get better over time doesn't just stagnate, it regresses.

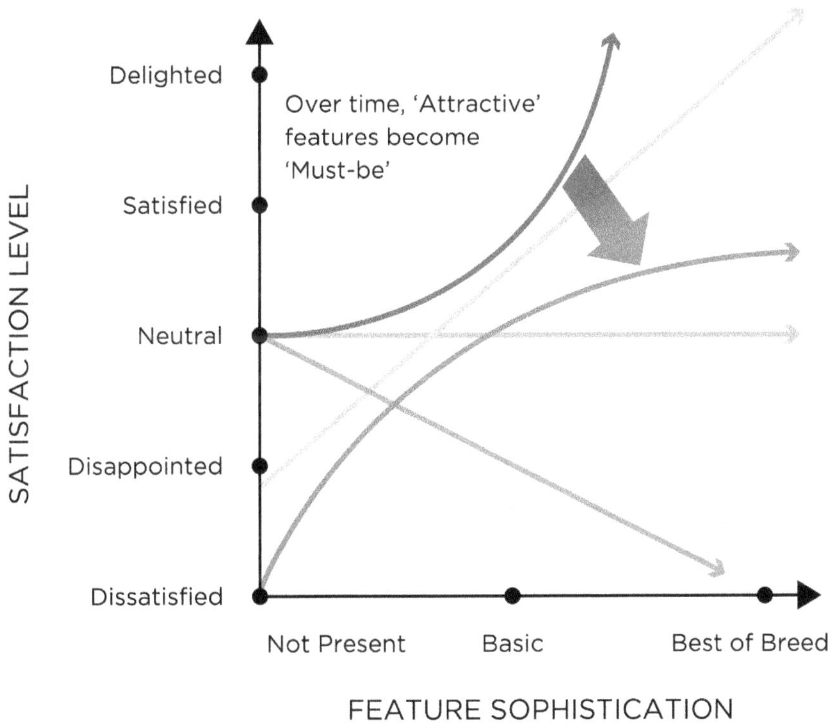

Figure 16.1 - Feature Satisfaction Over Time

Conversely, it's important to know when to *stop* improving certain criteria when it's well satisfied.

Ultimately, the pace of evolution in a market determines how quickly features get re-categorized.

Your product won't beat the competition by handling mandatory features better, but it can lose customers if these bases aren't covered. You need to make sure you always know what the "must-have" expectations are.

By this stage, you should have a good idea why customers are buying your product (Chapter #13), and how they evaluate the success it allows them to make. This should help make clear what your product's performance features are.

By digging deeper and keeping in mind the five categories of the Kano model, you'll be able to add value to your product time and time again, while ensuring that your bases are covered.

> *If you were a service company...*
>
> *This step would be about finding ways to further improve the services you deliver, and increase the likelihood of getting repeat business from customers.*

Techniques You Can Use

There are a lot of ways to improve the monetization potential and the engagement of a product. In this chapter, we look at different ways to source and evaluate value-enhancing product improvements.

- **Analyzing the Context of Feature Usage** will help you understand the triggers that lead to product usage, the expectations, and how well your product meets those expectations.
- **Understanding Customer Switch** will help you understand the gaps that prevent users from getting maximum value from your product.
- **Analyzing Value Drivers** will help you rank value-enhancing improvements based on customer input.
- **Learning from Feature Experiments** will help reveal which product features are essential, and which aren't.

- **Willingness to Buy Analysis** helps you evaluate whether your customers would be willing to spend money to access the features that you are thinking of building.

Once you come up with ideas for features, evaluate their potential with Feature Experiments or a Willingness to Buy Analysis. This will help you to ensure that customers find any features you add valuable.

Analyzing the Context of Feature Usage

> "When customers make requests for new product features, they are usually focused on solving just one problem and are not thinking of how their requested solution will impact other product or service functions."
>
> Tony Ulwick

Before starting to make changes to your product, you should understand current feature usage.

You should be very selective with any features that you add. Bloat and complexity are often easier to see in the rear-view mirror.

How are your product's current features being used? Are they easy to use? Do they contribute to your customers' success? In what contexts are they being used?

In *Intercom on Product Management*, Des Traynor points out three ways to improve existing features:

1. Making them better for the current users

2. Changing them so customers use them more often
3. Changing them so more people can use them

To learn how to improve a core feature of your product, you can use In-App messages (Chapter #12) to prompt users right after they use the target feature.

And to increase the frequency of use or the number of customers using a feature, you can ask the questions Dan Martell loves to ask:

> "What do you do three minutes before you use [Feature / Product]?" "What do you do three minutes after you use [Feature / Product]?"

These questions will help you learn about the triggers leading to product usage, the context of use, the expectations, and how well your product meets those expectations.

Analyzing the open-ended answers will help reveal opportunities for better embedding the feature in your customers' lives.

Understanding Customer Switch

> "When searching for traction, your best users are ones that once said '*Yes*' but now say '*No*'.[156]"

Vincent Huang
Springboard VP of Product & People

Every day, when prospects choose your product, or when they choose the competition over your product, or when customers churn, information about how well your product meets expectations is created.

We have already seen in Chapter #12 that the reasons why prospects make these decisions can help us improve our product's fit and sales funnels. Well, it turns out that those reasons can also be used to create new value for users.

Your product doesn't exist in a vacuum. It represents just one option within the range of products that prospects consider for addressing their needs.

Visibility, ad budgets, word of mouth, needs, expectations, and how well those expectations are satisfied, can all change over time—leading to changes in behaviors in vendor selection. In that sense, demand and needs are in flux.

Maybe when customers bought your product, it *was* the best solution for their needs. Maybe now, because of changes in their organization or aggressive marketing by the competition, they have realized that another product might better meet their needs.

To make sense of the flux of needs and customer choice, you need to understand:

- why your product is better than the status quo (the status quo is always the most popular option);
- why prospects choose your product over competitors';
- why prospects choose competitors' products over yours;
- why prospects choose indirect competitors over your solution;
- why customers switch away from your product;
- what competing products they choose when they switch (if any); and
- why they choose those competitors.

To understand why customers have chosen your competitors' products, you'll have to speak to their customers. You can find them through:

- case studies on their websites;
- product reviews on sites like G2, Capterra, etc;
- social media mentions; and

- technographics vendors like BuiltWith or Datanyze if the product has a digital footprint (e.g. analytics products).

To get a recent picture of their reasoning, focus on customers who bought in the last three months.

As with your own product, you should ask questions that help you to understand their decision-making process:

- *How did you first hear about [Competing Product] ? What did you know about it at the time?*
- *What was going on in your life at that time?*
- *Did you imagine what life would be like with the product? What were you expecting?*
- *What made you decide to sign up and try the product?*
- *Did anyone else weigh in on the decision?*
- *Did you evaluate other products?*
- Once you signed up, how did the product compare to your expectations?
- *Did you feel you had all the information you needed to get started?*
- *What made you decide to buy the product?*
- *What was the main thing that convinced you?*
- *Now that you have [Product], what can you do now that you couldn't do before?*

Alan Klement recommends always analyzing why customers choose your product, what trade-offs they make, and why they stop using your product together:

> *"If your existing customers are saying: "Hey, it'd be great if you had a Salesforce integration. I would mark that, but I wouldn't act on it until I had some signal that people were leaving because we didn't have a Salesforce integration."*

By segmenting the three data sets (why they choose your product, why they choose the competition, and why they abandon your product) you will start to see patterns emerge:

Why Customers Buy	Why They Leave	Why They Choose the Competition
Easy email automation	Clunky interface	24/7 customer service
Excellent deliverability	Limited reporting and analytics	Advanced A/B testing
Integrated website builder	Limited template design	Ecommerce integration
Multilingual interface	No Salesforce integration	Platform API
Powerful segmentation	Simplistic CRM	Push notifications
Wordpress integration	Unresponsive customer service	Salesforce integration

Figure 16.2 - Mapping of the Three Data Sets

To improve retention, focus on features that cause your customers to churn *and* choose the competition.

To improve acquisition and monetization, focus on features that convince prospects to choose other products over yours. Over time, this will allow you to steal market share from the competition.

Analyzing Value Drivers

> "So often people are working hard at the wrong thing. Working on the right thing is probably more important than working hard.[157]"

Caterina Fake
Flickr Co-Founder

Earlier in this chapter, we looked at the Kano model as a way to understand types of feature. The Kano survey, a standardized questionnaire designed by Dr. Noriaki Kano, can help to categorize features using customer input.

Although you can usually determine 90% of all possible product requirements with these surveys, Kano surveys are very lengthy, and this can make data collection challenging.

IBM researchers—experts who use Kano surveys to evaluate requirements—concluded that testing more than 20 features was an overwhelming amount of data, both for the customers and the researchers[158]. For this reason, I have focused on a different technique for this book[159].

MaxDiff, also known as Best-Worst Scaling, is a technique used to do conjoint analyses—statistical techniques used in market research to determine how people value different attributes.

MaxDiff surveys are a great way to compare many alternatives and capture data on trade-offs without overwhelming respondents.

The survey creates a single rank ordering of the most important features:

1. Feature A
2. Feature B
3. Feature C, etc

Data are calculated by showing users or customers four or five features at a time, and asking them to select the least and most important in their opinion.

When listening to music while commuting to work, what is most and least important to you?

Most Important		Least Important
○	Noise cancellation	○
○	Battery life	○
●	Volume control	○
○	Music recommendations	●

Figure 16.3 - Example of a MaxDiff Survey

To run a MaxDiff survey, I recommend using an established survey tool like Sawtooth Software's or SurveyGizmo's. Both have built-in functionalities to help analyze the survey data. While it's not impossible to analyze the results on your own[160], it can introduce risk in your analysis.

You want clear segmentation for MaxDiff surveys. The results won't be reliable if you survey across target profiles.

Because you need a statistically valid representation of the target population—150-300 participants for every segment you're exploring—you need to ensure that you can recruit this number of participants. Create the list of features you want to test. Run them by contacts or colleagues to make sure they're as clear as they can be. It should be nearly impossible for respondents to misinterpret these features when taking the survey.

Test at most 25 features, showing each feature at least three times to each respondent.

1. Battery life
2. Wireless headphones
3. Headphone comfort
4. Low-end response
5. Noise cancellation
6. Design

Figure 16.4 - Example of a Prioritized List of Features

It's important to note that, even though MaxDiff gives you quantitative data, the results are still extremely qualitative in nature. The analysis will tell you how important attributes are, *relative* to one another. It won't tell you whether they're important in general.

Context will determine a lot of the trade-offs people are willing to make, so it's a good idea to combine this analysis with a Willingness to Buy analysis (below).

With a large data set, you'll be able to compare responses per sub-segment to identify breakout opportunities.

Learning from Feature Experiments

> "Don't build anything unless you get validation first. Build the button, but not the feature. Track the results."

Sebastien Brault
Serial Entrepreneur

A common way to pre-test features is to set up a Fake Door demand test.

The general idea of a Fake Door experiment is to pretend to provide a product, feature, or service. For example, adding a button or menu item for the feature that you're thinking of building, without actually building it.

When users click the button, they're taken to a page explaining the experiment and how they can contribute by filling out a survey or taking part in an interview.

Fake Door demand tests can tell you if the idea sparks the interest of users. But there are a few challenges with this technique:

1. Clicking on a link or a button doesn't actually mean that the feature will be perceived as valuable. Curiosity clicks are unavoidable.
2. The button or link placement will affect test results.
3. Button or link labels can set the wrong expectations. If you intend to run a Fake Door demand test, definitely run a Comprehension Test (Chapter #12) beforehand.

What a Fake Door demand test can reveal is whether there is interest in *trying* a feature.

A perhaps more valuable way to learn about demand is to reverse this test, hiding or removing existing product features. You can design an A/B test that hides the feature for some users. If the feature is valued, its absence will impact usage. You will see an increase in support tickets and social media feedback. Those can be great indicators that the feature was valuable.

A less disruptive approach would be to ask the main question of the PMF survey (Chapter #11) after a specific feature gets used (*"How would you feel if you could no longer use [Feature]?"*).

As with the general PMF survey, the idea is that if at least 40% of respondents state that they would be "Very disappointed" if they could no longer use the feature, you can infer that this feature has market fit.

Following up with an open-ended question (*"What is the main reason for your answer?"*) can help reveal gaps. This will help you understand why the feature is valuable to some users, and not to others.

Surveys can help you make better product decisions, but don't surrender decision-making to a survey. They're simply there to help guide product decisions.

Sometimes reduction is the best way to make the existing value in a product more noticeable and effective. Don't be afraid to remove features when they don't move the needle.

Katryna Balboni of Appcues recommends making killing features a regular part of your product strategy[161] while Mind the Product co-founder Janna Bastow, recommends creating a 'kill list' of features[162].

Weigh the pros and cons. Ultimately, as Dave McClure says[163]: *"When you kill the wrong one, people will make noise and you'll be clued in to what actually adds value."*

Willingness to Buy Analysis

"What information would you purchase for a million dollars?"

John Cutler

This is the question John Cutler, product evangelist at Amplitude, asks customers to get right to monetizable value.

It does two things:

1. It gets the client to open up, and share his or her biggest need.
2. It forces the customer to make trade-offs.

Customers understand that it may be possible to get the information they need, but that it will cost more. This helps ground the discussion in reality—You can have this feature, but you'll need to pay.

It's one of the reasons why, years after company formation, Drift's product team still uses a form of dollar test to validate features. By putting a cost on features that they consider, they make sure that any features they build are monetizable.

David Cancel, Drift's CEO, explains: *"What happens when you do that is that most feature requests go away miraculously. They disappear. And so it lightens your load and all the decisions that you need to make. If you start assigning value to them and you're just being honest with them that it is going to cost more and if you value it you should be willing to pay for it."*

To analyze willingness to buy, pricing experts Madhavan Ramanujam and Georg Tacke recommend asking the following questions. Note that the questions should be asked in this specific sequence:

1. *What do you think is an acceptable price?*
2. *What do you think is an expensive price?*

3. *What is a prohibitively expensive price?*

The answers will help you understand whether the feature can be monetized, and will give you an idea of its pricing potential.

Willingness to buy conversations can be uncomfortable, but as we saw in Chapter #7, they are critical to understanding whether users have a real need for your product, or the feature that you are thinking of building.

If you're in B2C or your product has a large volume of traffic, you can decide to gate or limit access to the feature, asking users to upgrade to a higher-priced subscription, or pay a one-time fee to unlock it.

The idea is to force an upgrade decision:

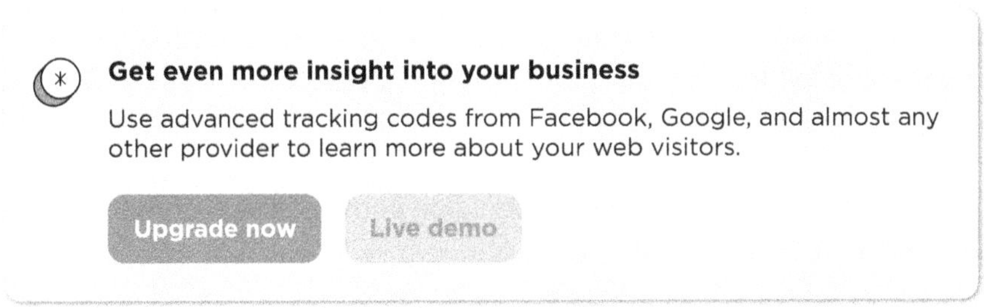

Figure 16.5 - Example of an Upgrade Prompt

In a way, this as a variation on the Fake Door demand test.

Since you haven't created the feature yet, it's generally not advisable to start collecting payments. Instead of letting users pay, consider linking to an explanation of the research you're doing, or a form to recruit candidates for customer interviews to flesh out the feature.

Making Progress

"A new feature has to retain users for that specific feature, have a scalable way to drive its own adoption, and has to improve retention, engagement, and/or monetization for the core product.[164]"

Casey Winters

To make progress at this stage, focus on one user profile or persona at a time. Don't try to please everyone with the feature you're thinking of building. You want to help your users get better at performing the Job.

Once you identify an opportunity to add value to your product, don't just build it. There's a gap between the concept of a new value-adding functionality, and its implementation; it usually takes several iterations to get the execution to the point where it delivers value. This delay is known as *time to money*.

Once a concept has been validated using some of the techniques covered earlier in this chapter, flesh it out:

- *What represents status quo?*
- *Whose behaviors are expected to change?*
- *How will they change?*
- *How will the new behaviors benefit users or customers?*
- *How will the new behaviors benefit the organization?*
- *What will customers say about the changes?*

Once you have clarity around what you're trying to achieve, you can build a very lightweight prototype to test the implementation with the intended audience for the feature. This is best done through user tests (Chapter #5).

Since you want natural and honest reactions, the prototype needs to appear real. You can use Axure, Keynote, or basic HTML to create the prototype.

In recent years, Keynote has become one of the best prototyping tools on the market. It can be used to create prototypes to test feature ideas on mobile, or with desktop computers.

If the new functionalities are intended to improve engagement or retention, you should recruit a range of users (e.g. novices *and* power users). If they're intended to improve acquisition or the sign-up and onboarding process, you need to recruit people who have never used your product.

It can be a good idea to combine user tests with interviews. If you do, schedule hour-long sessions with each participant. Your goals will be to:

1. understand their context and how the new value would fit in their lives; and
2. evaluate how well the implementation addresses their needs.

The first 10-15 minutes can be used to ask questions:

- *How would you describe your role as [Role]?*
- *What does success look like for you?*
- *Can you tell me how you deal with [Job to be Done]?*
- *Why did you decide to start using [Product]?*
- *Can you walk me through how you're currently using [Product] to perform [Job to be Done]?*
- *What's preventing you from [Specific Job Step]?*
- *Have you found ways to get more [Outcome]?*
- *What do you feel are the main limitations of [Product]?*

Follow the interview with a user test. Under Conducting User Tests in the Building Blocks section you'll learn about best practices for user testing.

Let users or customers familiarize themselves with the prototype for a few minutes. When ready, give them the first task.

As participants go through the tasks, ask about their:

- **Expectations**: *What would you expect this to be? What do you think would happen if you clicked this? How does that align with the way you do [Task]?*

- **Understanding**: *What do you think this is? What do you think this means? What do you understand from this?*

Your goal is to find gaps and friction points. In famous research, usability expert Jakob Nielsen demonstrated that five tests—with representative customers—can help reveal 85% of the issues[165].

It's better to do more series of tests than more tests in a single series. This will help progressively improve your implementation. You will learn about usability, language, and task-related issues. As a result, you'll ship much higher quality improvements that are much closer to the value customers expect, faster.

You're not making your product better if the things that you add don't have high usage. Iterating on new value additions is the best way of actually delivering new value to customers.

Case Study
How Hiten Shah and Marie Prokopets Improved FYI

> "Being forced to place many bets drains company resources as it floods the development pipeline with a torrent of ideas—each of which takes dedication and energy to pursue."
>
> Tony Ulwick

It didn't take long in the story of FYI for Hiten Shah and Marie Prokopets to realize that the most important feature of their document search product wasn't going to be the search.

While they were able to get users interested in their product, to get users to adopt it they had to, first, become world-class at integrations. Simply put, if the integrations didn't work perfectly, then they didn't get to have a business.

To get the integrations where they needed to be, they spent countless hours testing, refining, and iterating the integration process until it was optimal. After the integrations, document search and onboarding followed. Eventually, when the product had become effective for individual users, they began looking for the next thing.

Hiten says: *"Sequencing in product development is one of the wildest things out there. It used to be really easy where you didn't need to think about the sequence because there just weren't that many products on the market."*

The *next thing* came up when Hiten and Marie realized that a lot of FYI's growth was coming from their users' colleagues discovering the product.

It wasn't clear whether they were being told about it, or if they had simply seen the product in a tab during a meeting, but one thing was for sure, the behavior drove organic growth.

FYI didn't have the concept of a team, and there was no way to invite colleagues. Up to this point, they hadn't put any thought into building team functionalities. To Hiten and Marie, this was a sign. The discovery made them rethink and reprioritize their road map around the concept of *FYI for Teams*.

In their view, none of this would have worked if they had *started* with the idea of creating a team product.

To get to this point, they had to first build a world-class product for individuals that got traction for both work and personal use cases. Users also had to love FYI enough to be willing to tell others. All these improvements happened as iterations on the core product.

Hiten says: *"The way you think about the next thing is you start with what's the number one thing people are doing in your product. Once you figure out what that number one thing is people are doing in the product you go figure out why they're doing it. The next logical thing to do has everything to do with the thing users are already doing. It's the only way to make sure the next thing is as high usage as the rest of the product."*

Taking Action

1. Explore feature usage. Understand the context around it.
2. Generate customer engagement and monetization-enhancing feature ideas by analyzing support communications, usage context, and switching behaviors.
3. Test and rank features with a MaxDiff survey, Feature Experiments, or a Willingness to Buy analysis.
4. Once you have identified an opportunity to make your product more valuable, work with your users to smooth out the implementation.
5. Follow up on improvements after launch, to make sure that the additions deliver the expected value.
6. *Collaborating with others?* Share a PDF version of this chapter at **solvingproduct.com/chapter-16**.

17 / 26

Finding Other Segments for Your Product

Your product addresses the needs of a market segment. Use the following techniques to **find other segments** that could benefit from your product *as is*.

> "Once you've reached PMF, look for other audiences with similar problems.[166]"

Nate Desmond
Growth Marketer

Beyond improving your product, you can expand a product business in three ways:

1. By introducing the value your product currently delivers to new market segments;
2. By adding functionalities to attract new customers; and
3. By creating new related products around your core product.

It's important to understand that serving new segments can add significant complexity to your sales, marketing, and product management processes. It can also introduce new use cases and personas that you'll need to get familiar with.

We'll find opportunities to expand by exploring related Jobs and customer segments. Of the scenarios above, introducing your product to new segments will be the least disruptive to your business. It can be a good idea to start there.

> *If you were a service company...*
>
> *This step would be about finding new customer segments that stand to benefit from the services you're selling.*

Techniques You Can Use

Finding new segments to expand in can mean revisiting some of the information you collected in the earlier stages, and then testing demand in new segments.

- **Analyzing the Pull from Other Markets** will help you find patterns worth exploring in customer interactions and product usage.
- **Learning Through Series of Customer Interviews** will help you systematically evaluate customer segments and market demand.
- **Selling or Advertising into New Market Segments** will help you quickly test demand in different segments.

First you should analyze the pull from other markets. Then, using sales, ads, or customer interviews, you'll be able to gauge market demand.

Analyzing the Pull from Other Markets

> "If you have one customer in an industry, you can get 10. The outliers aren't anomalies, they are the future."
>
> Jason M. Lemkin

Chances are that by this stage you have already felt a certain pull from other market segments.

- *Have prospects from other segments signed up despite your messaging being focused on a different market? Do some of these user groups stand out?*
- *Have any of those prospects found real value in your product? Are there segments that received equal—or even greater—value from your product than your target customers?*
- *Do some of those groups perform better in terms of churn, engagement, or even NPS?*
- *Have users from other segments contacted your team asking for different features? Did they have a budget to pay for custom development?*
- *Has your team built a degree of authority or visibility that could be leveraged to ease your entry into a new market?*
- *Has your team gained knowledge or insights that could be used to help your expansion into a new market?*
- *Have customers recommended your product to prospects outside of your target market? Did those users find value with your product?*

These are some of the most telling signs that the market is trying to expand the scope of your product. They are examples of new groups of early adopters thinking that your product could help address their needs.

Maybe up until now you've been laser-focused on winning your core market—now it's time to change your focus, and have a look at the groups that are trying to get value from your product.

In Chapter #12, we talked about the importance of collecting and categorizing feedback and support conversations. Now's the time to revisit that data.

You want to identify:

1. the segments trying to get value from your product; *and*
2. what, if anything, is preventing them from getting that value.

Focusing on users outside of your target market, revisit:

- Positioning feedback (*"I'm probably not your target customer, but…", "I'm sure I'm wrong, but I thought…"*)
- The list of companies visiting your website if you're in B2B
- Unsolicited feedback and emails
- Feature requests
- Sales calls
- The profiles of users signing up
- The profiles of the users who cancelled or moved on that your team dismissed by saying *"They weren't in our target market"*
- Unusual product uses

When you look at all these interactions, *are there segments that stand out?*

Although you are trying to avoid edge cases and outliers, what you're really looking for are signals. Even small segments can be interesting. Segments can generally be grown.

For each of the groups you have identified, you want to understand the value sought, the gaps they see in your product, and anything else they feel prevents them from using your product. If you don't have enough data, then you need to dig deeper by conducting interviews (below).

Although the specific users that triggered these discussions have most likely moved on, there's still a lot of value in understanding which solutions they were considering, and what solution they chose.

Did they find a solution? How well does it meet their needs?

If your product now has everything that one of these segments needs to be successful, congratulations. You found an expansion opportunity. You might be able to grow that segment simply by adapting your messaging.

But even if you do find a similar opportunity, it's best to go through the entire exercise. Keep reading.

Learning Through Series of Customer Interviews

> "Cheating on customer discovery interviews is like cheating in your parachute packing class.[167]"
>
> Steve Blank
> Customer Development Creator

To evaluate markets, Geoffrey Moore, the author of *Crossing the Chasm*, recommends using the following criteria:

1. ***Is it large enough?*** You should make sure that you're not targeting a small or dying market. To be worthwhile, the market has to be large enough to generate at least $10M in annual revenue[168].
2. ***Can you access it?*** *Can you leverage some of the mechanics already in place to reach a large number of prospects? Would the*

cost of customer acquisition be prohibitive? Is there a clear path to be able to scale this segment?

3. ***Do you have a compelling value proposition?*** *Can you deliver significantly more value than the competition? Does your value proposition connect with this segment's needs and challenges?*

4. ***Do you already have the whole product?*** The whole product is the minimum set of requirements needed to sell to a customer segment. It can include features, integrations, partnerships, etc. *Is your product ready for purchase by this segment as is, or would you need to make changes to be able to get customers?*

5. ***Are there competitors?*** *How much competition is there? Would your product be differentiated in this segment? What alternatives will prospects consider?*

6. ***Can you leverage a leadership position?*** *Would winning this segment open up new opportunities? Would it help you build leadership, momentum, data or other assets that could be leveraged to enter other segments afterwards?*

These are six evaluation criteria—but I could have added another 10. The more data points you have, the better you'll be able to evaluate segments.

You could add customer budget, intensity of pain, estimated ROI, cost of acquisition, churn rates, or anything else that helps drive your decision. The important thing is to make sure that the segments you evaluate are homogeneous.

You can do a multi-criteria analysis to identify the best opportunities. Use the template at **solvingproduct.com/markets** to get started fast.

Once you've identified the top three or four highest potential segments for your product, you should do quick interviews with 5-10 prospects per segment.

Your objectives are:

1. to understand what Jobs they're trying to address; *and*

2. to figure out how well your current product meets their needs.

Understand the roles and responsibilities of the users you have identified in each segment. You can recruit extra participants by finding more people like them.

During the interviews, you can ask questions like:

- *What are your objectives this year?*
- *How will you be evaluated this year?*
- *What keeps you up at night? Why?*
- *What are your top three challenges?*
- *Can you tell me how you deal with [Job to be Done]?*
- *Could you walk me through the last time you did [Job to be Done]? Who else got involved? What tasks were involved?*
- *When was the last time you tried to find a solution to [Job to be Done]?*
- *What alternatives did you consider?*
- *What gaps did you perceive in those solutions?*
- *What would be the ideal solution for you?*

If prospects are not *actively* trying to address the Job, or if addressing the Job is not a priority, it will be difficult to build momentum.

If you're speaking to businesses, consider asking:

> Within the organization, who's responsible for [Job to be Done]?

If the answer is "no one", then the Job either doesn't exist or it's not a priority.

Now, if they say "someone else", take note of their answer, and consider how you might need to adjust your recruiting.

The interviews should help you to figure out how well your product fits each segment. *Would they be hiring your product for the same Job, or a different one?*

Selling or Advertising into New Market Segments

"As soon as we demonstrate PMF for a new market, we want the sales force to go out and find as many additional customers in that market as possible."

Marty Cagan
Silicon Valley Product Group Founder

At the onset when my ex-co-founder and I began work on Highlights[169], the idea was to create an analytics product to help SaaS businesses internationalize their products.

Because domestic markets tend to be much smaller for European businesses, we started doing customer discovery in Europe. After a few dozen interviews, a pattern began to emerge.

The businesses that had managed to capture new markets the fastest had... well... *just done it.* They had simply identified opportunities —sometimes based on signals, sometimes based on analysis—and started selling or advertising their current product in those markets.

Although this insight limited the value of the solution we were hoping to build, it came with a good lesson on market expansion.

At this stage, your team should be able to sell or advertise in at least one segment. This gives you metrics to benchmark your market expansion against.

Map your sales or conversion funnel and get clear benchmarks.

If you're acquiring customers through ads, start targeting the new segment with the exact same ads and messaging. *How does performance compare with your benchmarks? Is it 20% off? 50% off? What happens when users sign up?*

- **If they're engaging with the product, but your funnel underperforms**, the problem is your messaging.
- **If the funnel performs well, but users don't engage with your product**, then adapt your onboarding.
- **If both your funnel and your onboarding are performing but users don't engage**, the product might need more adaptation. Tread carefully, as this can lead to a feature loop[170], where features lead to the addition of more features.

Although you can also learn how to adjust your funnel or messaging by prompting users with timely In-App messages, sales might be a more effective way to learn.

You can start selling your product in a new segment, or get your sales team to start selling it. By starting with your original pitch, they'll quickly learn about gaps, objections, value propositions that resonate, and the particularities of the new segment.

Don't change your product—or the way you explain your product—until you're sure that features are missing.

If you plan to change your product to meet the needs of a certain segment, first you have to make sure that it's the best segment to expand in.

Making Progress

"If you don't have a clear strategy you are busy overcoming surprises instead of making progress.[171]"

Noa Ganot
Product Management Expert

For established businesses, capturing market shares is the name of the game. It's up and to the right, taking away market opportunities from the competition.

Many of the fastest growing businesses have taken a strategic approach to researching and growing their markets[172].

Because of the overheads involved in managing several segments, positionings, or feature sets, it's important to pick the right time to expand.

Before you consider expanding, make sure that:

- **You've captured the largest share of your original market**: *Are you at 30, 40 or 50% market share?* Don't stop until you dominate your market.
- **The vast majority of prospects have heard of your product**: *Are prospects talking about your product? How much awareness have you created?* In Chapter #22 you'll learn how to run a survey to find out.
- **You have taken away the best opportunities**: The most profitable, the fastest growing, the best customers. You want to make it an *unassailable* position. Let competitors fight for scraps.
- **You have resources that can be freed up without reducing your grip on the market**: You can service your core market while taking on new market segments.
- **You have the cashflow to build other sales or marketing teams**, support teams, and marketing pipelines.

This can't be stressed enough.

To make progress and expand strategically, Geoffrey Moore recommends using the "bowling pin" (or bowling alley) strategy.

The general idea is that once you knock over a pin—capture a significant share of a market segment—you can move on to adjacent markets... and then knock them over.

The key to success is to make sure that the next pins or segments you hit are related to the ones that you've already knocked down, so that awareness, word of mouth and case studies *travel* from one pin to the next. That way, you don't have to start from scratch every time you enter a new market.

Look for the easiest segments to capture that give you the greatest strategic benefit.

Which segments will open the most doors? Which will strengthen your leadership position? Which will help your finances the most?

Your goal here is maximum impact, minimum effort.

Case Study
How Poppulo Went from a Red to a Blue Ocean

"If you are the market leader [...] reinforce the current buying criteria, reiterating why you are the best at delivering those things."

April Dunford

Andrew O'Shaughnessy founded the email marketing platform Newsweaver in 1996. Soon after its launch, this small business from Cork, Ireland, began to win awards and was landing a wide range of clients, from large multinationals and government agencies to small and medium-sized enterprises (SMEs), charities and associations.

Even though Newsweaver was growing and profitable, Andrew and his team developed the habits of closely monitoring data and interacting with their customers.

One day, they noticed something interesting happening with a small, but engaged, segment of customers. After trawling through the data, the team realized that this segment was using Newsweaver for internal communications, sending announcements to their employees, internal surveys, etc.

This grabbed their attention. After further digging, Andrew and his team were surprised to find out that the internal communications segment was also one of their most profitable. To gain more clarity around this segment, they split up the product, creating *Internal Connect* to go along with *Customer Connect*, their original email marketing solution.

This separation proved effective. Soon, the team had a decision to make: *Could they grow faster, and more sustainably, by putting all their energies into one segment?*

In 2014 Andrew and his team decided to focus exclusively on the internal communications market. In 2017, they rebranded the entire company as Poppulo[173].

The change of segment transformed their business. They went from a Red Ocean—a hyper-competitive market like email marketing—to a Blue Ocean, a market with very little competition that they could, ultimately, own.

Keeping their ears to the ground paid off. Today, Poppulo has over 850 customers located in more than 100 countries around the world.

Taking Action

1. Analyze the pull from other markets. Look for signs that other early adopters are trying to get value from your product.
2. Define a set of criteria for strategically evaluating segments.
3. Use sales, ads, or customer interviews to learn from the segments that you're evaluating.

4. Look for the easiest segment to capture leading to the greatest strategic benefit for your organization.
5. Only consider going into other markets once you have positioned your business solidly enough to leverage extra capacity.
6. *Collaborating with others?* Share a PDF version of this chapter at **solvingproduct.com/chapter-17**.

18 / 26

Improving the Product to Acquire New Users

Your product addresses the needs of a part of the market. Use the techniques in this chapter to **improve your product** to **attract new users and customers**.

> "Your product should stop when the next step has 1) well-defined market leaders looking after it (e.g. Apple, Netflix, Expedia), and 2) you don't intend to compete."
>
> Samuel Hulick

At this point, *what's preventing you from acquiring **all** the customers in the market?*

- *Customer loyalty and habits?*
- *Buyers committed with the competition?*
- *Difficulty reaching prospects?*
- *Gaps in your product?*

Once you've reduced friction, improved your messaging and targeting, and improved your product's core functionalities, you'll want to turn your attention to attracting new customers—by convincing them to switch over from competitors, or by converting on-the-fence prospects.

It's not uncommon for businesses to copy their competitors' best features, in an attempt to create feature parity. But while understanding what the competition is doing should be among the inputs you consider when creating your product strategy, this approach can often backfire.

There's no guarantee that the competitors that you're emulating are targeting real opportunities. These new functionalities might ultimately reduce your product's attractiveness on the market by introducing bloat.

Maintain your leadership. Don't follow others. Focus on *your* product strategy and *your* unique growth recipe. Rank opportunities on the basis of what you have learned and are still learning.

To find the next thing, Box CEO Aaron Levie recommends asking[174]: *"If I were to start [Box / Company] today, what would I be focused on, what are the next opportunities?"*

> *If you were a service company...*
>
> *This step would be about overcoming objections to land more customers.*

Techniques You Can Use

You probably already have the information that you need to improve your product so that it attracts new users and customers. This step is about putting that data to use. Beyond Analyzing the Pull from Other Markets (Chapter #17), consider:

- **Analyzing Unprompted Feedback** will help you learn from the users who felt like your product couldn't meet their needs.
- **Learning from Customers "Hacking" Your Product** will help you to leverage outside innovation to expand your product.
- **Analyzing Need Satisfaction** will help you find outcomes that your product currently fails to satisfy.

Each of these analyses will reveal opportunities for improving your product and attracting new customers. Pick the approach that's most appropriate for your business.

Analyzing Unprompted Feedback

> "Hate is closer to love than indifference—you can't iterate around indifference, but you can around hate.[175]"
>
> Dave McClure

One of the many great things that happen when your business starts growing fast is that you begin to receive a lot of unprompted—or unsolicited—feedback.

It's something that many businesses have conflicting views about. On the one hand, unprompted feedback can:

- feel redundant;
- break team focus and concentration;
- force management to endlessly argue against ideas they already decided against; and
- be challenging to keep on top of.

You already have a plan. You want to execute on it and move forward. That's understandable.

On the other hand, there is real value in keeping at least some doors open.

People are generally motivated to provide unsolicited feedback when they are either very happy, or very unhappy, with a product.

As Instagram research manager Sian Townsend says[176]: *"The customer issues that aren't on your radar, that you're completely unaware of, can be the most important things you need to hear. [...] There's a reason doctors ask if there's "anything else you want to talk about?" at the end of your appointment. It often triggers the patient to talk about their most important issue."*

It's one of the reasons why, in the early days, Amazon founder Jeff Bezos made his email address available to everyone[177]. Even today, Bezos gets a lot of complaints, which he often reads and forwards to the appropriate people on his team with a single question mark, meaning *"what the heck is going on?"*.

This open-door strategy can help to reveal patterns, and increase the likelihood of serendipitous outcomes. It can also help you improve your product so that you acquire new users and customers.

Look at the roles and profiles of the users who have provided unsolicited feedback: *Are there users that **should have** been using your product?*

The users who have signed up, started using your product, realized that it was missing X, Y, or Z and moved on, but who went out of their way to give your team feedback, are people who were trying to get more—or different—value from your product.

Qualified prospects who never signed up, but still wrote in to give feedback, can also be good sources of insights.

Analyze the feedback that both types of users have provided: *Are there any patterns? Anything that fits your product strategy and could convince more people to adopt your product?*

Learning from Customers "Hacking" Your Product

> "If every customer is using your product "correctly", you'll never learn anything interesting about what to do next.[178]"

Aaron Levie

There's a reason why established businesses set up incubators, organize hackathons, and hold various types of innovation competitions.

There's a reason why companies expose some of their products' services via public application programming interfaces (APIs), and create app marketplaces.

There's a reason why it's generally a good idea to keep at least a few doors open for spontaneous feedback.

Outside innovation is good for business.

As smart and creative as your product team might be, they'll never be able to imagine *all* the ways your technology could create value in the market.

Ultimately, many opportunities might not be worth pursuing—but it's good business to be aware of all opportunities.

Beyond monitoring support communications (Chapter #12), consider keeping an eye on:

- New stories and use cases emerging from customer conversations
- New feature requests, including product integrations
- Unusual feature uses
- Increases in uncaught errors or internal search queries
- Popular public or private API integrations
- Public Zaps (Zapier) or product embeds if that's a possibility

Your goal is to catch the early signals that smart and creative people are trying to expand the functionalities of your product.

Many businesses, like eBay for example, have miscellaneous categories like "Everything Else". Monitoring similar *catch-alls* can help point to unmet needs.

The opportunities that you should explore further are those that:

1. are popular or expanding quickly in reach, or popularity;
2. flow from and align with the core value of your product; and
3. are perceived as adding value by a large subset of your customer base.

Features that meet these three criteria will often be worth building.

Analyzing Need Satisfaction

"Companies must know three things: what all the customer outcomes are, which of those outcomes are important, and which are unsatisfied."

Tony Ulwick

Tony Ulwick is the inventor of Outcome-Driven Innovation (ODI)®and the founder of Strategyn, a consulting firm that helps Fortune 100 companies to create successful innovations.

The ODI process helps Tony and his team uncover outcomes that are both important and unsatisfied. This, in turn, helps their customers address unmet needs through new or existing products.

In Chapter #4, we covered techniques to help you uncover and formulate desired outcome statements. At this stage, you can use ODI's quantitative survey method to figure out which outcomes your team should address.

To run this survey with the intent of creating a more attractive product, first you should gather all desired outcomes related to the core functional Job—including those that your product addresses and those that it doesn't.

For the survey to be conclusive, you'll need at least 150 participants[179]. These should be Job performers—the people who are striving to get the Job done—who have been recruited randomly. Participants should include prospects, your customers, and customers of your competitors.

Because of the volume and variety of the participants that you need for this survey, it can be a good idea to work with a research recruitment firm.

Before sending the survey, you should also test that your desired outcome statements are clear and can be understood (Chapter #12). This will help ensure that the results of your analysis are representative.

Although the ODI team will typically use the survey to evaluate *all* desired outcome statements—sometimes as many as 150—this can quickly overwhelm participants[180].

An alternative is to focus on the 15-25 most common desired outcomes, based on your initial research. You'll get better responses, although you will miss some of the opportunities.

For the survey, you should ask participants to rate each outcome for importance and satisfaction, on a scale of one to ten:

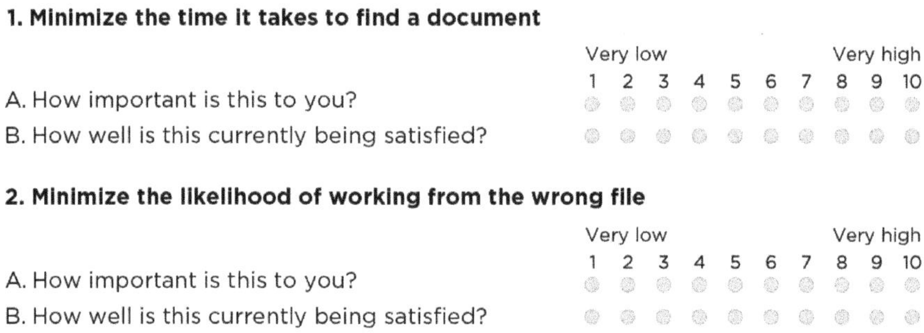

Figure 18.1 - ODI's Desired Outcome Survey

The data that you collect will allow you to assess desired outcomes one by one. To calculate the opportunity score of a particular desired outcome, you can use ODI's Opportunity Algorithm®:

Importance + (Importance - Satisfaction) = Opportunity Score

The higher the score, the more important the opportunity.

Dan Olsen, consultant and author of *The Lean Product Playbook*, has independently developed a similar approach, which uses an importance versus satisfaction matrix.

He recommends plotting desired outcomes on a 2x2 grid.

In his model, the bottom quadrants are considered not worth going after.

The top-right quadrant tends to include large opportunities that are very competitive. To win these opportunities, your solution needs to be at least 10 times better than what's currently on the market.

The top-left quadrant represents your best opportunities, where you can create value for customers.

Figure 18.2 - Dan Olsen's Importance vs. Satisfaction Grid

Dan says that the area (Satisfaction with the Product X Importance of the User Need) can be viewed as a proxy for the amount of value that can be created. The bigger the area, the more potential for value creation:

Figure 18.3 - Customer Value Estimates

By comparing the survey responses of prospects and your competitors' customers with responses from your customers, you can identify desired outcomes—which you can focus on to attract new customers. Opportunities will shift as new competitors enter the market and dissatisfaction gets addressed. You can update your research over time to track the evolution of markets and to identify new and emerging opportunities.

As Tony Ulwick says: *"Needs that are very important generally stay very important. What changes is the satisfaction level."*

Track satisfaction and the opportunities will reveal themselves.

Making Progress

> "Oftentimes, that first guess is usually not going to get us to the outcome, because to be honest, if it does get us to the outcome, then the outcome is probably not hard enough."
>
> Dan Touchette

No matter what is the source of your innovation—ideas, unprompted feedback, hacks, desired outcome surveys, etc—you need to make sure that whatever you add to your product drives the right behavior.

Building functionalities with the aim of attracting new customers can be dangerous. If these new features don't land you more customers, then they will simply add bloat to your product, and may even turn away some of your current customers.

Thankfully, you can learn before building.

If new features were requested by past users or customers, then reach back, giving the users a timeline and telling them that these functionalities will become part of a paid plan.

Do they get back to you? Do they delay? Will the new functionalities address their needs? Do they have any objections?

If the features don't get them back in your product, or get them to upgrade, then keep testing.

Create a new landing page identical to your current landing pages. Use the exact same targeting as you have used for user acquisition. Add the new functionalities and their benefits. Evaluate performance. *Does it actually increase sign-ups? Does it drive more conversions?*

Don't build new features to attract users without first validating that this will change behaviors. Adding features that don't move the needle will make your product more complicated to use.

Case Study
How LANDR Expanded Its Market

"Chase customers, not channels."

Unknown

In 2014, LANDR became the first ever instant music mastering service. Historically, only artists with recording contracts could afford to master their songs. But with LANDR, any artist, anywhere, could master music at a fraction of the cost of studio mastering[181].

LANDR's mastering tool was disruptive. Not only did it use artificial intelligence (AI) to improve and optimize the sound, it mastered tracks in less than two minutes.

The simplicity and versatility of this tool helped attract a wide range of customers, from DJs to record labels, and all the way to music composers and engineers.

As the customer base grew, various use cases began to emerge. From album mastering to sharing and promotion, it was clear that creators wanted to do more with their music. Groups of users and customers were trying to get around some of the limitations of the product. Many users were writing in to support, asking for extra features and enhancements.

The company could have decided to add more functionalities to their mastering tool at the risk of breaking the simplicity of the product. Instead, they decided to strategically expand their market by following the life cycle of a song. In 2016, they added collaboration tools. In 2017, they added music distribution and promotion functionalities. In 2018, they added music samples to help creators create more music.

In the course of a few years, LANDR transitioned from being a single-feature product to being a full creative platform addressing a range of related Jobs for music creators.

The platform LANDR created greatly improved their ability to acquire customers. Now, users can sign up to master, distribute, or promote their music. Eventually, they discover the other tools at their disposal, and stick around for the entire platform.

What else are your users trying to achieve?

At the time of writing, LANDR had acquired more than 3 million users, and was releasing 20,000 songs a month, with 12M tracks mastered since launch.

It's safe to say that adding complementary tools greatly helped expand LANDR's market.

Taking Action

1. Source acquisition-enhancing improvements by analyzing the pull from other markets, sifting through unprompted feedback, analyzing need satisfaction, or learning from customers "hacking" your product.
2. Clarify the scope of the improvements that you're hoping to make. Create a timeline.
3. Reach back to the requesters asking them to upgrade to get early access to the improvements.
4. Test demand through landing page tests or willingness to buy analyses (Chapter #16).
5. Don't build new functionalities in the hope of acquiring customers without first validating behavior change.
6. *Collaborating with others?* Share a PDF version of this chapter at **solvingproduct.com/chapter-18**.

19 / 26

Uncovering Opportunities to Create New Products

You're starting to max out growth from your product. Use the techniques in this chapter to **uncover opportunities to create new products** for your users.

"Any new product has to capitalize on unique strengths of the business.[182]"

Lew Cirne
New Relic Founder & CEO

Your team has ideas.

The customer data you're getting is pointing to a lot of unmet needs on the market.

Competitors are adding products of their own.

Many of the most successful organizations on the market have several products—*shouldn't yours too?*

At this stage, the temptation to expand your product line is strong.

However, the more products, product configurations, or code bases that your organization has to maintain, the less quickly it will be able to move, and the more distracted teams and executives will become.

If your team can only move slowly, and lacks clear focus, then it will be slow to learn and adapt.

For this reason, your team's initial answer to the idea of adding new products should always be "No".

Although you should constantly be scouting for new opportunities, creating altogether new products should always be the last option on your list. You should only consider adding products when there is undeniable proof that your business will be better for it.

As you'll see in the ProfitWell case study at the end of this chapter, there are times when expanding the product line can lead to great results. Most times, however, new products lead to wasted efforts that yield little to no new value[183].

Tread carefully.

> *If you were a service company...*
>
> *This step would be about figuring out your customers' other needs to strategically expand your service offering.*

Techniques You Can Use

It's a good idea to jump back to the Idea Stage at this point.

Although you may have a good understanding of your customers' needs and of market dynamics, our assumptions can easily lead us down the wrong path. As we have seen already, any new product idea should be guilty until proven innocent.

- **Customer Discovery Interviews** or **Contextual Inquiries** (Chapter #4) will help you identify or confirm the existence of another Customer Job.
- **Validating Through Preselling** (Chapter #7) will help you validate the opportunity.

New product opportunities should be treated with the same level of scrutiny that allowed you to reach PMF with your original business idea. Make sure you cover your bases by revisiting the steps covered in the Idea Stage.

Making Progress

"Managers have come to expect that more than half their innovation initiatives will fail. To compensate, companies commonly invest in dozens of initiatives and hope that those that succeed will recoup the investments made in those that fail. This undisciplined approach is not only wasteful, it also directs resources away from opportunities that are truly worthy of pursuit."

Upon his return to Apple in 1997, Steve Jobs famously laid out all Apple's products on a meeting room table[184].

Looking at the display, Steve and his team concluded that 30% of Apple's products were incredibly good. And about 70% of them were either pretty good, or they were things that Apple didn't need to be doing, businesses they didn't need to be in. To move the company forward, they pared down their road map, and refocused their energy on fewer products.

In 2014, Basecamp (then 37signals) moved back from a multi-product strategy to focusing on a single product based on very similar reasoning[185].

Rand Fishkin, co-founder and ex-CEO of Moz, another company that had a multi-product strategy, says: *"Looking back over the last few years of product growth rates, there was an uncanny correlation – as if each new product we added to the mix subtracted a little from the growth of every other product we offered.[186]"*

The products they had added—like Followerwonk, a Twitter analytics product—had been successful on their own. But sold under the umbrella of Moz, producers of SEO software, they *took away* from their growth[187].

In Rand's opinion, to succeed with a multi-product strategy your initial product needs to have enough momentum, viability, and traction to stand on its own.

Because multiple products can dilute your brand and hurt your growth rate, businesses should only consider adding new products when they have the resources to make it work, and when their core product can't be expanded without diluting its effectiveness.

To make real progress in expanding your product line, make sure the new product addresses a distinct, but related, Customer Job.

Your customers should view the new product both as an extension of your first product, and as a logical addition to your product line.

If the products don't overlap in function, there will be little to no synergy between them.

To assess the potency of new product concepts, GoPractice Founder & CEO Oleg Yakubenkov also recommends asking[188]:

- *What added value does the new product create for the target audience?*
- *Is this added value enough to make users switch from competitors' products?*
- *Does this new product exist in the same value chain?*
- *What is the potential of this new business?*
- *Is it big enough?*

A new product won't gain ground simply by association. Bing, Microsoft's search engine, is a relatively small player in the search market[189], despite its parent company's distribution power and large user base.

Make sure you give time and space to the new product, to allow it to reach maturity. If you don't, then your products will compete for resources and attention, and will trigger conflicts around product strategy.

Case Study How ProfitWell Expanded Its Product Line

"If you are going to expand, the key is to look for what's uniquely adjacent and possible for **you**, based on the position you've developed. For example, how much easier was it for

Amazon to launch the first successful ebook platform, given they were the number one seller of books online?[190]"

Evan Williams
Serial Entrepreneur

Patrick Campbell founded ProfitWell (formerly Price Intelligently) in 2012.

Their original product, Price Intelligently, helped businesses to improve their pricing strategy by allowing them to capture willingness to pay data from customers.

Although Patrick's vision had always been to create a product business, what they soon realized was that customers didn't feel comfortable making pricing decisions on their own. Patrick's team could create more value for customers by combining tech and services.

Since their pricing research relied on cleaning and analyzing large sets of survey data (work that consumed a lot of resources), Patrick's team was actively looking for better ways to capture the financial, top of the funnel, and engagement data needed to do the work. It wouldn't be easy to get access to all those data points, but it had the potential to drastically improve their business.

The idea was still on their minds when, months later, Patrick was helping a customer who was about to IPO with their pricing. He was shocked to realize that the company had been calculating MRR churn wrongly.

The company's CEO had managed several businesses. Their team was experienced. Yet their data was off.

After digging around, Patrick's team realized that many organizations had similar problems. More and more data pointed towards a need on the market.

Patrick knew that adding new products would be challenging, but he also knew that their TAM was small. The market they were serving—subscription and recurring revenue businesses—had at most 100,000 companies.

To build a $100M company, they would need to increase their Average Revenue per User (ARPU). Selling multiple products to the same customers could help them do that.

In 2015, the company launched ProfitWell[191] (now ProfitWell Metrics), a free subscription metrics dashboard.

Although the original idea wasn't to launch a free product, their research had indicated that many businesses were unwilling to pay for analytics products[192]. *Metrics* would help attract customers and inform their next opportunities.

Within the next few years, ProfitWell launched *Retain*, a product designed to help reduce churn from payment failures, and *Recognized*, an audit-proof revenue recognition product. Both products leveraged their unique expertise and the large dataset they had collected through *Metrics*. They both delivered on clear outcomes businesses were willing to pay for.

Although managing four products could have been a challenge that was too big to tackle, all of ProfitWell's products were targeted at the same customers, just for different roles within the organizations.

As Patrick says: *"Companies don't take multi-product strategies on until they're $100 million companies, and we're a $10 million company. [...] If we were targeting different types of companies and different types of buyers, I think it would be a very dumb decision."*

A multi-product strategy can work, but for it to work, there have to be clear synergies between the products, the users or the buyers.

Taking Action

1. Evaluate your organization: *Do you have resources and capacity that can be freed up to tackle the creation of a new product?* Only

consider building new products if you have enough capacity.

2. Get back to the Idea stage to uncover Customer Jobs via Customer Discovery Interviews or Contextual Inquiry Interviews.
3. Identify a Customer Job that you can provide added value on, and that can be perceived as an extension of your main product or a logical addition. Think expansion pack, not an altogether different opportunity.
4. Validate the opportunity with both current and new customers.
5. Only move forward once you've found an opportunity that *adds* to your business's product line.
6. *Collaborating with others?* Share a PDF version of this chapter at **solvingproduct.com/chapter-19**.

Stage 5:

Maturity

Can We Find More Growth?

"Customers are always beautifully, wonderfully dissatisfied, even when they report being happy and business is great. Even when they don't yet know it, customers want something better, and your desire to delight customers will drive you to invent on their behalf.[193]"

Jeff Bezos
Amazon Founder & CEO

At the Maturity stage, growth is expected to slow down.

If you've done your job right, a large share of the market knows about your product, you have taken the most interesting opportunities, and your team has become experts at executing your current strategy.

Now the biggest opportunities for transformative growth will come from business developments, new innovations, and mergers and acquisitions.

The product is successful and at maturity. You've won, *right?*

Now you can sit back, *exploit*, and expect the business to last another... *18 years?!*

In 1958, the companies that made up the S&P 500 had an average life expectancy of 61 years. In recent years, the average life expectancy has fallen to under 20 years, and it's still falling[194].

The position of incumbents has never been more fragile.

Sure, customers know about your company, *and* you have revenue and a solid user base, *and* your product is ahead of the competition—but things can change quickly, and sometimes very subtly, in technology.

Case Study Escaping Experience Rot at VWO

"The advantage you have yesterday, will be replaced by the trends of tomorrow. You don't have to do anything wrong, as long as your competitors catch the wave and do it RIGHT, you can lose out and fail."

Ziyad Jawabra
Management Consultant

Ashwin Gupta is in charge of growth at Visual Website Optimizer (VWO), a product created by Wingify in New Delhi, India in 2009.

VWO's core product is used by marketing teams to run growth and product experiments.

The teams that use the VWO platform often have pipelines of experiments to run each month. They log in, do their tasks, and log back in the next day to see the results.

Ashwin says: *"When you look at the dashboard, you've got 90% of users logging in. Things are great."*

But when speaking with customers more generally one day, Ashwin was surprised to hear about some of the *hacks* that users had come up with to get around what they felt were product limitations. On thinking through the stories that he had heard, it was clear that some features were missing.

When he dug into the issues, Ashwin realized that some users had been growing dissatisfied with the product. He was stunned. None of that had been reflected in their use of the product.

His team was monitoring the data daily. People were logging in, completing their tasks, and using the product. Yet, there was a bubble of dissatisfaction brewing.

Through in-depth conversations with users, Ashwin's team eventually realized that VWO users *had* to run experiments as part of their work. Many of them were forced to use the product. They were logging in and setting up experiments—but they weren't satisfied with the product.

Ashwin's fear was that, once this bubble of dissatisfaction grew big enough, users would jump at the opportunity to use a competing product if an alternative appeared.

He had to understand how to either pop this bubble, or reduce it significantly.

The Challenge

> "Your biggest risk isn't occasional failure it's sustained mediocrity.[195]"

Luke Wroblewski
Google Product Director

As organizations mature, they tend to shift from being problem-or customer-centric to being solution-centric.

Teams become more specialized; they start thinking about their own goals and realities, sometimes to the detriment of the larger organization. People become motivated to sell more of their unique expertise, and what their team does.

Research becomes its own function. Teams start relying on others for learning about their users and customers. It becomes difficult to justify doing your own research.

With hundreds or thousands of customers and a Board to satisfy, a lot of things need to be maintained, and the stakes are much higher. Code has to be production quality. Copy needs to be reviewed before roll out. Design needs to fit within the brand guidelines. Things start to slip through the cracks.

As a result, customers end up as a kind of third party sitting on the outside, with competitors increasingly focused on one another, losing track of what their customers want.

> *"The bigger your company is, the harder it is to get out of the building."* – Zoran Kovacevic, TripActions Product Lead

Product teams complain about their lack of autonomy, the time it takes to make decisions, and the overall lack of innovation.

It's incredibly difficult to try to cause dramatic change in a large and financially successful company.

Mature companies are almost nothing like startups. Their staff are driven by different motivations, they have different expertise and skillsets, and they don't view the world the way the company's founding team once did.

How do you drive new growth when the business is focused on operationalizing its current model?

The Opportunity

"When you confuse the Job to be Done with your solution, you are tying yourself with one cycle of innovation."

Des Traynor

The general theory for products is that they are first introduced to fill an unmet need, they become more valuable over time, the market is exploited, and then eventually, the product is retired, as it is no longer perceived as valuable by its customers[196].

Although physical products tend to follow similar paths, *why would digital products need to meet the same fate?*

Adobe, founded in 1982, created its flagship product, Photoshop, in 1988[197]. The product was publicly released in 1990. It has gone through several major transitions from shrink-wrapped software to cloud and mobile—but it's still going strong today. While the designs, functionalities, and revenue models may have changed, the product still fulfills the same Jobs for its users.

Technology products don't *need* to be retired. Their specific implementations might though.

Things are always changing. Problems mature. Use cases mature. Technology matures. What is differentiated today might become table stakes tomorrow. Businesses have to constantly reinvent themselves.

Anytime technology changes, Des Traynor recommends asking: *"Does it make it cheaper, faster, easier for your customers to make progress in their lives?[198]"*

As we've seen in the previous section, in order to keep growing it's important to find a balance between expanding your product line and breathing new life into your existing products.

Growth rates typically slow down at the Maturity stage. To keep growing, you have to keep pushing the boundaries. Your company culture needs to get to a point where it tolerates both failure and the process of exploration.

Do more research, get qualitative and quantitative research teams talking, don't assume you know your customers, and don't let red tape limit your ability to ship and iterate.

As Jeff Bezos says: *"If you double the number of experiments you do per year, you're going to double your inventiveness".*

At Maturity, we focus on:

- Compounding growth by running rapid product, growth, and revenue experiments (Chapter #20);
- Maximizing product fit and effectiveness (Chapter #21);
- Assessing remaining growth opportunities and improving user acquisition (Chapter #22);
- Maximizing revenue and profitability (Chapter #23).

If you were a service company...

This phase would be about improving profitability, the way work gets delivered, sales, and finding new ways to grow.

Compounding Wins

"The only way that you're going to win is by testing a lot, lot more things, and being lucky in finding something that sticks. The entire logic is to have a very high pace of testing, being very good at measuring the outcomes, and just moving very fast, and something is going to work."

Guillaume Cabane

At this stage, the best way to find success is to make use of the entire organization and to speed up testing.

In a presentation in 2014[199], Satya Patel, Twitter's ex-VP of Product, demonstrated the impact of the testing culture at Twitter:

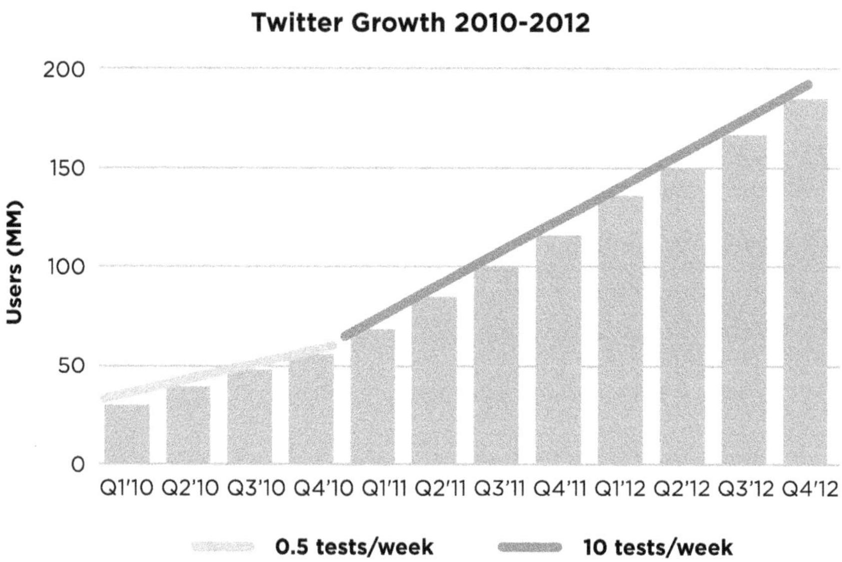

Figure VI.1 - Twitter's Growth 2010-2012

In 2011, when Twitter went from running one experiment every two weeks to running more than 10 experiments a week, growth significantly sped up. Up to a point of diminishing return, the more tests they ran, the faster they grew.

It's important to acknowledge that experiments are based on assumptions, and that assumptions are often wrong.

The performance of a rapid experimentation process depends on:

1. the quality of the insights and research, which help the team come up with better hypotheses;
2. the speed at which they're able to run tests and experiments; *and*
3. their ability to learn from their experiments.

Combining qualitative and quantitative research will help your team to come up with the best experiments possible.

Research will help improve your team's base knowledge, while experiments will accelerate learning and reduce uncertainty.

In the aggregate, experiment ideas sourced from the entire organization will perform better.

While there will inevitably be some misses, following the experimentation process covered in Chapter #20 will help you make real progress.

Onwards!

20 / 26

Compounding Growth Through Rapid Experiments

Your business is maxing out. Use the following techniques to **compound growth** by running **rapid product, growth, or revenue experiments**.

"If you want to be successful as a company, the culture should be of experimentation. Experimentation, to be successful, should be based on user insights."

Karl Gilis
AGConsult Partner

It takes a certain level of maturity to run effective experiments.

To avoid shipping experiments for the sake of shipping experiments, teams need to focus on delivering outcomes. They also need to be willing to embrace failure to make progress.

On average, 80% of experiments fail to deliver the expected outcomes, but with the right method, 100% of experiments can help you learn and progress.

With the right mindset, experiments can help teams to make increasingly better decisions.

To create this mindset, assemble a multidisciplinary team—often a marketer, a product manager, a data analyst, and engineers—and let them work out their own process.

Unless your organization is entirely focused on growing through experimentation, it's a good idea to split off the growth team to avoid competition between backlogs.

You should focus on one or two core goals at a time, aligning with your North Star metric or the AARRR steps (Chapter #12) that you're focused on. Your goals should be big, your experiments small and nimble.

Once you know what you're trying to achieve, you need to establish a high-tempo cadence of testing.

Since the average growth experiment across organizations has a one in five chance of working, the more *quality* experiments your team is able to run, the faster you'll learn, and hopefully, grow.

But there's a method to creating this velocity. Sean Ellis (Chapter #9), recommends following a four-step process:

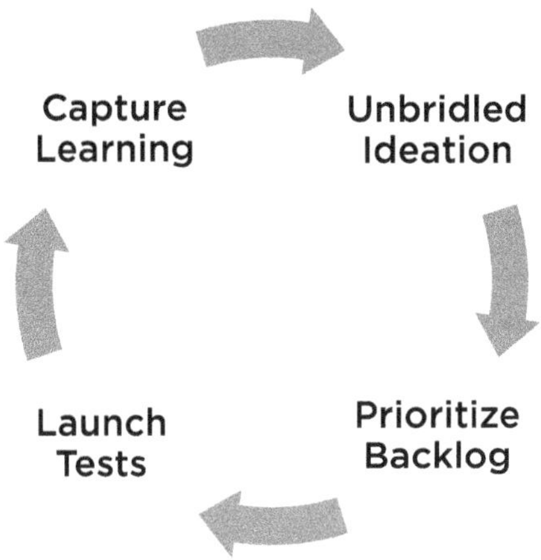

Figure 20.1 - Sean Ellis' Rapid Experimentation Process

1) Unbridled ideation: To create inclusivity within the team, generate better ideas, and always have a large pool of experiments to pick from, it's a good idea to solicit opportunities from the team, but also the entire organization. Testing many concepts helps reduce politics, and makes team members feel like they're part of the process. Transparently sharing experiment results and holding team members accountable for performance reinforces objectivity.

2) Backlog prioritization: Ellis created the I.C.E. score[200] to help rank ideas. In his model, each person within the team assigns a ranking from one to 10 along three criteria:

1. **Impact**: *If the experiment is successful, what's the potential impact? More revenue? More sign-ups? More referrals?* Impact always needs to be in relation to the goal of the experiment.
2. **Confidence**: *What's the likelihood that the experiment delivers the expected impact? What evidence do we have to prove this?*
3. **Ease**: *How easy is it to run the experiment? Will it require a lot of engineering resources? Or is it a simple A/B test of marketing copy?*

Some organizations will want to change the relative weight of each of these criteria based on their own growth theses. Growth expert Guillaume Cabane recommends taking prioritization a step further by converting impact projections into dollar amounts[201]. Using Guillaume's approach, teams are able to make revenue growth projections for their organizations.

Each experiment's I.C.E. score can be used to guide prioritization. Hosting a weekly growth meeting will increase agility and help set a regular cadence for the team.

3) Test launch: During the week, teams take time to brainstorm and dive deeper into the experiments that they have committed to implementing.

If you're starting out, start small by running one or two experiments a week. As you learn and iron out your experimentation processes, gradually increase the number of experiments that your team runs, and how ambitious the experiments are. Starting with a good backlog will allow your team to build their experimentation muscles before they begin to increase test velocity.

Don't let past experiments blind you. Things change. There are hundreds of reasons why something didn't work in the past. Revisit old hypotheses, tweak their variables, and rerun the experiments when it makes sense.

4) Operationalizing learnings: Lastly—and this step is the one teams often overlook—the team has to learn from every experiment it runs.

What was the goal? Why did it work/not work? What can be learned from the experiment?

Involve the whole team in the analysis. Talk through the results and assumptions made. A lot of times, the tests that *didn't* work lead to the biggest breakthroughs.

Making experiment results transparent and accessible helps to keep everyone in sync. It also ensures that your experimenting process remains focused on your goals, not on running series of experiments.

As we'll see in Chapter #25, it's often important to promote and evangelize cross-functional processes like high tempo testing in order to get top-down support and reinforce the value of the experimental mindset.

To get started fast, download the experiment prioritization template at **solvingproduct.com/experiments**.

If you were a service company...

This stage would be about creating experimental processes to improve your services, your funnel, and your profitability.

Techniques You Can Use

There are hundreds of types of experiments that you can run (product, value proposition, branding, etc). But there are only a few ways to evaluate your experiments.

- **Learning Through A/B Testing** will allow you to compare options against each other to determine which one performs best.
- **Learning Through Off-Brand Testing** is similar to running an A/B test in anonymity—off-brand tests are the digital equivalent of blind taste tests.

You need to establish rapid experimentation processes so you can quickly evaluate your product and market assumptions.

Learning Through A/B Testing

"If your definition of success is product progress then 90% of your experiments will end in failure.[202]"

Tristan Kromer
Innovation Coach

When doing research online, it might look like A/B tests are about technology—but they're not.

Today, most A/B tests are run using technology, but A/B testing has actually been around since the 18th century[203].

A/B testing is simply the idea of showing different options to similar audiences, and observing their behaviors. It's how prescription drugs are tested before they reach the market[204].

You may already be familiar with the concept of A/B testing under other names: split testing, A/B/n testing, or bucket testing.

Many businesses refrain from running A/B tests because of the amount of traffic their app or site gets (complex B2B for example), or because it can take a long time to get statistically significant results, but I'd argue that this is missing the point. If an A/B test can help increase the confidence that you have in making a decision, it can be deemed valuable.

That said, statistical significance—the likelihood that a relationship between two or more variables is caused by something other than chance—is something you should try to make use of once your business reaches maturity.

So, *what makes a good A/B test?*

There are three parts to a successful A/B test:

1. **A homogeneous segment**: Randomly selected, representative of your audience without noticeable biases.
2. **The experiment**: Forget complex or multivariate—many variables—tests. Learn about the most important thing, first.
3. **The success (or failure) criteria**: *What will tell you whether this experiment is a success or a failure?*

Peep Laja says that the average A/B test lasts 28 days[205]. This obviously depends on how much traffic you get, how discrete the action you're evaluating is, and the level of confidence that you are seeking.

It's a good idea to calculate the required sample size before testing. There are many online tools you can use to calculate sample sizes[206].

As a rule of thumb, you want at least 350 key actions—clicks, sales, conversions, etc—per variation (more if you plan to segment the results afterwards) before confirming test results.

The tests have to run long enough to overcome seasonality (e.g. summer vs winter, weekday vs weekend). For this reason, you should run tests for full weeks at a time stopping at the 7-, 14-, 21- or 28-day mark, watching out for outliers like holidays, unexpected mentions in the media, product releases, etc.

To get a homogeneous segment of users or customers, you can use an A/B testing platform like Optimizely or VWO. These tools randomly assign visitors or users to variants. Alternatively, you can decide to build your own tool, or use a randomly assigned user or customer attribute like a user ID to target representative slices of your audience.

Your A/B tests can be anything:

- Products
- Value propositions
- Features (positionings, copies, options, values, etc)
- Landing pages (offers, headlines, images, social proof elements, layouts, call-to-actions, etc)
- Emails (timings, templates, subject lines, personalization items, copies, etc)
- Sales script (sequences, arguments, value propositions, prices, etc)
- Branding elements
- Pricing, etc

The important thing is to **test, at most, one element at a time**.

You can test several variants against one another (A/B/C/D/etc), or against the control, your original version. But the more variants you test, the more traffic you need to send to each version, and the longer your test will take.

Small, incremental changes will obviously have a bigger impact on high traffic sites or products.

Last, but not least, you need a clear criterion for success or failure. This is best formulated as a hypothesis:

> The new onboarding sequence will increase our 7-day activation rate by at least five percent.

The clearer your hypothesis is, and the more aligned with business metrics your target is, then the easier it will be to test and compare, and to communicate the results with your team.

A/B tests help you to see what happens in a real-world context—much more than user tests or any form of lab testing.

It's important to remember that, as Hotjar co-founder and CEO David Darmanin, says[207]: *"Testing is for confirming winning ideas, not finding them."* To understand true causation, you'll need to conduct extra analyses, doing user tests (Chapter #5) or prompting visitors for feedback (Chapter #12).

Peep Laja recommends stopping an A/B test when you have 1) a big enough sample size, 2) a long enough test duration, and 3) statistical significance (95% or higher).

If your site has low traffic or gets few conversions, make sure you get a big lift before calling a test a success.

It's a good idea to always be running some kind of A/B test. Just make sure that your tests don't overlap with the same users.

Learning Through Off-Brand Testing

> "The question was simple, if this wasn't Toyota, would anybody even care?[208]"

David J. Bland

Although Off-Brand Testing is a type of A/B test, I think it's worth separating it out.

While A/B tests generally use your company's branding and official channels, off-brand experiments are run in anonymity.

As mentioned in the previous chapter, mature organizations usually have more to lose by running experiments than startups.

Off-brand tests allow them to run experiments while minimizing the risk to their brand equity. It's also a way to avoid skewing perception due to brand association. Toyota[209], Dell, and NatWest[210] are examples of large companies that have run off-brand experiments to gauge market demand.

With off-brand testing, the product is presented using a no-name brand or without any branding.

As with A/B tests, off-brand experiments need homogeneous segments, an experiment, and success or failure criteria.

Because of the complexity of creating no-brand versions of products, off-brand experiments are mostly used to gauge market demand, for example evaluating conversions on landing pages.

This type of test can be used to reveal if there is merit in an idea independent from an established brand, whether there might be an opportunity for a breakout product, whether a different value proposition could work best, or if other segments could be of interest to the organization.

To run an off-brand test, first determine what you are testing:

- a product;
- a segment;
- a value proposition; *or*
- branding elements.

You should create a landing page, and confirm interest through sales (Chapter #16) or sign-ups. If you're trying to compare performance against your current product, use your existing benchmarks as comparison points.

You can capture traffic with your current ad targeting if you are running ads, or by creating new ad targeting to reach the desired audience. If you intend to do that, consider first testing the quality of sign-ups (Chapter #12).

By segmenting results and breaking them down by sub-segments, you may be able to find early adopters who feel the pain more acutely than others.

Making Progress

"If all we did was split test everything, we'd end up at porn."

Sean Ellis

Because of the high velocity, and the fact that you could be running product and growth experiments forever, it would be easy to run an endless stream of experiments that only slightly move the needle.

At this stage, it's a good idea to build in processes to create a bit of distance from your work.

In his book, *Shape Up*[211], Basecamp's head of strategy, Ryan Singer, explains why Basecamp follows six-week sprints with two-week periods of downtime.

Not only do those two weeks allow teams to close the loop on outstanding work, they also allow them to create distance from the work, allowing them to better evaluate the progress made.

Your team should *feel* the business metrics, and be completely honest about whether they are making progress, or if they are, in the words of Karl Gilis, just *"tweaking bullshit"*.

When you start seeing a high level of test failures or non-results, Kieran

Flanagan recommends switching the focus to more complex growth opportunities and taking bigger risks.

This can be a good stress test. Optimization helps you find the maximum (local maxima), giving you the best from your current model. Innovation can get you to the next level.

Set clear goals, find the highest potential experiments to run, nurture the experimental approach in your organization, and gradually increase test scope and velocity.

If you stick with the process long enough, growth will follow.

Case Study How Rocketrip Got Diverted From Its Goal

> "Getting people to think about the problem space as some situation we're going to experiment on, we're going to create hypotheses, and we're going to be able to do whatever we can to solve that solution, but we don't know what the solution is. That's a hard concept for people to understand."
>
> Dan Touchette

Dan Touchette was director of product at Rocketrip, a platform designed to help companies save on business travel by incentivizing employees to spend less on travel.

When using Rocketrip, employees were given a price to beat, based on the expected cost of travel. Every dollar saved under that price got redistributed evenly between the employee and the company, making saving a shared affair. For this to work, however, employees had to change their travel shopping behavior. If they didn't see the price to beat while they shopped, their behavior rarely changed.

One quarter, Dan's team was asked to increase the number of users who saw the price to beat while they shopped. The goal was aggressive—they had to increase the rate by at least 50%.

Because Rocketrip used a browser extension to display the price to beat, and few users were signing into the extension, the team's first instinct was to try to increase the sign-in rate. They spent weeks and weeks iterating and refining the sign-in flow, trying to get employees to log in.

Through continuous experimentation, they managed to get two, three, even four percent improvements. More users were signing in, but the changes weren't reflected in the number of shoppers who saw the price to beat. They still had a long way to go to meet their goal.

One quarter in, it was becoming clear that users didn't care about signing into the extension.

Dan and his team started to wonder: *"Why do we actually need them to sign in in the first place? Can we figure out who they are, and present them a price to beat regardless of whether they're signed in or not?"*

Their goal had been to increase the number of users who saw the price to beat. Along the way, they had become so focused on their experiment pipeline and improving the sign-in flow that they had lost track of their real objective. They had made a lot of progress improving the sign-in rate, but the shopping behaviors hadn't changed much.

That quarter, Dan and his team learned an important lesson: The end goal should always be kept front and center; focusing too much on your experiment pipeline can lead you astray.

This is what Jeff Bezos calls *process as proxy*. He says[212]: *"Good process serves you so you can serve customers. But if you're not watchful, the process can become the thing. This can happen very easily in large organizations. The process becomes the proxy for the result you want. You stop looking at outcomes and just make sure you're doing the process right."*

Taking Action

1. Establish processes to collect product, growth, and revenue experiment ideas from everyone in your organization.
2. Use a framework like Sean Ellis' I.C.E. score to rank your experiment backlog.
3. Run A/B tests or Off-Brand Tests to evaluate your experiments.
4. Create processes for capturing and operationalizing learnings from the experiments you run.
5. Periodically re-evaluate the effectiveness of your experimentation processes to make sure they deliver actual outcomes for your business.
6. *Collaborating with others?* Share a PDF version of this chapter at **solvingproduct.com/chapter-20**.

21 / 26

Maximizing Product Fit and Effectiveness

Your product serves the needs of different segments and user types. Use the following techniques to **improve your product's fit and effectiveness**.

"Curiously, sometimes experimentation leads to arrogance. It's way too easy to jump to conclusions and develop a false sense of security when a number of experiments appear to confirm your hypotheses. You may even believe you reached the "One

Truth". You didn't. There's still a lot you don't know."

Claudio Perrone
PopcornFlow (Continuous Innovation & Change) Creator

Experimentation is only one part of the equation.

Experiments help you to explore and compare options, but often you can only infer why they either worked or didn't.

As PartnerStack VP of Product Daniel Shapiro says: *"I think we've gotten a little overly dependent on highly analytical and rapid testing as a crutch to deeply understand the customers. [...] What that really is, is you're not understanding your customer. You're just kind of understanding the symptoms and the reactions to features. You're not understanding the why behind what's motivating them."*

To accelerate growth, you should combine in-depth research—to understand problems more richly and generate ideas—and experimentation—to explore and test new concepts.

Products (and businesses) are moving targets. At this stage, it's still possible to improve your understanding of your customers' journeys by exploring acquisition, activation, revenue, retention, and referral mechanics.

Although the analyses that you focus on should align with your company's priorities, *all* organizations can benefit from understanding their customers' journeys at a deeper level.

As Douglas W. Hubbard says: *"If you want an epiphany, look at a high-value measurement you were previously ignoring."*

> *If you were a service company...*
>
> *This stage would be about improving customer retention by perfecting your services and service delivery.*

Techniques You Can Use

Reaching the Maturity stage doesn't mean that your product is perfect. In fact, thinking that your product is good enough—or worse, that it's perfect—is what tends to get companies in trouble. You can use the following techniques to find areas to improve:

- **Key Task Success Analysis** will help you evaluate how well users are able to perform key tasks in your product.
- **Learning from On-Site Research** will help you understand how your product fits into your customers' lives.
- **Value Fit Analysis** will help you monitor how well your product meets customer needs.

It's a good idea to set up processes to perform ongoing Value Fit Analyses. When you have time, consider doing On-Site Research, or a Key Task Success Analysis.

Key Task Success Analysis

> "If you're not world-class at integrations, and your whole product's dependent on that, you're screwed. So, one big piece is we had to get great at that, not just good at it, and every day we push that ball forward."

Hiten Shah

As your product has matured, it should have become quite obvious which actions and workflows matter more.

Since these key flows and actions are responsible for the value that users get from your product, you need to make sure that they're as polished as they can be.

There are three main ways to assess tasks:

1. **Success**: *Can users achieve their goals with your product? Can they complete their tasks?*
2. **Time**: *How much time does it take an average user to complete the task?* Time is often viewed as a proxy for ease, but it isn't always.
3. **Perceived ease of use**: *How hard is it to complete the task?* Ease is completely subjective. It can vary depending on users' backgrounds and experience.

Up to this point, you have been able to evaluate task success—task time even—through user tests (Chapter #5) or via visitor recordings (Chapter #10).

As a general rule, you can consider a task to have been a 'direct success' if the user completed it using the expected flow, an 'indirect success' if the user completed it using alternate flows, and a 'failure' if the user was unable to complete it.

According to research by Dr. Jeff Sauro[213], the average task completion rate across products is 78%. This means that, across products and experiences, 22% of tasks fail.

Many user testing platforms like UserTesting, Usabilla, or Maze can help you measure task time and success.

Although both measures are useful, perceived ease of use can give you an important benchmark to iterate against.

The Single Ease Question (SEQ) questionnaire is the best tool to evaluate ease of use. It's a single question questionnaire, generally administered right after a task to evaluate a user's feeling toward the task they just attempted. It asks:

> "Overall, how difficult or easy was the task to complete?"

A seven-point scale—labelled at the end points—makes user input quick and easy:

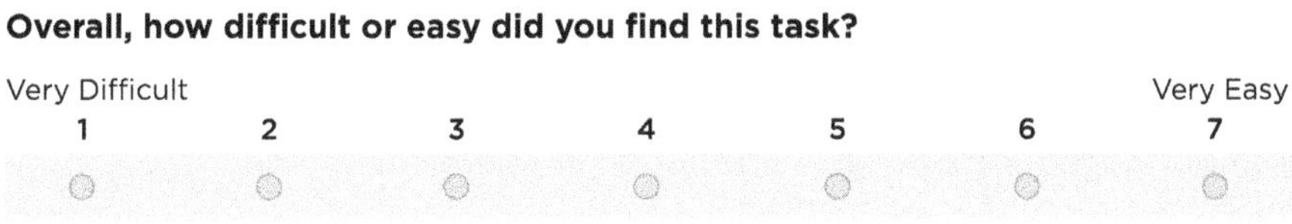

Figure 21.1 - The Single Ease Question Questionnaire

Post-task questionnaires should be short—three questions at most—to avoid breaking your user's flow.

In spite of the simplicity of the questionnaire, responses are strongly correlated with other usability metrics like the System Usability Scale (SUS)[214].

The SEQ score for a task is the average responses of the respondents. The average SEQ score across tasks is 5.5[215].

Scores can be broken down by segments, lifetime value, or any other user attributes.

Evaluating different tasks will help you identify the weakest parts of your product. Benchmarking the scores over time will help you track progress across iterations.

Since the SEQ questionnaire is not a good diagnostic tool, and users have difficulty separating the complexity of completing a task from the problems they experience while completing it, it's a good idea to ask a follow up question:

> "What is the primary reason for your score?"

The reasons for scores below five (out of seven) will help point out issues and friction points in your product's workflows.

Alternatively, customer experience expert Karl Gilis recommends asking *"How **difficult** was it to [Task]?"*

Although this open-ended question will generate lower scores than SEQ questionnaires, the answers will be a treasure trove of insights.

You can expand your research by targeting users who have just completed key tasks in your product with automated In-App messages. If you do, consider tracking the evolution of scores over time.

Learning from On-Site Research

"Always try to learn what other apps are your core customers using on a daily basis. This will allow to design similar experiences and remove any friction or create uncomfortable learning situations.[216]"

Eugen Eşanu
Laroche.co Designer

Users have certain expectations when they start using your product.

Their mental models—their frame of reality or thought process about how the world works—are the result of their beliefs, their use of other products, their culture, and their expectations for how the specific Job ought to be done.

Mental models allow us to predict how things work. It turns out that the closer your product *mirrors* your users' mental models, the more satisfied they'll be when using your product[217], and the easier it will be for them to build habits with it.

Creating this kind of alignment can have a big impact on retention, and can produce a strong competitive advantage for your company.

Analyzing mental models can help you to reveal gaps, and to point out mismatches between the product and customer expectations.

This is one of the reasons why, in the early days of Intuit, co-founder Scott Cook spent a lot of time in Staples office supply stores waiting for customers to buy Quicken[218]. Whenever someone bought the product, he would ask to follow them home to see how they use the product. This led to many great insights that helped guide product direction.

To understand how well your product fits in your users' lives, first identify:

- your product's usage frequency (monthly, weekly, daily, hourly, on-going, etc);
- your core users (be it many user types or profiles, or a single user for a simple consumer product); *and*
- the core activities you're trying to study.

If usage occurs less often than once a week, you may have difficulty getting useful data by going on-site. If that's the case, a diary study[219]—a research method designed to collect qualitative information by having users record entries about their daily lives involving the experience being studied—could yield better results.

You should recruit 5-10 participants per role or profile studied, and spend at least a few hours in their office or in their home. You can use the recruitment guide under Building Blocks to help source participants.

Since inviting yourself into their office or their home is a significant ask, it's probably a good idea to focus on users who are already getting a lot of value from your product. They'll be more likely to want to help once they understand that you are trying to make the product better for them.

Field studies are a bit like unscripted user tests, during which you observe people in their natural environment.

To put users at ease, make sure they understand that you're not testing them.

Let users go through their regular tasks and processes lightly probing them about their workflows, reasoning, triggers, and the challenges that they are facing.

Where are users struggling the most to get the Job done? Why are they getting off track? Are there steps that could be eliminated? How could the product get more of the Job done for them?

You'll want to ask questions like:

- *Why is this task important?*
- *Why did you do this step before that other step?*
- *What are you trying to achieve with [Task]?*
- *Why is this the best way to achieve [Task]?*
- *Do you always do [Task] this way?*
- *Are there times when you use different solutions to get the Job done? Why?*
- *What other responsibilities do you have before, during, or after using [Product]?*
- *What are the most central tasks that must be accomplished when [Job to be Done]?*
- *What solutions (products, services, etc.) do you use in this process step?*
- *Over time, what changes have you made to the way you get the [Task] done, and why?*
- *What have you done over time to [Job to be Done] more quickly? Why did you feel you had to do it? How did that help?*

Your goal is to map and understand:

- their thinking as they go about performing the core Jobs;
- how your product fits in the larger context of their life, or their work;
- the context in which they use your product (keeping an eye out for Post-it notes or anything else they use in conjunction with your product);
- other tools or products that they use;
- the challenges they face and how they overcome them; *and*
- triggers that lead to product use, and what follows their use of your product.

Take pictures when appropriate. Pay attention at all times. You might be surprised by what gets said, or what can be observed.

Analyzing workflows and comparing the behaviors of participants will help you find ways to improve and simplify your product, and add more *delighters* to your road map.

Keep your eyes (and ears) open.

Value Fit Analysis

> "Customers are loyal to the Job to be Done, not to the solutions they use.[220]"

Mike Boysen
Jobs to be Done Canvas Creator

Markets are accelerating.

As a result, businesses have to become more responsive to the market. If a business catches a wave too late, it stands to lose momentum—and customers—and it runs the risk of having to play catch-up.

The problem is that companies can easily miss signals. According to research[221], many organizations only do customer research a few times a year. That's simply not enough.

Although the market you're in tends to dictate how often research data needs to be analyzed, data capture should be continuous.

To make sure the market doesn't pass you by, set up at least two distinct continuous processes for capturing customer expectations.

Those could be:

1. Monitoring sign up and cancellation decision-making processes using Switch interviews (Chapter #12); and

2. Capturing open-ended responses to the PMF survey (Chapter #11).

Drift uses the same survey for important features (*"How would you feel if we discontinued this feature?"*). Responses give them a real-time feel of the value delivered by individual features.

Similarly, VWO uses the Customer Satisfaction Score (CSAT) to assess touch points along the sales cycle and customer journey (*"Overall, how satisfied are you with [Step]?"*). The survey results help them catch issues early.

Although you may decide to capture value fit data through other means, your goal will always be the same: to track the evolution of user and customer expectations over time.

It's a good idea to go through the data every other sprint, slicing it up by profiles, time periods, acquisition channels, etc. Keep an open mind. Better yet, get fresh pairs of eyes on the data.

It is normal to be less attuned to nuances when data don't seem to change much month-over-month. Fresh eyes can help to identify new patterns. This can also help build more empathy in the team.

Companies like Amazon, for example, have their own version of the Andon Cord[222]—a pull cord or button that workers can activate to stop the production and warn management in case of significant issues—from lean manufacturing[223].

At Amazon, there's a cultural norm that everybody's expected to *pull* the Andon Cord when something's wrong. A lot of technology companies could benefit from this concept.

It's a good idea to sign up to your product every couple of months. Try different workflows, test different actions, and evaluate the experience as a new user would. Smart new hires can also help point out gaps. It can be a good idea to capture their insights before their opinions get biased by the group.

Every year, the team at Amplitude runs a 'Kill the Company' (KTC) exercise[224]. The team imagines how they would beat their own company if they were to leave and start a competing organization.

There are many ways to test and monitor the value fit. However, all approaches depend on being able to be objective and see your product as it really is today on the market.

Making Progress

> "Companies who understand their customers better, and in a deeper way (than their competitors) build better products and bring those products to market much more effectively."

Daniel Shapiro
PartnerStack VP of Product

This step is about improving your product's fit and effectiveness.

To make progress and avoid going off track, mark any new discoveries as assumptions, pick a North Star metric, and run experiments to evaluate whether your findings truly improve product effectiveness.

Learning through SEQ questionnaires? Iterate against SEQ scores. Run experiments to make the score go up.

Learning through On-Site Research? The metric that you use will depend on what you are trying to improve. *Are you trying to improve a certain feature's adoption? Habituation? Reengagement?* Pick the metric that best captures task success or engagement.

Introduce changes progressively, running A/B tests (Chapter #20) to test the impact of the changes you're making.

Keep iterating and improving the ways in which your product fits into your customers' lives. Make your product's position unassailable.

Case Study
How the Market Changed for Basecamp

"If we don't create the thing that kills Facebook, someone else will."

Mark Zuckerberg
Facebook Co-Founder & CEO

If you've been working in technology these past ten years or more, you probably heard of Basecamp, or of its co-founders Jason Fried and David Heinemeier Hansson.

The company, originally named 37signals, launched its flagship product Basecamp in 2004. At the time, they were one of the first SaaS project management applications on the market.

They created a strong brand—and a cult following—with the help of their thought leadership on their blog, their best-selling books (REWORK, REMOTE, and Getting Real), and their strong opinions.

With over 130,000 customers[225], a profitable business, and a product loved by its users, no one could argue that Basecamp hasn't been a huge success. However, since Basecamp's initial launch in 2004, the market has really grown up around them.

With hundreds of project management apps on the market vying for a share of the market—including talented product teams and well-funded organizations—Basecamp's core product has had to deal with changing customer expectations.

The company that often spoke about 'ignoring the competition'[226], was built in different times under different premises.

They improved the product for their customers, made technological choices that worked for their business, and focused on their own perception of the market. But over time, the landscape changed, competitors leveled up, and channels like search and online advertising became major acquisition drivers for their competitors.

Basecamp grew through strong word of mouth, but they didn't advertise or spend time on their search engine positioning. And although Basecamp learned about their users, they probably didn't spend enough time studying the market to learn how to turn non-users into users.

Feeling the pressure over the years, they had to start thinking about how to market themselves again—using new channels, positionings, and value propositions to reflect new customer expectations.

They caught the market changes in time. In the last few years, they have started updating their strategy. They have hired search optimization consultants[227], created a free offering[228], and strengthened their marketing leadership[229].

Even the best organizations have to adapt when the market changes.

Taking Action

1. Get clarity on the key tasks that users perform in your product.
2. Set up processes for a Key Task Success Analysis, or conduct On-Site Research.
3. Create hypotheses based on findings. Run experiments to improve your product's fit and effectiveness.
4. Set up processes to continuously gather data on your product's value fit.
5. Avoid complacency.

6. *Collaborating with others?* Share a PDF version of this chapter at **solvingproduct.com/chapter-21**.

22
/
26

Assessing Remaining Growth Opportunities

You've been acquiring customers for a while now. Use the techniques below to **assess remaining growth opportunities** and **improve user acquisition**.

"It's important to diversify the kind of people you're talking to. Especially the customers, and see how they reacted to the product, what they thought about it, what made them actually use the product in the first place, what problem they were trying to solve, what were they doing before the product, was there another product in place or they were doing it manually."

Ashwin Gupta

It's almost inevitable that, at some point, user acquisition starts to slow down.

Either prospect quality will decrease, the effectiveness of your acquisition strategies will drop, or the lead pools that you've been targeting will grow numb to your messaging.

When that happens, you can experiment with new acquisition channels (Chapter #15), introduce your product to new markets (Chapter #17), or focus on maxing out your customer acquisition efforts.

> *If you were a service company...*
>
> *This stage would be about sizing up market demand, and finding new ways to get customers.*

Techniques You Can Use

You can assess the user acquisition efforts of your business by either zooming in, or zooming out. Both approaches can help reveal additional opportunities to grow your customer base.

- **Analyzing the Segments Within Your User Base** will help reveal the growth potential of the segments within your user base.
- **Assessing Brand Awareness** will help you look at the market at large to assess the remaining market opportunity, and understand whether you've saturated the market.

Segmentation will help refine your business operations. Assessing Brand Awareness can be useful when it feels like growth is starting to slow down.

Analyzing the Segments Within Your User Base

"A lot of products are one-size-fits-all. And it doesn't work super well for anybody. And nothing is done about it."

Indi Young

Up to this point, you've most likely been building your product to address the needs of your HXC (Chapter #9), a group of *best fit* customers, or personas prioritized by your team.

But, just as there are variations in your user base, there are also variations in the profiles within the groups you're targeting—accountants from Ohio won't all share the exact same needs or processes.

At maturity, one-size-fits-all isn't optimal.

There could be hundreds of sub-segments of users using your product. Some users within these segments may be completely satisfied with your product, while others might be looking for a replacement.

By creating experiences that better match the needs of these sub-segments, you'll be able to:

- reduce churn and dissatisfaction in neglected segments;
- increase usage and revenue across your user base; and
- define more tailored acquisition strategies to grow the most promising sub-segments.

But just as there are different ways to cut a cake, there are also different ways to segment a user base.

Good segments are homogeneous, mutually exclusive, have predictable behaviors, and can be reached through marketing and sales efforts.

The earlier in the customer journey that you are able to segment users, the better you will be able to adapt the experience to the specific needs of each segments.

So, what you're looking for is the earliest signal–leading indicator that allows you to predict behaviors across segments.

Good segmentation criteria might be company size for a chat product, or user roles for a sales tool, or number of subscribers for Mailchimp (as we'll see in the upcoming case study).

There are four main ways to segment users:

1. With **implicit data**: Implicit data is information that's inferred from other available data. As an example, sign-ups originating from organic channels tend to have higher purchase intent and convert better. Applying this theory to acquisition channel data could help with segmentation.
2. **Explicit data**: Explicit data is information captured through a form, a survey, or a setup process. Users understand that they are being asked questions, to which they give answers.
3. By **user or buyer persona**: Personas can be very powerful when they are based on *provable* theories (e.g. with real causation).
4. With a **behavioral model**: Behavioral segmentation leverages transaction and engagement data to create *profiles*.

To determine which segmentation criterion your business should use, you should evaluate the correlation between different events and user attributes the way we did in Chapter #14.

You're looking for criteria that are most likely to correlate with purchases, engagement, or long-term retention.

You can test different recipes by combining criteria (e.g. persona AND revenue). It's often a good idea to focus on information that's unlikely to drastically change in the near-term, for example:

- Employee headcount

- Revenue
- Vertical
- Business model
- Location(s)
- Tech stack
- Web traffic
- Use case
- Acquisition channel
- Landing page value proposition
- Persona
- Role
- Job title, etc

What criteria seem most predictive?

For each of the most predictive criteria, explore the resulting segments: *How different are they from one another?*

You're looking for, at most, five to seven groupings. Your segments should be mutually exclusive, cover most—if not all—of your customers, reveal underlying needs, and ideally be reliable long-term.

No matter which recipe you choose, it's important to stick to a single segmentation model.

Select the most promising segmentation model. Break down your metrics by segments: *are behaviors noticeably different?*

If you don't understand what drives these differences, then consider exploring segments one by one through customer interviews (Chapter #13).

If you're not already collecting all the information you need, then look for ways to collect it through the sign-up process, the onboarding flow, or data enrichment using external services like Clearbit Enrichment[230].

Once you are capturing the right information, you'll be able to experiment with workflows to influence the behavior of the users in each of your segments.

Assessing Brand Awareness

> "When our research indicated that 50% of people had heard of Showmax, then we knew we had "saturated" the market in terms of awareness, and could effectively move into performance marketing from there.[231]"

Barron Ernst
Zenly Senior Product Manager

How much growth is left in your market? Are the markets that you're in saturated?

The more prospects are aware of your product and your competitors' products, the more competitive acquisition strategies tend to be.

Since your product is viewed as one option within a set, it needs to be differentiated if it is to stand out.

David Cancel calls this the Procter & Gamble stage[232]. At this stage, companies need to focus on brand building and differentiation to gain market shares.

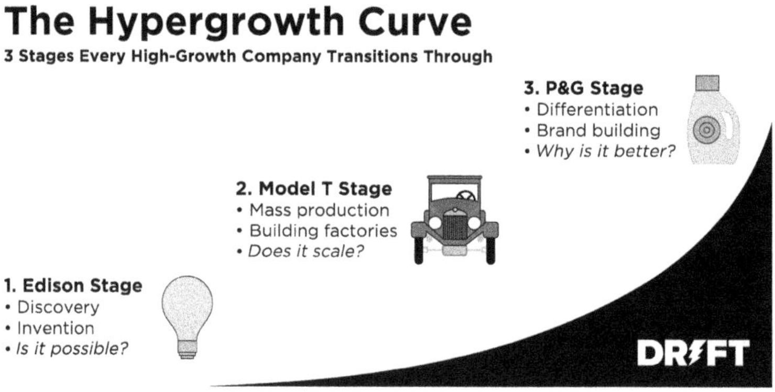

Figure 22.1 - The Hypergrowth Curve

To understand where you stand, it's a good idea to assess how much growth is left in the market. *Are there still unaware prospects? Should you focus on getting customers to switch from the competition?*

To work out what proportion of the prospect pool is aware of your brand, start by sizing your target market. *How many customers are there? How many of those customers are your customers?*

If you can find your competitors' customer count—perhaps through their annual reports, S-1 filings, or fundraising announcements—then you can begin to get a feel for how much opportunity is left in the market.

Taking this a step further, you can create an anonymous survey asking prospects within the market which products they have heard of.

> "Which of the following products have you heard of?"

By listing the top 10-12 options on the market, and ordering them randomly, you'll get good data on brand awareness in your market.

For each positive response, ask a follow up question:

> "What do you understand [Product] does?"

The answers will help reveal the messages shared on the market.

Is your positioning clear? How different are your competitors' positionings? How many prospects surveyed know none of the products on the market?

For this type of research to be effective, recruit randomly in your target market. Respondents can include your customers, your competitors' customers, and prospects who are not yet aware of your brand or your competitors' brands.

400 respondents should start giving you reliable data. If your market has less than a few thousand prospects, then don't waste your time. Your sales team or your CRM should be able to tell you which prospects have heard of your organization.

To get more than 400 respondents and avoid associations with your brand, the survey should either be done Off-Brand (Chapter #20), or conducted through a market research agency. These agencies will help incentivize participants and will make sure you get a large enough sample size.

If you intend to do your own recruitment, avoid any affiliations with your organization and focus your efforts on the market's watering holes.

You can consider market awareness *saturated* when 50% or more of prospects are aware of your product or your competitors' products.

Above 50%, focus your messaging on differentiation. Under 50%, focus on awareness.

Making Progress

> "Your product should sell itself, but that does not mean you don't need salespeople."
>
> Aaron Levie

To make progress at this stage, first you need to define the right segmentation strategy for your business.

Assessing segments one by one will help to reveal new opportunities for growth. This should help you to come up with ideas and experiments for extending your market share and growing performance.

Are there segments worth growing? Can this be done by improving communications? Can you adapt your communications to improve monetization or retention in certain segments?

At this stage, defining strategies for each of the segments you serve can help you find new growth and improve your grip on the market.

Case Study How Mailchimp Uses Onboarding to Segment Its Users

"The goal is to create a delightful experience. It's to create a first impression that is so personalized, so useful that you're delivering value in that first touch, or that first couple of touches. That's super important."

Guillaume Cabane

As an early entrant to the email marketing market, Mailchimp had managed to build a strong brand, generate a lot of awareness, and acquire more than 85,000 users and customers.

But to increase their footprint in the market still further, in 2009 Mailchimp decided to add a free tier to their product. Within a year of 'going Freemium', their user base had jumped to 450,000 users[233].

Marketing agencies managing newsletters for Fortune 500 companies with millions of subscribers were signing up, hardware store owners who had recently discovered email marketing were signing up, and a wide range of prospects falling between were also signing up.

To better address the needs of its user base, Mailchimp decided to work on segmentation. There were hundreds of user profiles. They couldn't simply ask: *"Are you a hardware store or a marketing agency?"*

Instead, they decided to first ask users if they had a subscription list. If they did, they would ask how many people were in it.

Based on these two data points, they were able to determine the appropriate next steps. One segment might get emails about a WordPress plugin to help set up a sign-up form on a blog, while another might receive advanced segmentation tips.

Samuel Hulick, who did consulting work for Mailchimp says: *"Even just asking a little insightful question like that can give you a relatively good idea of what the outcomes that the sign-up is looking for are, and then, as much as you can, personalize the ensuing experience around those outcomes."*

A lot of information can be inferred from the data points at your disposal, including where users signed up, the time of the day, the time of the year, which landing pages they came from, and which posts they read. You don't need to ask explicit questions to segment users. You can often get valuable segmentation data in more indirect ways.

As Erika Hall says[234]: *"Often asking a question directly is the worst way to get a true and useful answer to that question."*

Over the years, Mailchimp's functionalities and marketing have changed significantly. As a result, their segmentation has also changed. They're able to make increasingly precise recommendations and grow revenue per user by helping each of their customers maximize their use of the product.

Like Mailchimp, you can use your onboarding process to ask questions (e.g. *What expectations did you have for our product? How can we help?*) and experiment with segmentation.

You will get people who are new to your product all the time. They will all have their own unique perspectives and expectations. Onboarding is the perfect place to test different messaging and value drivers.

Taking Action

1. Evaluate behaviors in your product in relation to purchases, engagement, and long-term retention.
2. Define a segmentation strategy for your business, assessing each segment independently to find new opportunities for growth.
3. Run a survey to measure brand awareness on the market and evaluate remaining growth opportunities.
4. Define experiments to test your segmentation and grow your market share.
5. *Collaborating with others?* Share a PDF version of this chapter at **solvingproduct.com/chapter-22**.

23 / 26

Maximizing Revenue and Profitability

Your business is mature. Over time, you have managed to iron out most business processes. Use the techniques below to **optimize revenue and profitability**.

> "Profitability isn't an event; it's a habit."
>
> Mike Michalowicz
> Author of Profit First

When it comes to monetization, most businesses underperform. Maybe their price points are too low, or their plans don't align with customer expectations, or they simply can't accept payment in certain parts of the world.

No matter what the reason, the ability to collect payments and maximize the value of all transactions is a great enabler for organizations.

More money means more engineers, more cash spent on acquiring customers, and a greater share of profits for the company's owners.

At this stage, optimizing profit and your ability to generate more revenue makes a lot of sense. Shareholders may even be demanding it.

> *If you were a service company...*
>
> *This stage would be about increasing contract value, and adding payment options to be able to land more customers.*

Techniques You Can Use

Optimizing revenue may require experimentation and testing, but as you'll see, the processes to follow are straightforward: tweak revenue levers and check profitability.

- **Analyzing One-Time & Recurring Payments** will help you find the leaks in your payment processes.
- **Learning from Pricing Research** will help you find the optimal price points for your products and for each of your plans.

Both analyses are essential. They will help to maximize your company's revenue and profitability.

Analyzing One-Time & Recurring Payments

"It's much easier to double your business by doubling your conversion rate than by doubling your traffic."

Jeffrey Eisenberg
Buyer Legends CEO

From a Western perspective it may be easy to assume that everyone has access to a credit card, which they can use to buy products with.

But payments truly are Pandora's box. When you start digging into online payments, you begin to understand how complex some of the issues are.

As examples:

- Debit cards are the preferred method of payment online in France[235].
- Most payment methods in Brazil only work domestically[236].
- You need to establish a local entity in Indonesia to be able to collect payments. The local currency also can't be repatriated offshore[237].
- Some countries like Argentina tax their citizens on foreign currency transactions[238].

This means that if your business has grown internationally, your product might have been turning away good prospects and customers—without you even realizing it.

Amidst total sales and payment data, it's easy to miss subtle issues, but delinquent credit cards or payment methods are a major cause of payment failures and churn. For regular credit cards alone, there can be more than 130 reasons why prospects experience payment failures[239].

Because payment is fairly straightforward in the United-States, and because most major payment gateways like Stripe, PayPal, and Braintree have been optimized in part for the US market, it's a good idea to benchmark against your US payment flow.

Looking at your analytics for the US market—or your highest converting market—evaluate:

- the percentage of site visitors visiting your pricing page;
- the percentage of pricing page visitors initiating the purchase process (e.g. Add to cart);

- the percentage of users beginning the purchase process and then the ensuing process step by step;
- the percentage of users converting; *and*
- the percentage of users whose payment was accepted (e.g. successful payments).

By analyzing this process as a funnel, as seen in Chapter #12, you will be able to pinpoint issues. This will also give you comparison points for analyzing your other markets.

Get the same data points for each of your highest potential geographical markets[240]: *Are there significant outliers? Conversion rates well below the average?*

When visitors drop off before beginning the payment process, issues are often related to language, pricing or currencies.

When they make it all the way to the payment flow, the main problems tend to be the payment methods available. If you haven't done so already, it can be a good idea to start thinking about localizing payments (e.g. offering pricing in another country's currency). Localization has been proven to improve conversions by 11 to 18%[241].

Once you have identified a few outliers, you can start running experiments to address issues one by one. Payment gateways like Adyen will swap out payment methods to help increase conversions.

For subscription businesses, sometimes you'll be able to capture the first payment, but run into problems when recurring payments begin.

For this reason—and because it's estimated that 20 to 40% of churn is caused by delinquent credit cards[242]—it's a good idea to conduct the same analysis for recurring payments.

By first setting a benchmark for recurring payment success in your core market, you'll then be able to compare success per country.

Through this analysis, you can identify issues associated with payment processors, credit card expirations, payment limit failures, and false fraud prevention.

Only 5% of *delinquent* churners ever re-subscribe[243]. You may be leaving a lot of money on the table.

Learning from Pricing Research

> "A customer's price ceiling isn't set by the value you deliver. It's set by their **perception** of the value you deliver.[244]"

Dan Adams
AIM Institute Founder % President

In long-standing research published in Harvard Business Review[245] based on the economics of 2,463 companies, pricing experts Michael V. Marn and Robert L. Rosiello demonstrated that a 1% improvement in price resulted in an 11.1% increase in operating profit.

Although their research dates from 1992, more recent research[246] has corroborated their results.

The reason is simple. Unlike other levers like acquisition or retention, pricing has a *direct* impact on profitability.

Charge more, earn more. Profits.

Yet, ProfitWell found that, on average, businesses spend less than ten hours per year working on their pricing strategy[247].

The reason for this is simple. Price setting and optimization doesn't have a *natural home* in organizations.

Sometimes pricing is the responsibility of marketing, sometimes it's finance, and sometimes it's sales. Everyone has an opinion on this topic, which makes making real progress difficult.

As general benchmarks, if more than 10% of your users leave for pricing reasons (churn/cancellation), or if less than 15% of your revenue comes from expansion[248], then your pricing probably needs some work.

Getting pricing right first means making sure that you price for value, not cost. Don't base your pricing on what competitors are doing. And definitely don't base it on guesswork.

There are two key challenges associated with analyzing and iterating pricing:

1. **You need stable product value**: For this reason, it's usually best to hold off on optimizing pricing until you have reached PMF and have a good understanding of your unit economics.
2. **Evaluation cycles can be long (especially for subscription-based businesses)**: You need to factor in seasonality and full subscription cycles if you want to understand the impact of any changes that you make.

Pricing is not an absolute. The market that you're in, your packaging, and your pitch all impact perceived value and willingness to pay.

To optimize your price point(s), it's a good idea first to try to understand price sensitivity—how much the market is willing to pay for your product.

Price sensitivity tends to be a range rather than a single value.

The best way to evaluate price sensitivity is by using the Price Sensitivity Meter (PSM), which was introduced by Dutch economist Peter van Westendorp in 1976.

You can run this survey with both prospects and customers. It can be useful to capture more information from respondents (e.g. roles, personas, subscription plans, etc), as this will help to refine your segmentation later on.

The four questions of the survey are:

1. ***At what price would you consider the product to be so expensive that you would not consider buying it?*** This first question points to a price point that's too expensive for the customer.

2. ***At what price would you consider the product to be priced so low that you would feel the quality couldn't be very good?*** The second question points to a price point that is too cheap for the customer.

3. ***At what price would you consider the product starting to get expensive, so that it is not out of the question, but you would have to give some thought to buying it?*** The third question gives you a price point at the high end of acceptable prices.

4. ***At what price would you consider the product to be a bargain—a great buy for the money?*** The fourth question gives you the low end of the range of acceptable prices.

You can either use open-ended questions and let respondents fill in amounts, or you can ask them to select values from a range. It's important to ask the questions in this sequence.

The first two questions force respondents to anchor themselves to an acceptable price range, while the last two help to narrow down answers around an optimal price range.

Once a statistically significant number of people has answered these four questions, you can start plotting the answers on a chart, so that you can determine the optimal price band and find the optimal price point.

Van Westendorp survey results are usually plotted on a chart that combines all four data points. The section at the center of the chart represents the range of acceptable price points:

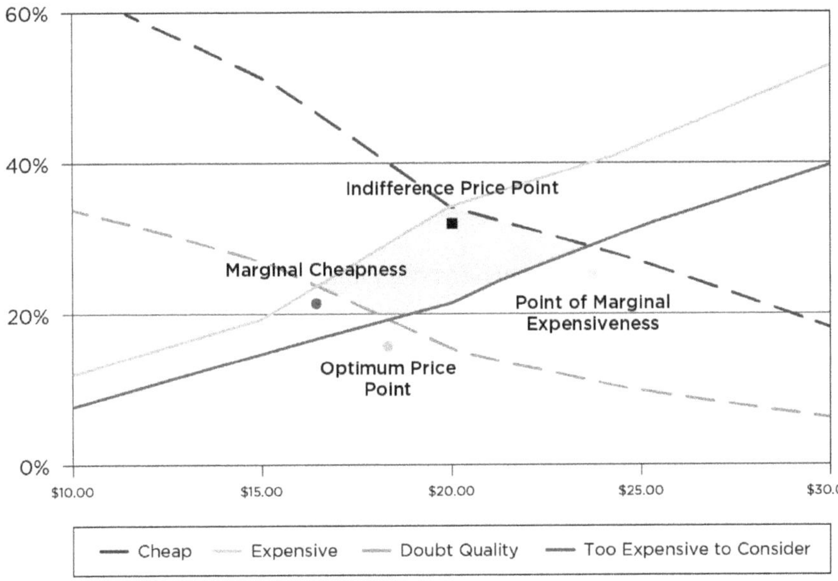

Figure 23.1 - Example of Price Sensitivity Meter Results

The intersection of the 'Too cheap' and 'Too expensive' lines—the point of marginal expensiveness—is often the optimal price point.

As pricing expert Madhavan Ramanujam says[249]: *"An acceptable price is the price that people are super comfortable paying. No friction, they just love your pricing because it's a steal. If you're pricing for growth, maybe you can price in the acceptable area. Expensive is the price that they would actually pay you, but they don't like it. Neither do they hate it, but it's the price usually that's aligned with value. The prohibitively expensive is the price that they'll pretty much be laughing you out of the room. Asking that question gives you some sense of where you can actually be someday, but not at the moment."*

You can also use the PSM to evaluate the perceived value of certain features—by comparing the price points given by participants when you include (or remove) certain features from product packaging.

Slice and dice any changes you make. You should introduce any pricing changes through an A/B test (Chapter #25) so that you can compare the conversion rates (the percentage of buyers), revenue (customer lifetime value and revenue), and churn rates (the percentage of churners) associated with pricing changes that you have made.

As you experiment and learn from pricing, you should also consider experimenting with:

- payment cycles (one-time, monthly, quarterly, yearly, etc);
- price plans (up to five plans, more plans often mean more money);
- segmentation (per-seat, per feature set, per persona, etc); *and*
- discounting based on longer commitments.

Pricing is an important lever. Do the research, experiment, and move your business forward.

Making Progress

> "Requirements are actually Hypotheses and your Projects are really just Experiments. Realizing this should be liberating.[250]"
>
> David J. Bland

Maturity means more complexity in terms of user and customer behaviors, more use cases covered, and more reliance on your product.

If you make sweeping changes, you run the risk of breaking things that are already working in your product, or in your business.

To make real progress, you should create strong hypotheses that are based on research, run experiments on segments of your user base, and *only* commit to the changes once the experiments have been proven to have a sustained positive impact on your business.

At LANDR, one of our hypotheses was that removing the lowest tier price plan (Basic) would increase Monthly Recurring Revenue (MRR) by at least 15%. One late summer day, it was decided that we would move forward with the experiment.

To avoid creating an inconsistent experience, we decided to hide all mentions of 'Basic' from the app and the website for all users. The idea was to compare time periods to see whether the experiment had a positive impact on business.

Very quickly, MRR increased by more than the 15% we were aiming for—it looked like the experiment would be successful.

In months two and three of the experiment, however, churn began to increase for the more expensive subscription tiers (the plans customers had chosen instead of Basic). Sure, we were able to collect more money upfront, but this increase in churn was hurting our business more than the increase in revenue was helping it.

Soon we had to bring back the lower tier plan. The experiment failed, but what we learned from it helped to inform our next pricing experiments.

Making progress at this stage means leveraging new information to run more successful experiments.

True progress only happens when experiments create sustained positive change in user or customer behaviors.

Case Study
How Book'n'Bloom Expanded Internationally

"The fact that credit cards in Colombia were local and not international should have been flagged much earlier instead of signing up 300 customers, and then realizing none of them could pay."

Claus Rosenberg Gotthard

Claus Rosenberg Gotthard has been an entrepreneur since the early 90s. In 1998, he moved to Russia, where he founded Scanclean, a company that soon became Russia's leading contract cleaning company with over 700 employees.

A few years after Scanclean's acquisition in 2005, Claus was exploring new business opportunities.

Noticing that many small businesses were struggling with the shift to mobile and social media, Claus had the idea of allowing small local businesses to operate directly from Facebook. Book'n'Bloom, a Facebook-integrated business management platform was born. To get the business off the ground, Claus and his team decided to focus on hairdressing salons, a very promising market at the time.

Having done business in Denmark, Russia, Cyprus, Greece, and Spain, Claus knew the importance of international markets in business growth.

Although Greece had been a good place to build this product, the economic crisis made it a difficult market to grow in.

To get good traction data, show that the business could scale, and start selling in some of the largest markets, Claus relocated the business to Spain, a market that was more representative of real market conditions.

Almost immediately, users began signing up and using the product—and they stuck around, meaning that customer acquisition costs could be recovered in just a few months. Spain had been a good choice. Now it was time to expand by targeting peripheral markets.

The idea of expanding into Colombia was first brought to Claus' attention by a partner who had been trying to get Book'n'Bloom to expand there for over a year.

This country had a growing economy, there were a lot of small businesses, there was strong demand for hairdressing services, and mobile phone penetration was high. As a market, it ticked a lot of boxes.

Initially, the market didn't disappoint. The acquisition costs were low, product usage was high, and users were willing to pay. What the team didn't realize right away was that a lot of users either couldn't convert, or that their payments were failing.

At the time, most people in Colombia only had debit cards for their businesses, and most of credit cards could only be used locally. Book'n'Bloom couldn't get paid. Payment hadn't been an issue before, and the team hadn't thought of looking at credit card usage specifically.

Claus says: *"On the surface, Colombia looked like a good market to expand and test our internationalization...with a decent card penetration...but what was not clear was that these cards were not for international payments."*

Book'n'Bloom's expansion into Colombia cost the business time and money. They could have recovered with the remaining $8M they had raised, but their main investor, a VC fund in London, ran out of money.

These setbacks forced Claus to get back to fundraising, and to rethink the product.

Although internationalization will still be a key part of Book'n'Bloom's growth strategy moving forward, the lessons learned will help better inform their market selection strategy.

Taking Action

1. Get benchmarks for your conversion and payment funnels.
2. Analyze your payment and conversion funnels from various per-

spectives.

3. Capture willingness to buy data from the market and your customers.
4. Run cyclical experiments to optimize your pricing strategy.
5. *Collaborating with others?* Share a PDF version of this chapter at **solvingproduct.com/chapter-23**.

Retros-
pective

24 / 26

Adjusting Learning Goals

"For every fact there is an infinity of hypotheses."

Robert M. Pirsig
Author of Zen and the Art of Motorcycle Maintenance

Part of my personal fascination with customer research and growing product organizations comes from the fact that, across organizations, things tend to be both very similar and very different.

In some ways, people are extremely consistent (there are universal truths across cultures that stay the same), but humans are also constantly learning, changing, and adapting to their reality.

Because people change, and because businesses and markets also change, we're never actually done with learning about our users and customers.

Indi Young says: *"The mental model is always incomplete because there's always more to find out. It's an ocean we can't boil. There's always more ocean."*

Strategy is a conversation that's always happening.

Your business ships new functionalities. Competitors react. Customer expectations get reshaped. Competitors ship their own improvements. The market changes and evolves again. Within this, teams change, budgets change, tools change, mindsets evolve.

People are trying to get better all the time. They're trying to lead more meaningful lives and spend more time with friends and family.

As *Shaping Things* author Bruce Sterling explains: *"Any "solved problem" that involves human beings solves a problem whose parameters must change through time."*

To hope to grow and capture a large share of the market, you need to be continuously learning and re-visiting your hypotheses. You can't rest on your laurels.

Your model won't ever be complete, but the more you learn, the more confidence you'll have in the decisions that you make.

Continuous Learning = Continuous Growth

> "Teams that build continuous customer discovery into their DNA will become smarter than their investors, and build more successful companies.[251]"
>
> Steve Blank

This book could go on forever. There are thousands of ways to learn from your users and customers to move your business forward.

Unfortunately, without a plan and the desire to bring continuous learning inside your organization, it is difficult to create true predictable growth.

To keep learning, you'll want to move from project-based customer research to continuous research—scouting new opportunities, and re-visiting assumptions when new information comes into light.

You should use the scientific method to test ideas, expose assumptions, and refine your hypotheses. Unfortunately, unlike scientific experiments, customer research rarely uncovers absolute truths.

While the best way to ensure continuous learning inside organizations is to have product teams do continuous product discovery, there are other ways to gradually build your organization's capabilities, starting with:

1. Hiring (and empowering) a product discovery coach or freelance researchers;
2. Zeroing in on the most valuable elements of the customer research process and hiring consultants to deliver on that expertise;
3. Hiring for expertise once the business case for continuous learning has gained traction;
4. Creating a center of excellence to help share information and standardize practices across projects and product teams;
5. Adding product discovery to your product development processes; *and*
6. Making customer research and testing acceptance criteria for new product development.

Your goal is to establish processes which help you learn how to overcome hurdles, which reduce uncertainty, and which point out gaps in your knowledge.

The value of continuous learning is huge. NFX managing partner Gigi Levy-Weiss explains[252]: *"Assume that in every iteration a learning organization gets 10% better than a non-learning one. The compounding effect post 10 iterations makes it 2.5x faster than the non-learning competitor."*

Finding Gaps in Your Answers

> "A lot of organizations prefer to talk about testing rather than research because it sounds definitive and finite. (We passed the test! We're done!) If you are running a company or building a product, you have to commit to continuous learning.[253]"
>
> Erika Hall

To keep growing, you have to be able to point out gaps in your organization's knowledge, flag assumptions, and challenge hypotheses.

Unfortunately, we don't know what we don't know... There are assumptions that we perceive as truths, and truths that we perceive as gaps.

The best way to bring knowledge gaps to the surface is by ensuring that your team's assumptions get flagged as assumptions.

Doing this often means establishing processes to help make sure that co-workers point out each other's assumptions. This can be done by:

- **Inviting comments and feedback on backlog items**: Sian Townsend, a research manager at Instagram, recommends keeping a list of the top ten feature requests and customer issues[254]. Making these lists accessible to everyone in the organization will help fuel discussions and reveal false assumptions.
- **Creating a culture of *radical truth* and *radical transparency*[255]**: To help reduce the role of ego in decision-making processes, team members at Drift are expected to point out assumptions in their colleagues' work. Not only does this help surface assumptions, it also forces team members to think through the assumptions they make in their work. Although the practice can be taxing, Drift's

unique culture[256] helps reinforce the behavior.

- **Speaking in terms of bets and confidence**: As we saw in Chapter #2, Jeff Patton recommends assessing confidence in terms of bets. Whenever the team has an idea, validates a hypothesis, or uncovers new facts about users or customers, Jeff recommends asking team members what they would be willing to bet on the new information. *Would they be willing to bet their lunch? Their day's pay? Their car? Their retirement savings?* Answers should help reveal true validated learning, or a lack thereof.
- **Writing down beliefs**: John Cutler recommends getting team members to formally express their beliefs around the product vision, the product value, or the markets, by asking them, one by one to fill in the blanks: "Our direct competition is [______].", "I think the real reason why we win new customers is because [______].", and "If we focus on meeting [a specific customer need], and do that extremely well, we will have some leeway when it comes to [less important challenges].".

Fill your learning backlog with the assumptions that come out of these exercises.

Hypotheses can be prioritized using a Hypothesis Prioritization Canvas like Lean UX co-author's Jeff Gothelf's[257]:

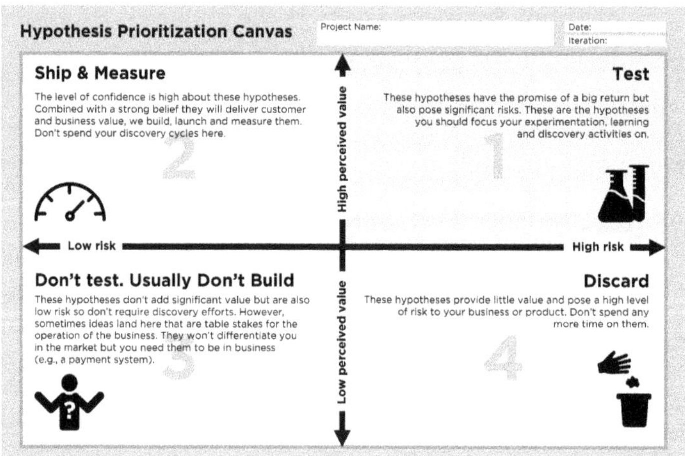

Figure 24.1 - Jeff Gothelf's Hypothesis Prioritization Canvas

This is a simple 2x2 matrix designed to help teams assess the relative risk and value of validating each of their hypotheses.

Your research and experiments should focus first on high risk/high value hypotheses.

Fill up your learning backlog and move on!

Case Study
How Sachin and His Team Refined Their Market Assumptions

"We start to test the personas. We start to test different segments and markets. We try to test different go-to-market approaches. We're always testing a new thing, but we're refining who our audience is, who we speak to, what message resonates with them. And we keep getting more and more focused. This happens every single day, but it also happens at the macro sense. Every year, I look at what we're doing as a company. On one end, the vision and the breadth becomes way bigger, but from a tactical standpoint, it becomes more and more laser-focused every year."

David Cancel

When Sachin Rekhi began work on what would eventually become LinkedIn Sales Navigator, it was clear that they were going after sales professionals; they just didn't know what kind of professionals.

They had an idea of the type of value propositions they wanted to bring to market, but they didn't know who those value propositions would resonate with the most.

To work this out, they decided to do waves of customer interviews, and explore different customer segments, one at a time.

As the discussions evolved, the vision changed from 'LinkedIn is building a sales tool for sales professionals' to 'LinkedIn is building a ***B2B*** sales tool specifically focused on B2B ***sales reps***'.

The target was becoming clearer, but Sachin's team didn't stop there.

Digging further, they decided to target ***enterprise*** sales reps. They wanted to build a product that would work with the largest sales teams and organizations on the market.

And by speaking to those teams, they realized that certain industries—tech and financial services—had stronger needs for the product.

Through series of customer discovery interviews (Chapter #4), they iterated and clarified their targeting. The product was no longer for sales reps—it was for sales professionals working for enterprises in **tech** or in the **financial services** industries.

While their original hypothesis had been in the right ballpark, it wasn't detailed enough to be actionable. But they successfully used research to increase precision.

Sachin says: *"It's super important to spend time on increasing precision, thinking about your iteration not as just validating and pivoting, but instead as adding meat and substance to the understanding of that hypothesis."*

The bulk of your time in product discovery should be spent on increasing precision, not diverting from your original hypotheses.

Don't pivot unless you really have to.

Making Progress

> "Speed of learning creates speed of growth."
>
> Aaron Ross and Jason M. Lemkin
> Authors of From Impossible to Inevitable

If you've ever worked in an early-stage startup, you have most likely noticed that a lot of the people who thrive in times of great uncertainty have usually gone or are leaving by the time that the company grows beyond 100-150 employees.

Some of these people love the rush of starting anew. Some feel that the more structured environment stifles their creativity. Some, like Demoto's co-founders (Chapter #1), have moved on to starting their own businesses.

Those are all very real and valid reasons for leaving, but I'd argue that the vast majority of people who leave organizations at this stage are leaving because their skills aren't being properly utilized.

As businesses grow in size and in maturity, the key employees who helped make it successful tend to transition into leadership or management roles. They're then made accountable for achieving business objectives and executing on a plan.

But executing against a plan is very different from helping to discover the business model.

The truth is, companies still face unknowns, even in these later stages. But the responsibility for figuring out those unknowns gets split off across teams and departments. Too often, this *R&D* gets buried under delivery work, or the work becomes so scattered across teams that new learnings go unnoticed.

To continue innovating while growing, you need to take a systematic approach to generating new learnings.

Lightspeed venture partner Aaron Batalion recommends mapping learning goals around the Known/Unknown matrix[258], which is based on Donald Rumsfeld's famous saying[259]:

Figure 24.2 - Aaron Batalion's Adaptation of the Known/Unknown Matrix

In this model, executives hire staff to execute against *Known Knowns* and *Unknown Knowns*, while founders—or the people who've shown the most abilities in de-risking market or product assumptions—focus on the *Known Unknowns*, the risks that have the potential to kill or hinder the company's progress.

Once a problem gets moved from a *Known Unknown* to a *Known Known* with a clear solution, then new people get hired to execute against the problem.

Aaron says: *"The best teams consistently focus on the known unknowns".*

If you're facing a lot of uncertainty, or your team is making a lot of assumptions, learn. If there are few assumptions, delegate.

Document processes and findings, hire new staff to execute on known problems, and focus on the next unknowns.

Continuous learning is a superpower you want to develop. This framework should help you continuously learn and de-risk projects, even as your business matures.

Collaborating with others? Share a PDF version of this chapter at **solvingproduct.com/chapter-24**.

25 / 26

Making It Work in Your Organiza-tion

"There are only two sources of com-petitive advantage: the ability to learn more about our customers faster than the competition and the ability to turn that learning into action faster than the competition."

Jack Welch
General Electric (GE) Former Chairman & CEO

My career really began when I became a user experience analyst at Aero-plan, a loyalty program in Canada.

At Aeroplan, it was normal to do extensive user research before beginning work on a project. Usability analysts tested both prototype and complete versions of products with target end users. Goals and metrics were set before projects began and were monitored after launch. And I naively believed that all organizations worked that way.

When I began consulting afterwards, and over the following three years, I came to the realization that, businesses *talk* about being customer-centric more often than they actually *are* customer-centric.

While doing research for this book, I was stunned to discover that:

- 48% of businesses don't run any tests or experiments[260];
- 68% of companies speak to less than 10 customers per month[261]; *and*
- 42% of companies don't even survey their customers or collect feedback[262].

Patrick Campbell explains[263]: *"Put simply, we love to retweet articles about customer research, we love to give advice to people about customer research - but we're not doing customer research."*

Most businesses don't proactively try to learn about their users. They don't test or validate their products before launch. They don't try to disprove their hypotheses. They rarely get out of the building to speak to customers.

In other words, companies are doing the most expensive kind of testing—shipping to real customers—without realizing the risk they're taking on.

As OpenView managing director Scott Maxwell says[264]: *"The problem is that no one believes they have false knowledge of the customer."*

There are many reasons for this:

- Organizations don't know *how* to be customer-centric.
- Their Definition of Done[265] doesn't include validation, user testing, or customer research.
- Product teams are expected to deliver output (products or features), while executives are responsible for ensuring outcomes.

- Key stakeholders feel like there's nothing they can learn from users or customers.
- The organization is too set in its ways to change.
- The product backlog is already set for the next three, six, or 12 months.
- Customer research is perceived as being a waste of time,
- Teams are not given time and space to try new things.
- There's red tape. It's difficult to speak to customers.
- Stakeholders are afraid that doing research will come across as a sign of weakness or lack of confidence.
- Stakeholders are afraid that research will prove they were wrong and cause others to question their ability to make decisions.
- Gatekeepers are actively trying to limit the scope of customer research for fear of it diminishing their ability to influence decision-making.
- The organization has been successful without proactively learning from its end users and doesn't feel the need to *rock the boat*.

There are a lot of reasons why businesses don't become customer-centric. Usually, these reasons can be boiled down to either company culture or lack of executive support. It's surprising how many hurdles can disappear when executives support an initiative.

This is what helped create a supportive environment for customer-centric strategies at Aeroplan, and in most of the organizations where I've seen it work.

In this chapter, I lay out at a process for diagnosing the organizational culture, building internal capacities, and driving the adoption of customer research—all critical steps if you are to bring continuous learning into your organization.

Diagnosing Your Organization

"Every company in the world will tell you they are customer-driven. They'll believe in the principle. They'll even have framed posters on the wall about it. [...] But I've learned that none of that means anything unless you actually make the structural decisions to ensure it."

David Cancel

To make changes, you first have to understand the state of things.

If you're not yet inside the organization—maybe you are considering a job or you're about to start—then you can learn about the internal dynamics by asking questions like[266]:

- *How does the team decide what to build?*
- *Can you walk me through a recent mission and talk through the decision-making process?*
- *How does [Company] measure success?*
- *How does the product team measure success?*

Hesitations, diversions, and fuzzy or dismissive answers will tell you a lot about the company's internal decision-making process, or at least, their openness to talk about it.

If you are already working in the organization, or if it's your business, evaluate:

- **Company focus**: When a company lacks focus, meetings run longer and decisions get delayed, people get frustrated not having a clear strategy, and teams have different, sometimes conflicting, definitions of success. *How focused is the organization?*
- **Decision-making effectiveness**: *What's the general theme behind decision-making? Are most decisions made on the basis of logic or emotions? How many people get involved in decisions? Are subject-matter experts asked to contribute? Who gets final say?*

How do decisions map back to assumptions? How is the team learning from past decisions?

- **Outputs vs outcomes**: *Are teams more focused on problems or solutions? How are new features and improvements evaluated? How much work is put into delivering outputs?* People innately want to think in terms of outputs (deliverables). It's easier to plan your work if you are thinking in terms of outputs. But if you're truly being customer-centric, you should be managing to outcomes.

- **Collaboration effectiveness**: *How much collaboration is there between teams? Does the product backlog get influenced by the work of non-product teams? Do the sales, marketing, customer support, and customer success teams feel included in the product work? Do teams get their own goals or are goals shared across teams?*

- **Source of the voice-of-the-customer**: *Who 'owns' the customer relationship? How is empathy developed throughout the team? Is feedback first-hand, second-hand, or third-hand? Are sales, customer success, or customer support staff perceived as the voice-of-the-customer?* Companies too often think that because sales teams are close to the customers, they know what customers want—but it's not always the case.

- **Source of innovations**: *What's preventing someone in the organization from proposing a new project? A new feature? How much red tape is there? Are the employees' ideas solicited and evaluated? Can teams influence the backlog? How much ego is involved in the ideation process?*

- **Psychological safety**: *Can people speak their minds freely? Can they raise objections? Can they make mistakes without fearing punishment or loss of status? How comfortable are team members with sharing bad news with management? Do team members tend to withhold information? Is there a network for people to learn from one another?* Information should always flow up in organizations. There's usually a reason when it doesn't.

- **Company culture**: *What are some companies that teams and management respect and want to emulate? What are some of the distinctive traits of those companies? How much alignment is there between what executives say, and what they do? What behaviors* *get people promoted? What behaviors get people fired? What attributes tend to be valued above others? Cost? Speed? Quality?*

- **Openness to change**: *Are executives supportive of changes and experimentation? How hard is it for you to try something new? For your team? For the organization? How long does it take to be able to try something new? How many people need to get involved?*

Asking these questions will help you get some clarity around the issues that your team or organization may be facing. They should help you pinpoint some of the factors that may be limiting the adoption of customer-centric strategies. You can download a copy of the question list at **solvingproduct.com/questions**.

Easing in Customer Research in the Organization

> "We have this belief that we can manage change, but the reality is we all change on our own terms, on our own time[267]."

Teresa Torres
Product Discovery Coach

No matter where you start from, you'll need to use change management tactics to ease customer research inside your organization.

A lot of the challenges that you will face are common across organizations.

If your organization is used to thinking in terms of features or output, you'll have difficulty getting people to start thinking in terms of bets, problems, Jobs and experiments, while embracing failure.

If your organization has a very hierarchical structure, it's quite likely that many executives will have got their current positions because of their past successes. Unless they acknowledge customer-centricity as a key to their success, you'll most likely be going against their egos.

If the leadership team has had little to no exposure to customer research, it won't have a clear frame of reference for assessing its potential value; they'll have a hard time seeing its tangible benefits.

Research cannot be optimally effective unless it becomes a part of the product development process—from initial market exploration, all the way to defining a strategy, testing concepts, and evaluating finished products. Because of this, full adoption should be your goal.

Your first step is to understand how the people in charge make decisions, and what sources of information they rely on.

The best-case scenario is often top-down support with bottom-up mobilization—that is, support from the executive team, combined with passion from the team to learn and execute customer-centric strategies.

Find a champion. You will be much more effective if the founders or the leadership team are supportive of the initiative. *Can you find competitors who are doing customer research?* If you can show that competitors are doing research, this can really help sway decision-makers.

If you can't get top-down support right away, consider bringing in customer research as an experiment. Oftentimes, people who are resistant to change will be open to running a one-time experiment.

Start with a small team. Set a goal for the team to have changed its behavior by the end of the experiment. Look to co-create the best process, adapting it to your organization's unique context. The experiment should help you uncover the specific challenges for your organization.

You will need enough time and repetition to improve your processes. If you can find a way to do the research on your own, or with a small team to show the value of customer insights, then you'll be able to speed up adoption.

It's difficult to convince people of the value of customer research when they don't know what the output looks like. For this reason, it's best to focus on delivering quick wins. The more clearly you can tie research to ROI for the organization, the more buy-in and momentum you should be able to build.

When you begin to get results, you should start democratizing research by including more people—influencers, managers, engineers, etc—in your research processes. Unfortunately, you can't transfer empathy from one person to another. You'll need to find ways to bring colleagues along in the research.

Find ways to create connections. Position research findings in terms of things that teams care about. For example, if a team cares about churn, position the insights in terms of churn reduction.

Observing user tests, visiting customers on site, taking part in interviews, or discussing experiment results with data can all help build empathy and bring team members along in the research. Bringing others on board will help solidify your case for customer research. Keep working at it. Bringing customer research inside an organization is no easy feat.

Case Study
How Dr. Sam Ladner Drives Change Internally

> "I've never met anybody from any team that hasn't been transformed by meeting real people in their environments. Some of them are shocked at how much they've changed after the meetings."

Dr. Sam Ladner

For the past decade, Dr. Sam Ladner has been leading user research in some of the largest tech companies on the market (Amazon, Microsoft, and Workday). A major challenge that she has faced in those roles has been in developing empathy within the teams she works with.

Over the years, Sam has come up with a set of strategies for enhancing empathy.

First, she begins by assessing the organization's familiarity with human-centered principles. She does this by trying to understand how teams make sense of user behaviors.

If they make *homo economicus* rational inferences, then familiarity is likely low, because it indicates they are focused on the concrete and "rational" aspects of human behavior, rather than the deeply felt and even subconscious nature of why humans do what they do. If they try to understand the humans behind the behaviors, then they tend to be more in tune with human motivations.

To help develop empathy, Sam looks for opportunities to bring customers into the office.

For example, when she started working at Microsoft, she noticed that it was very common for people to observe usability tests remotely or behind a glass; product teams were always kept at a distance from the users. It was easy for people to leave the room, check their emails, or tune out certain parts of the conversations.

At the time, the gaming industry was facing a lot of issues around inclusion. Sam wanted to leverage an important upcoming gaming panel for women, and help build awareness around the issues that women were facing. Her goal was to make sure teams heard first-hand from the participants.

Sam writes in her book, *Practical Ethnography*: *"You can read all the research reports you want, but to sit there and listen to somebody tell you about how they love gaming and how they've been chased out. You can't ignore it. It changes you."*

When somebody is physically sitting in front of you talking about an experience, it's very hard not to listen.

Bringing users in without any of the previous separations helped build empathy with the team. They were able to get a more *nuanced* understanding of the realities of their customers. This proximity changed them, and it changed the way they made decisions afterwards.

Finding Opportunities for Customer Research

> "Focus on the things that no one owns, but that are visible by all."

Darius Contractor
Airtable Head of Growth

A lot of parallels can be drawn between how people and expertise are brought into organizations.

First, they start out with little to no credibility. The champion—or the hiring manager—believes the addition will benefit the organization. The expertise or the new hiree then has to work to build credibility, one person at a time, until enough trust is built for their opinions to influence decision-making.

Now, if we look back at the last time you joined a team or an organization, would you recommend:

- *Challenging core assumptions the day you walked in?*
- *Going against key influencers' opinions right away?*
- *Working on the most complex projects or challenges before first establishing trust and relationships?*

Of course not. Those are all setups to fail[268].

With customer research (and new roles really), it's a good idea to find white space— opportunities that aren't owned by anyone, where you can *add* to the understanding of the business and demonstrate value.

To do this, you should:

1. **Identify key stakeholders**: Prepare a list of champions, supporters, influencers, key staff, and potential blockers looking to derail your process.

2. **Meet one on one**: Meet all key stakeholders privately. Try and understand their goals, their world views, and their focus areas. Ask questions like: *"What are your current priorities?", "What are your duties and core responsibilities?", "How do you define success for you or your team?", "What do you feel are the biggest opportunities for growth for the company?", "What do you feel we should be doing more of?", "What do you think are the greatest challenges to our success (internally and externally)?", "Is there anyone else I should speak to?"*;

3. **Analyze the situation**: List out assumptions, projects people are currently working on, what they're looking at, and any sacred cows or untouchables you stumble on. Analyze the company's current position and opportunities.

4. **Find white space**: Using this book and your findings, identify an opportunity to use research to drive new growth for the organization. As much as possible, make sure that the resulting knowledge *adds* without challenging core assumptions.

5. **Socialize the research topic**: Start building relationships. Identify other influential groups in the company. Expose them to your plan and research area. Adjust based on their feedback. People are much more positive when they are in the know. They'll be more supportive if they feel like their input was taken into consideration.

The more political your organization is, the more important private conversations will be.

Pick a gap worth exploring, and define a clear research question.

Defining the Research Questions

> "I don't believe in any one right way or one process because I think context determines the sequence."
>
> Bob Moesta

Innovation expert Tristan Kromer created the Question Index[269] to help sort out the type of questions that product teams need to address:

	Market	Product
Generative	- Who is our customer? - What are their pains? - What job do they need done? - Is our customer segment too broad? - How do we find them?	- How can we solve this problem? - What form should this take? - How important is the design? - What's the quickest solution? - What is the minimum feature set? - How should we prioritize?
Evaluative	- Are they really willing to pay? - How much will they pay? - How do we convince them to buy? - How much will it cost to sell? - Can we scale marketing?	- Is this solution working? - Are people using it? - Which solution is better? - How should we optimize this? - What do people like/dislike? - Why do they do that with our product/service?

Figure 25.1 - The Question Index

In his model, questions are either about the product or the market. They can be evaluated through:

- **Evaluative research**: You have a clear hypothesis (e.g. people will buy our product). You want to know whether the hypothesis is true or false; or
- **Generative research**: You don't fully know what you're looking for. You're trying to generate new ideas or understand the problem space.

Is your question about the market, or about the product? Do you have a falsifiable hypothesis you can test?

Clarify the research question. Write down the decision(s) that the answers will inform. For example:

Question:

- *Who are our most valuable customers?*

Decisions:

- Features we should focus on
- Markets and customer attributes that we should focus on with our user acquisition

Once the question is clear, refer to the appropriate section in this book. *Timebox* your research and start learning.

For a research activity to be meaningful, the research has to take significantly less time than building a product. So, be careful which technique you choose.

Building Consensus Within the Team

> "What confuses researchers is they think if they present logical facts that are irrefutable then obviously people have to listen to it. Somehow, they're continually surprised over their careers that people aren't listening to their irrefutable facts, not understanding that these decisions are not being made on the basis of irrefutable

facts.[270]"

Steve Blank

Everyone on your team and in your organization will approach research findings with their own beliefs and biases, including:

- assumptions about what customers value;
- hypotheses about where the market is going;
- theories about technology trends;
- opinions about competitors' strategies; *and*
- beliefs about the why customers buy and use your product.

Maybe your colleagues' beliefs are right, maybe they're wrong, but their assumptions and biases will influence the way they make sense of new information. They may be looking at different data points than you are, and reaching different conclusions about what's best for the product.

Acknowledging subjectivity is key.

When you bring in new information and the team wasn't part of the research process, the reaction is often almost binary. They either:

- trust the results and the process blindly; OR
- disregard the results.

You can view this as the difference between reading a book, and having someone tell you about a book. *Was the book good?* Hard to say.

There are a lot of nuances in customer truths. Telling the rest of the team what you have learned can create what Rob Fitzpatrick calls a de facto "the customer said so" trump card. If you're not the ultimate decision-maker, this can create a strong reaction, which leads to stakeholders dismissing the insights:

> "They're not in our target market." "It's only one data point." "[Future Plan X] will solve this."

To be effective, **all learnings must be *shared* learning**.

You'll be fighting an endless uphill battle if you don't bring colleagues along with the insights.

Thousands of micro-decisions are made each day by designers, marketers, engineers, and support staff. These decisions should be based on your organization's latest beliefs. And if those beliefs are based on second-hand experience, team members will lack the nuances and conviction to reinforce the decisions.

If the team's beliefs don't change with the insights, you'll constantly need to re-convince new hirees. Even if you can keep a good record of the learnings, show the impact of the information, and back it up with more data points, you could get pushback every time a new leader comes on board.

One of the most important problems for a product leader is getting their team to empathize with the customer.

Alex Schiff says: *"Every day, dozens of "first draft" choices need to be made by engineers and designers, and the more you can get them to empathize with the customer, the closer those first drafts will be to something you can ship, and the faster you'll get things out the door."*

Early on, it's easy to share what you learn because the product team and the company are pretty much the same thing, but as a company grows in size and in complexity, the need for documentation, mapping, and information sharing also grows. As Jim Kalbach says: *"If you have a big complex solution and a big complex organization your need for mapping is going to be high."*

Here are the most impactful ways to bring the team along:

- **Taking part in the research**: Having team members take part in the primary research, sitting in on user tests and interviews, and reading survey results helps them draw their own conclusions. If you're analyzing the results collaboratively, there's often no need for a lengthy report or analysis period.
- **Holding *sensemaking*[271] workshops**: Instead of giving the insights to the team, organize collaborative workshops to help them take

ownership of the learnings. This can be done by consuming insights as a team and discussing their meaning. People tend to disagree on what they heard from the customer. A group will often generate insights more quickly. The insights will also be shared and internalized more effectively this way. It's a great way to build consensus.

- **Sharing short updates**: User research expert Steve Portigal recommends sharing short updates with highlights, anecdotes, and descriptions via email. This can help create momentum, fuel discussions, and give everyone a feel for the voice of the customer.
- **All-hands and meetings**: For larger organizations wishing to bring the team at large aboard with findings, it can be a good idea to have the head of product present every week or so, for 15 to 30 minutes, to highlight what the team has learned. These should focus on information that fits the company's priorities, to avoid diverting attention away from the core goals.

It's a good idea to use these techniques in conjunction with artifacts that are designed to help summarize the findings.

Artifacts that are the easiest to update and the fastest to consume will work best. For example:

- **Customer journey maps (CJMs)**: A customer journey map can help a team sync up on their understanding of the progress that prospects and users need to make in order to discover and start using a product. Customer journeys can involve segments, use cases, or feature sets. Because they represent the current understanding of the journey (which won't ever be perfect), they need to be continuously improved and refined. Customer journeys come in many shapes and forms. The general idea is to visually show goals and touchpoints in relation to the awareness stages.
- **Personas**: Personas are fictional representations and generalizations of a cluster of your target users who exhibit similar goals, attitudes, or behaviors in relation to your product. Personas can help you to understand and communicate the motivations and reasoning of your prospects. Effective personas are focused on goals and behaviors. For personas to be actionable, teams need to start addressing the problems and opportunities from their perspective. *"What would [Mitchell] do?"* Although personas have lost a bit of their popularity in recent years[272], they can still be a very useful tool for sharing and summarizing learnings.

- **Mixed solutions**: Unfortunately, once created, CJMs and personas tend to collect dust. The insights they help centralize are valuable, but they tend to be kept far away from the line of action. For this reason, a whiteboard summarizing the latest set of beliefs often works best. This can be a good way to keep the team focused on the metrics, the objectives, the key personas, the customer journey, and the opportunities. To make it work, focus on information and insights that can drive decisions. Iterate on the content of your whiteboard until consumption of the information has become part of your team's weekly—even daily—habits.

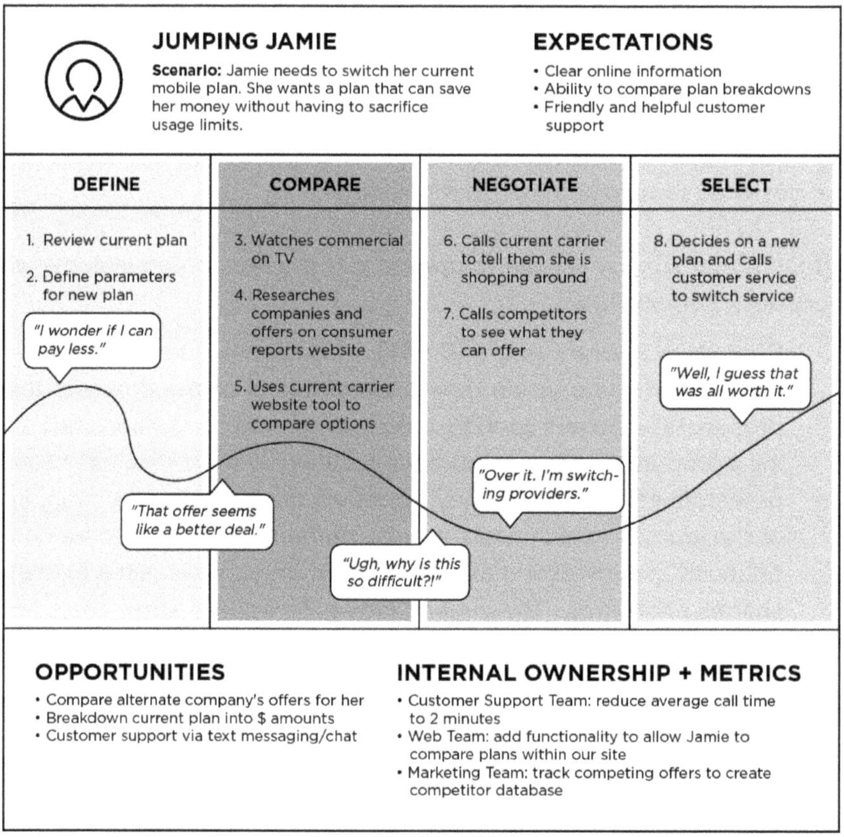

Figure 25.2 - Example of a Customer Journey[273]

Product leaders often have one of the most cross-functional roles in the organization. For this reason, it often makes sense for them to be point person for the propagation of research findings in the organization.

Whether there is or isn't a distinct user or customer research team in the organization, someone needs to make sure that insights are shared and consumed across the business.

Case Study
How Statflo Creates Alignment

"Nothing is more certain to cause a project to fail than a misunderstanding of the problem you are solving.[274]"

Lenny Rachitsky
Product Management Expert

As Statflo kept growing, the co-founders decided to split up the product by feature sets, and hire several more product managers.

Although the split helped create focused backlogs, each with their own goals and missions, the product teams' knowledge no longer overlapped. Very quickly, it became evident that product managers were getting different—sometimes conflicting—feedback from their users. It was becoming difficult to keep everyone synced up on priorities.

> *"It's very easy for us to kind of silo and split off. The best way to find out about that is when a product manager goes on vacation and someone needs to take on their stuff, and then they realize they don't know it. It's completely isolated. It's completely separate."*

To make sure product teams had the same knowledge, and were aligned on the same vision, Ian set up a whiteboard in a meeting room.

On it, the team mapped the customer journeys and listed burning issues from sales, support, and design.

Because the whiteboard was in plain sight of the entire organization, everyone could follow the evolution of the business on their own.

Each week, product managers met. During the meetings, they would refine the journeys and update the question lists based on new discoveries and feedback that had come in during the week.

Priorities changed. New questions emerged. New tasks got created. Sharing a single map of the experience forced consensus: *What do we agree on?*

Product managers would pick up items to dig into each week based on the gaps and assumptions they had ran into. They would speak to users, join the customer success team on calls, and conduct user interviews.

These new learnings would then help refine their shared understanding and point to the next areas of research.

Making Progress

> "The machine consists of two big parts—the culture and the people. If the outcomes are inconsistent with the goals, something must be wrong with the machine, which means that something must be wrong with the culture and/or the people."

Ray Dalio
Bridgewater Associates Founder

Making progress creating a more customer-centric culture means fighting a battle on two fronts:

1. Generating value and helping move the product forward though research (the work); *and*
2. Evangelizing the value of the work to grow your internal support group (the process).

It's easy to get frustrated when you are doing great work (the work), but have difficulty getting enough support (the process) to get the resources you need.

Unfortunately, both parts of the equation are necessary; they should be built and iterated on in parallel.

And since teams rarely get it right the first time, you need to have enough time to iterate, learn, and find the right fit within your organization.

Oftentimes, teams will compare their results against what they hear from other organizations, which may be much further along than they are in terms of customer-centricity. They become vested in a fixed end-point that never fully materializes. It makes them devalue the progress they made, and can lead them to revert to old patterns.

Product development expert Jabe Bloom calls this gap thinking:

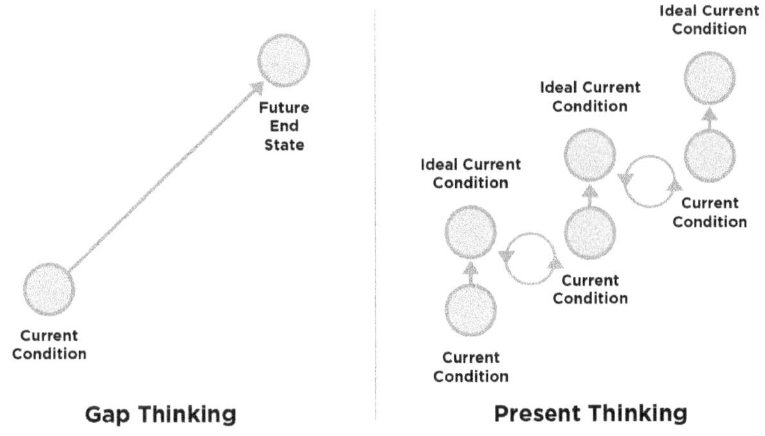

Figure 25.3 - Gap Thinking vs. Present Thinking

To focus on *present thinking*, Gabe recommends asking the following questions[275]:

- *Where are we?*
- *What do I need now?*
- *How do I improve the current way of working?*

Building up customer research will be an iterative process. You'll need to learn as much about the process as you learn about the organization.

With enough patience and effort, the path will eventually reveal itself.

Collaborating with others? Share a PDF version of this chapter at **solvingproduct.com/chapter-25**.

26 / 26 Conclusion

"Whoever gets closest to their customer wins."

Bernadette Jiwa
Author of Marketing: A Love Story

Throughout *Solving Product*, I've shown you 65+ ways to move a product business forward with customer research.

Depending on where you started this journey, you may believe that a few, all, or none of the techniques covered in this book represent actual opportunities for your business.

The fact is, whether you believe in these opportunities or not, you should realize that many of those opportunities are going away, fast.

As David Cancel says: *"The Internet has done one thing over time, and it's finally compounded to this point where it removes all friction out of the market. In every market."*

As friction goes away, markets open up. Everyone is able to compete globally on an almost equal footing. Competitive advantages fade away[276], functionalities get commoditized, and power shifts to the customers, who now have thousands of competing products to pick from.

How will your business compete tomorrow? How will your product differentiate itself? How will you keep customers when their expectations increase?

The ground to compete on is shrinking. Customer-centric strategies can help unlock new growth and create sustaining differentiation.

Eventually, all businesses will need to be customer-centric to compete. It might take 2-10 years depending on the industry, but it's coming.

As marketing expert Bernadette Jiwa says: *"Whoever gets closest to their customer wins."* This quote may have never been truer than it is today.

We're spoiled with the amount of data we can look at, the ease we have in communicating with customers, and the research tools at our disposal. The opportunity is there for the taking. *Will you run with it?*

A Few Caveats

> "If you start a strategy meeting with data, most people will agree what should be done next. If you start it with ideas, be prepared to debate and disagree.[277]"

Peter Caputa IV
Databox CEO

As we're closing out this book, there are a few things I think are important to bring up one last time:

1) The Speed at Which You Make Decisions Matters

One of the most important things in a business is the decision-making process—how people work together, how they align on decisions, how those decisions get communicated across the organization, and how the organization learns and adjusts when decisions are wrong.

In some ways, you can compare the ways that people and organizations make decisions.

Effective decision-makers will Observe the environment and situation, Orient themselves based on *best-available* information, data, and their own mental models, conclusively Decide after weighing the pros and cons of various alternatives, Act, and Adjust based on feedback.

The faster—and more decisively—that people are able to make decisions, the more effective they will be.

For organizations, it's often better to make wrong decisions quickly, learn, and recover, than it is to take too long to make good decisions. Except, as I hope this book demonstrated, you don't need to be making bad decisions in the first place.

2) Learning for the Sake of Learning is a Waste

You may also have noticed throughout this book that some of the analyses got repeated in different forms.

For example, the Idea, Startup, Growth, and Maturity stages all include a research activity that is designed to help us refine our customer targeting. None of these steps are redundant. The change of context makes new analyses possible; with more customers and more data, you can do more things.

Insights and findings represent a point in time in the evolution of your business. They should be seen as your best understanding of the situation *at a given moment*. You could try to go through all the analyses in this book in one go, but ultimately, most of your learnings would go to waste.

Contexts change, customer expectations change, and strategies change too. As a result, learnings become outdated.

Don't look too far ahead. Be deliberate about what you want to learn.

To make real progress, you need to focus on the risks, gaps, and assumptions at hand.

Learning for the sake of learning is a waste.

3) The Wheel Doesn't Need to be Reinvented

It's common for organizations—even teams within the same organizations—to try to reinvent the wheel when doing customer research.

They believe that their situation is unique, or that their product faces greater uncertainty than other products, because their business model, industry, or feature set is different from those products. This leads them to try and find new ways to get customer insights.

In doing so, they fail to realize that they are actually introducing risk into their research.

People behave pretty consistently. While the context in which we operate changes all the time, the actual Jobs we do stay mostly the same.

The best techniques and methods for learning from users and customers have emerged over time—and they are the techniques included in this book. For *Solving Product*, I tried to stick to proven techniques as much as possible.

Customer research will continue to evolve as the field keeps on growing, but the solutions we have today already help answer most product or business problems. They just need to be used more.

Parting Words

> "When in doubt, start with the customer."
>
> Robert Martichenko and Thomas J. Goldsby
> Authors of Lean Six Sigma Logistics

Henry Ford once said that: *"The competitor to be feared is one who never bothers about you at all, but goes on making his own business better all the time."*

One of my secret wishes for this book is to inspire you to become this competitor. I hope you go on to create a company that relentlessly learns from its customers and makes every interaction count.

This, to me, is a true win-win-win situation:

1. Your customers' satisfaction increases.
2. Your business fends off stagnation.
3. Growth accelerates.

As you've seen throughout this book, driving growth from the customer is within your reach. None of it is rocket science.

Stay humble, challenge your assumptions, and remember that the answers *almost* always come from the customers.

This book should help you unlock all the insights you need to make your business a success.

If I haven't answered a specific question you had, or if you'd like to dive deeper into a certain topic, I invite you to visit our website (**solvingproduct.com**), or to contact me at **etienne@solvingproduct.com**.

Thanks for reading *Solving Product.*

-Étienne

Building Blocks

Building Blocks

"When we started out with this kind of product and had a really risky opinion about what it should be, we just didn't know how to test it. We didn't think we, Hiten and I, could do testing. We didn't have someone on the team that was used to doing this kind of work, so we put it off.[278]"

Marie Prokopets and Hiten Shah

Although *Solving Product* is fundamentally a book about growth, it's also a book about customer research.

It's my belief that many product organizations haven't adopted the techniques in this book simply because they are not sure how to do the work, or they are scared of doing it wrong.

Many qualitative and quantitative research experts rightly point out the importance of statistical significance, creating testable hypotheses, recruiting the right participants, and steering clear from cognitive biases.

So far, this book has focused on the importance of making progress and reducing uncertainty.

In this section, we take a closer look at the practice of doing good research and analysis.

This section covers:

1. Finding Early Adopters

2. Recruiting Prospects for Interviews
3. Recruiting Users or Customers for Interviews
4. Setting up Customer Interviews
5. Conducting User or Customer Interviews
6. Defining Tasks for User Tests
7. Conducting User Tests
8. Creating Effective Surveys
9. Defining Your North Star Metric
10. Acting on Customer Insights
11. Making Customer Insights Actionable

To ensure the quality and validity of the insights you collect, I strongly recommend reading through the recruitment, testing, and interview processes covered hereafter.

1. Finding Early Adopters

> "It's important to understand that (being an early adopter) it's not a personality type, so we get lost, especially in the tech scene, people assume that 'people who are early adopters and get the new iPhones are the same people that go and try the new coffee shop' and that's not true."

Brant Cooper
Co-Author of The Lean Entrepreneur

The early adopters you'll serve will be uniquely related to the opportunity or Job you intend to address.

These will be people who are trying to get the Job done faster, more conveniently, or with better results.

Looking for early adopters is a good example of the Rubik's Cube dilemma discussed earlier (Stage #1). You can either start looking for Job performers and try to find the early adopters within that group, or you can look for signals that people want new or better solutions and take it from there.

This guide is about the latter scenario. The best way to find early adopters is through expressed needs—needs that people are aware of, for which they are actively looking for solutions.

To find these people, you have to go to the places where they will be looking for solutions. These include:

- **Forums and communities**: As discussed in Chapter #4, real markets will generally have many watering holes. You can find forums and communities by conducting searches for "[Market] + forum", or "[Market] + community".
- **Quora**: Quora is part forum, part social network. It can be a really useful tool for research. Users are directly asking questions, seeking advice. You can easily find people and message them.
- **Groups**: LinkedIn and Facebook groups are great ways to find expressed needs. Chances are that if someone is a member of *The Future of Recruiting* on LinkedIn, they'll be on the lookout for something new.
- **Blog posts**: If you can find blog posts on the topic you're exploring, you can generally find early adopters. *Maybe the author? Maybe the people sharing the content? Maybe the people commenting?* How-to posts are often expressions of needs. Their comment threads can be very revealing.
- **YouTube**: YouTube is the home of How-to videos. The same general idea applies there.
- **Personal ads**: Craigslist, or even personal ads in newspapers can be good places to find expressed needs. Airbnb used Craigslist to find its early adopters[279], and many followed in their footsteps[280].

- **Reddit**: Many users also visit Reddit looking for solutions or seeking advice. You can find early adopters there, or on Product Hunt, Hacker News, GrowthHackers, etc. Read through the comments to find the right folks.
- **Twitter**: People share things on Twitter that they often wouldn't share on LinkedIn or Facebook. There, you can find pains, needs, Jobs, etc.
- **Product reviews**: Amazon and specialty e-commerce sites can also be good platforms to find expressed needs. Looking at reviews, comments, or reading lists can help reveal early adopters.
- **Related problems**: If you have a good understanding of the problem space, you can find early adopters through related products or services. For example, if you were exploring Jobs around translation, companies like Adyen, helping businesses internationalize their payment gateways might point you to good candidates. As mentioned in Chapter #5, case studies and testimonies can often tell you exactly who to speak to.
- **Open customer service**: Feature request boards are great places to find unmet needs and home in on early adopters who are looking for solutions.

To help you find early adopters via expressed needs, imagine you were exploring a solution around A/B testing (Chapter #20).

To find early adopters, you might go to sites where data and marketing people hang out. A community like GrowthHackers—focused on agile marketing—can point you to hundreds of potential early adopters.

By looking at the question threads, you may be able to find the right people:

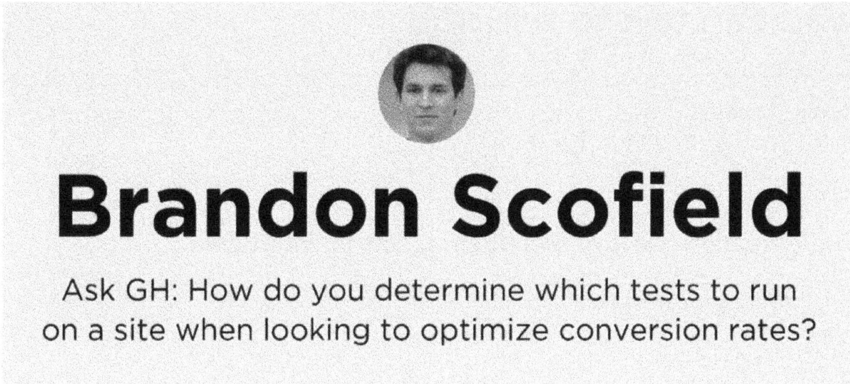

Figure BB.1 - Example of an Explicit Need

Very quickly, you will also find out:

- which questions get traction;
- which users are interested in the answers;
- which influencers are knowledgeable on the topic; *and*
- how prospects express their needs and what topics they care about.

Explore several watering holes. Add the contacts to your list, and keep searching. The search process itself will be revealing.

2. Recruiting Prospects for Interviews

> "Finding your qualified users outside of your existing customer base is always a challenge; where you want someone who's fresh to your products, but they still need a lot of industry knowledge and a lot of background before

you can talk to them."

Nate Archer
Ada Senior Product Manager

There are many ways to recruit prospects for interviews:

- Through referrals
- Via cold calls
- In your network
- By targeting certain events or communities
- By working with research recruitment firms
- Via social media, etc

While all these approaches can help you find good participants, the most precise and most effective way to recruit prospects is through cold outreach.

Sending cold emails—unsolicited emails without prior contact—not only teaches you how to find and reach prospects, it helps you reach the exact profiles you're looking for, thus limiting the risk of learning from the wrong people.

Depending on how much research you do up-front, the quality of your email script, and the type of prospects that you are targeting, you may be able to convert as many as 30% of your cold emails into customer interviews.

To get interviews, you need to be relevant and credible. Prospects need to be motivated to speak to you about the Job, problem, or opportunity that you are researching.

You are already learning if they're not interested in speaking to you. To recruit prospects, you need:

1. an email script;
2. a high-level value proposition (Chapter #6);

3. a lead-in; *and*
4. the right email addresses.

If you're still in the early days (Idea stage), then use a broadly defined Job, desired outcome, or value proposition. A looser proposition has a higher likelihood to connect. Prospects will build their own perception and invent the product in their minds.

Here's a sample script that I've used many times before:

> Subject Line: [International growth]
>
> Hi [Max],
>
> [I enjoyed your two-part series on employee retention. I had also tried to find a job in Hong Kong when I was living there. I know it's not easy.]
>
> I'm contacting you because I have a software company trying to improve [how businesses expand internationally].
>
> I'm not looking to sell anything, but since you have so much expertise with [international growth], I'd love to get your input to make sure we don't build the wrong thing.
>
> Can I schedule a quick call with you next week? [Monday or Tuesday]? Let me know, thank you.
>
> Étienne

To get started fast, you can download an editable copy of this script at **solvingproduct.com/template**.

Keep your email short. Make it easy to respond to. The cold emails that get the most responses are short and to the point. You have to be humble and remember that *you* need their help, not the reverse.

The right email script will drastically improve your response rate.

To make your emails effective, it's important to personalize them. This will help establish rapport with the prospects, and lift your emails above the spammers'.

You have to spend time researching prospects one by one. You can't skip this step. Your goal is to add a personal note or lead-in in *every* email's introduction—to show that you've done your research, and that any time that they spend with you won't be wasted. As you probably know, we're all short on time.

Here are the most effective lead-ins ranked from most to least effective:

1. **Personal success**: a job promotion, an award, an achievement
2. **Company news**: related to them, their department, or a significant company achievement like a fundraising event
3. **A shared experience, acquaintance, hobby, or interest**: ideally something beyond work
4. **Recent posts**: on LinkedIn, Medium, or on their own blog
5. **Company accomplishments**: 5-star ratings, reviews, releases, etc
6. **Recent LinkedIn or Twitter updates**

You can decide to add more personalization, but don't overdo it.

Once you have your email script, your value proposition, and your lead-ins, all you need are email addresses.

Tools like Clearbit Connect or Hunter will help you find almost any email addresses.

I use Clearbit Connect. It's a browser extension that sits inside Gmail. It gives you 100 free credits per month, and it's 97% accurate according to research by Yesware[281].

It's as simple to use as typing an organization's domain name, searching for the name of your prospect, and copying their email address. Once you have enough prospects, you can start sending emails.

You can decide to send emails manually, but that's a lot of work. Tools like Mailshake, Yesware, or Streak will allow you to send mass personalized emails, manage pipelines, track replies, and send follow up emails.

Start slowly. Don't send too many emails. Make revisions to your script and follow up.

Getting the right prospects to agree to customer interviews can take a bit of time. If your script or your targeting isn't connecting, start again from the beginning of this section, improving your messaging.

If you're willing to pay for customer interviews, you can use tools like Zintro, Ethnio, AYTM (Ask Your Target Market), Clarity, or UserInterviews to get qualified candidates. Many of these tools will handle recruiting, scheduling, and incentive payments.

Although using these platforms can simplify recruitment later on—especially if you need participants often—early on, prospects should genuinely care about the Job, problem, or opportunity you're exploring.

If you incentivize participants, you'll miss a critical part of the picture.

3. Recruiting Users or Customers for Interviews

> "You can learn valuable things by asking the right people the wrong questions. If you're talking to the wrong people, it doesn't matter what you ask."
>
> Erika Hall

It's generally easier to recruit from your user base than it is to recruit prospects. For one, your users and customers have had at least some exposure to your brand and product. They also stand to benefit from any improvements that you make on the basis of the insights they share.

To get started recruiting users or customers, first figure out which specific profiles or behaviors you're looking for. *Are you looking for people who have stopped using your product? People who use certain features each week?*

- *What profiles are you looking for?*
- *What goals, problems, opportunities, or behaviors should they share?*
- *What level of familiarity with the product should they have?*
- *What level of comfort with technology should they have?*
- *How well should they know the industry that they're in?*
- *What profiles are you trying to exclude from your research?*
- *Are the profiles and behaviors you're recruiting for 'observable'? Can you find the exact profiles you need using the data at your disposal?*

The more context that you have around their use of the product or behaviors, the easier it will be to recruit them. If you can infer behaviors using data that you already have, you may not even need a screener, a survey designed to weed out *wrong-fit* participants.

The most effective ways to recruit from your user base are through your website or product, or via email, targeting specific behaviors or profiles.

If you want to recruit a wide range of participants, consider using pop-ups on high-trafficked posts or sections of your site, or recruiting via your social media platforms. If that's your intent, know that you will need to screen for the right behaviors.

It's common to incentivize participants, by rewarding them with gift cards, product credits, or cash. As a rule of thumb, the incentive should be equal to the participant's average wage for the duration of the research, including travel time.

The more niche your product is, the more expensive recruitment tends to be. I once had a client who was building software for lawyers. The cost per usability testing participant was $300. The total cost quickly added up.

Note that even a $25 Amazon or OpenTable gift card might attract *professional* participants, who routinely seek out opportunities to get paid for taking part in research.

Be vague about the research topic, and weed out wrong fits with your screener. Participants should care about the study beyond the incentives that you are offering.

You can use the section below on Creating Effective Surveys to create your own screener. The general idea is to break down your ideal participant profile into different characteristics, and then coming up with questions that allow you to test for those characteristics. You have to be clear about who you want to speak to, and who you want to avoid.

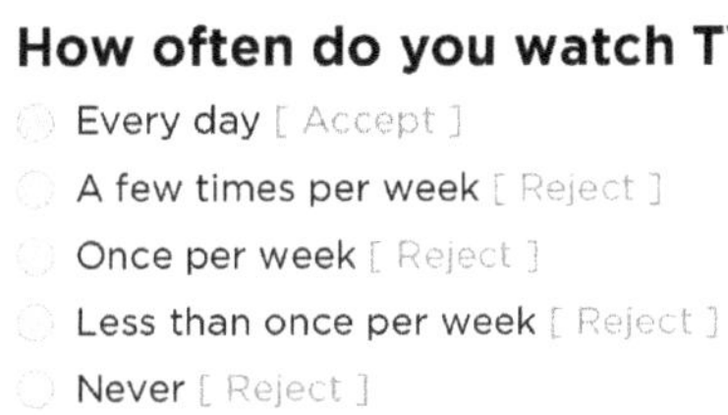

Figure BB.2 - Example of a Screener Survey Question

You want to screen for behaviors, not demographics or preferences. Consider screening for:

- **Behavior frequency**: *Please tell us how often you [Task / Behavior]?*
- **Goals**: *What is the main reason why you use [Feature / Product]?*
- **Familiarity with technology**: *How often do you do these activities online?*
- **Willingness to share personal information**: *This test will require you to share openly about [Topic], do you agree to share honestly about this topic?*

Make sure it's clear to your participants that filling out the screener doesn't guarantee that they will be recruited for the study. Don't waste their time. Start with your most important questions.

Provide clear and distinct choices that don't overlap. Make sure you include a "None of the above," "I don't know," or "Other" option. Disqualify wrong-fit participants as quickly as you can.

If you can infer the behaviors that you're recruiting for with your data, use a message like the following to recruit participants via email, In-App messages, or pop-up messages:

> Subject Line: Help me make [Product Name] better
>
> Hi [Julie],
>
> We're working on new functionalities to improve [Functionality Group]. I noticed that you seem to be getting value from [Functionality Group]. I'd love to get your input to make sure we don't build the wrong thing.
>
> Can I schedule a quick call with you next week? [Monday or Tuesday]?
>
> Let me know, thank you.
>
> Étienne

Sample and recruit participants randomly. Make sure the messaging you use doesn't feel creepy.

If you're using a screener, change your call-to-action:

> We're looking for savvy [Users / Customers] to help us refine [Functionality Group]. Would you be interested in taking part in our research? Simply fill out this quick [X] question survey: [surveylink.com]

Only mention the incentives if you have difficulty recruiting at least 5-10 percent of the users that you contact.

For in-person studies, it's a good idea to follow up by phone before confirming invitations This will help make sure that you get great participants.

> "I have a few more questions. I just want to confirm that you're a good match for our research. Could you walk me through how you typically decide what to work on?"

Eventually, you should turn user and customer recruitment into a continuous process.

Consider automating some of your recruitment messages once you know that they work. Create a database of potential participants and give someone on your team the responsibility for recruitment.

4. Setting Up Customer Interviews

"Every meeting either succeeds or fails. You've lost the meeting when you leave with a compliment or a stalling tactic. While we might spot something as blatant as "Let's talk again after the holidays... Don't call me, I'll call you," we accept the more subtle versions every day."

Rob Fitzpatrick
Author of The Mom Test Author

Customer interviews can be done face-to-face, over the phone, or via conferencing software like Skype or Zoom.

- Face-to-face interviews allow you to get more focused attention. They give you an opportunity to learn about the ultimate context of use of your product. They can help you get better cues, being able to observe the interviewee's body language.

- Phone or conferencing software interviews can be faster. They allow you to target very precise roles and behaviors across regions or countries. But because of notifications popping up, colleagues showing up, and all types of emergencies, interviewees may be more distracted than during face-to-face interviews.

No matter the approach you choose, you should make sure you can keep your interviewee's attention throughout the entire discussion.

To achieve this, and because you want to learn about the interviewee's unique world view—not their employer's, their friends', or their team's—it's best to interview one person at a time.

Group interviews make people defensive. It forces them to maintain a certain image, which often prevents them from opening up.

If you're uncomfortable meeting with a high-ranked prospect (e.g. in B2B), consider getting them out of their office for lunch or coffee to even the odds. A neutral location will make you feel more comfortable.

The biggest challenge when starting out is being able to get valid data consistently. You need to create a structure and a script that will capture consistent information around your key assumptions.

As a rule of thumb—and this depends on how talkative your prospects are—you can squeeze as few as three to five questions in a divergent or generative interview and as many as 15-20 in a convergent interview.

Because of this, it's important to always keep in mind what your main questions are. You should plan for a meeting structure like this:

1. **Introduction & warm up (two minutes)**: Greetings are exchanged. You can use icebreakers or warm-up questions to make the interviewees feel comfortable.
2. **Qualification (three minutes)**: You ask questions to understand the role and situation of your prospect. *Do they fit your target profile?*
3. **Open-ended questions (20 minutes)**: The bulk of the time allotted to the interview falls in this stage. Your goal is to understand their view of the world.

4. **Closing (five minutes)**: To move the relationship forward, and to gauge the prospect's interest, you try to close them on another meeting, referrals, or a purchase (Chapter #7).
5. **Note review (ten minutes)**: After the meeting (and without the prospect), review your notes to make sure you've not lost any of the key insights.

Before the discussion, you should also make sure that you've researched the prospect thoroughly. This shows respect, and means you can avoid asking questions that could have been answered by a Google search.

During the introduction & warm-up phase, you can ask questions about the interviewee's home city, a hobby, a mutual acquaintance, a blog post, or anything else that can help you establish rapport.

You can then transition into a simple intro:

> Thanks for taking the time to [Meet / Speak] with me.
>
> We're a young company working on [Value Proposition]. We're currently trying to learn as much as we can. We'd like to understand your needs and reality to avoid building the wrong thing.
>
> I have roughly [X] questions for you today.
>
> Before we begin, I'd like to stress that we don't have a finished product yet and our objective is to learn from you—not to sell or pitch to you.
>
> Does that make sense?

During the qualification phase, you try to understand their role and situation. This will allow you to identify patterns between any roles, conditions, and the opportunities that you uncover.

Don't feel like you need to talk or fill the silence. You can ask questions like:

- *How would you describe your role as [Role]?*
- *What does success look like for you?*

Then follows the meatiest part of the discussion: open-ended questions. Ask open-ended questions, follow emotion, encourage complaints, ask follow up questions, and don't forget to empathize.

The last phase is about closing. Depending on the stage you're at, you should close with:

- a new meeting to explore the situation further;
- referrals to confirm the existence of the market and have discussions with more prospects; *or*
- pre-sales.

As you go through the interviews, it's important to have a script and to stick to it. While it's okay to adjust the phrasing or add questions, remember that you have to be able to compare the data points.

Refer to the appropriate sections of this book to build your interview script, and then get started doing interviews.

5. Conducting User or Customer Interviews

"Listen, not to respond, but really listen to understand."

Simon Seroussi
Feather Product Manager

Time to get started doing interviews. The first thing to understand is that interviews are *not* discussions. You can't evaluate the success of customer interviews in the same way that you would evaluate the success of discussions. Interviews are not about being liked, having an enjoyable discussion, or leaving on a high note.

The best interviews are 90% listening, and 10% talking. You have to learn to stay quiet. Initially, this makes many interviewers quite uncomfortable.

You'll learn very little from close-ended questions that lead to quick yes/no answers like: *"Do you like your job?"*.

Closed-Ended Questions Begin with...	**Open-Ended Questions Begin with...**
Which...?	Why...?
Who...?	What...?
When...?	How...?
Where...?	
Can also start with...	**Can also start with...**
Is/Are...?	Tell me about...?
Do/Did...?	Explain...?
Would/Will...?	Describe...?
Could/Can...?	
Was/were...?	
Have/Has...?	

Figure BB.3 - Closed vs. Open-Ended Questions Cheat Sheet

90% of everything you learn will be the result of asking open-ended questions, following emotion, and digging for the truth.

You are looking for facts and insights, so it's critical to get interviewees to open up. To get interviewees to do this, ask follow up questions like:

- *What do you mean by that?*
- *Can you explain that a little more?*
- *Why do you say that?*
- *How do you feel about that?*
- *Sounds like there's a story there, can you tell me more?*
- *Tell me more about...*

Avoid mentioning your idea or what you're working on as much as possible. Don't try to land customers with interviews. If you do, then you will stop learning, and you'll appear needy. At this stage you're just trying to find helpful, knowledgeable people.

Beware that **everyone** lies. This could be because:

- they don't trust you—they might think you're planning to compete against them; *or*
- the real answer doesn't make them look good; *or*
- it's not the image they're trying to create; *or*
- they're being overly optimistic.

Rob Fitzpatrick says that: *"Anything that involves the future is an over-optimistic lie."*, and that *"People will lie to you if they think it's what you want to hear."*

People generally want to be liked. Once interviewees detect that your ego is on the line, then their answers will stop being what they really think.

You want to ground your innovation in *truths* and *reality*, not lies. This will get a lot easier when prospects feel comfortable and are willing to open up. The more comfortable interviewees feel, the more talkative they'll be, and the better the information you will get.

Create a welcoming atmosphere. Build relationships. Make sure prospects understand that you're not planning to compete with their organization, and that everything they say will be kept confidential. You need to overcome their defenses to get to the truth.

I strongly recommend recording these interviews. You can use your phone, your computer, or a recorder for this. Make sure prospects agree to being recorded (you need to ask), and communicate that the recording will only be used for internal reference.

I prefer relistening to the interviews afterwards than interrupting the flow and holding back the discussion by trying to take notes. The truth is that you'll miss 50% of what's being said during the interview if you are taking notes.

Sometimes it will make sense to bring a partner along for the interviews. In those situations, one person can lead the discussion while the other takes notes. This can make your team appear more credible, and will definitely accelerate share back with the team. But any more than two interviewers will intimidate participants.

Don't judge. Make sure you smile during the interviews, even when it's over the phone. People can sense that.

Being non-judgmental, empathetic, and friendly helps prospects to open up and feel more comfortable talking about their reality.

Keep the discussion casual. Don't interrogate. It has to feel like a discussion with a friend. Whenever an interviewee starts complaining, listen. People will be more specific with complaints than praise. Specific examples will really help you learn about their goals and the challenges they're facing.

Keep your questions short. Oftentimes, the longer the question, the shorter the answer.

Practice active listening. Nod and look directly at the interviewee. From time to time, make interested "hmm hmm" sounds. Empathize.

Use silence and broken questions—starting to ask a question and letting your speech trail off (e.g. *"Why do you..."*)—to get interviewees to talk. People are naturally uncomfortable with silences. They tend to want to fill silences with words.

Most times, questions should emerge from the previous questions, the same way they would in regular conversations. But, if you feel like the interviewee is just going through the motions, you can decide to drastically switch topics between questions. By doing this, interviewees are forced to refocus on the discussion.

Avoid putting many questions in the same question. The interviewee won't know which question to answer. Break them into different questions.

Don't put answers into questions. For example: *"Do you think Apple is the most innovative company in the world?"*

Avoid answering questions about your product. As Steve Portigal says[282]: *"Once you answer those questions then you become the expert, and it's almost impossible to return to research mode. In research mode, they're the expert and you're interested and curious."*

You can repeat the answers back to your prospect for further clarifications and to confirm your understanding. Do this by saying: *"So, what you're saying is..."*

You can also challenge pre-existing hypotheses by referencing "other people." For example, *"I've heard from other people that ______. Do you agree?"* It's easier for people to disagree with an anonymous third party than to disagree with a person in front of them.

Keep an eye out for body language. Strong reactions, posture, body positioning, language, tone variations and eye movements can tell you a lot. *Do they seem nervous? Tentative? Bored?*

If so, try to restore your rapport and reassure them (*"This is very helpful"*). You can also decide to ask what made them roll their eyes, sigh, laugh, frown, smirk, etc.

If you sense hostility, stay calm, take a deep breath, and try to get the interview back on track. Restate the goal of the interview, and ask a general, open-ended question.

Prospects who are leaning forward, asking a lot of questions and who really get involved in the discussion are interested. Prospects who are easily distracted, look through their emails or messages, slouch and talk without answering the questions are almost certainly not interested.

If you're meeting face-to-face, have a look at your surroundings. Office walls and sticky notes can be gold. They can tell you a lot about what prospects care about.

Watch out for compliments. Compliments can be very misleading and can derail your interview process. Focus on facts and what people *actually* do or have done in recent past. The best predictor of future behavior will always be current or past behavior.

Unless you try to close someone, it's hard to really know if the meeting went well. Your ask will depend on which stage you are at, so refer to the appropriate section in this book, and make sure you try to close them.

Conclude by summarizing what you learned. You can ask the interviewee to confirm some of your observations. Consider concluding by asking: *"Is there anything else you would like to tell me about what we discussed?"*

Write down your notes and impressions right after the interview to make sure you don't forget anything.

Then, with the benefit of distance, listen to the interview once more. By relistening to the interview, you'll be able to:

- assess your performance as an interviewer; *and*
- evaluate the quality and validity of the information collected.

Now, share the recordings—not your notes or a summary of the interview—with colleagues or team members.

Sharing summarized versions of the interviews will limit your team's interpretation of the customer data; they'll have a hard time helping you identify lies and half-truths. You'll also have more difficulty getting them to buy in, as discussed in Chapter #25.

6. Defining Tasks for User Tests

> "How well we communicate is determined not by how well we say things, but how well we are understood."
>
> Andy Grove
> Intel Corporation Former CEO

Creating great tasks for user tests is both an art and a science.

The tasks that you select need to be unambiguous, and free from interpretation. This is especially important for *unmoderated* user tests—when participants are on their own. For these tests, you won't have the opportunity to clarify any of the scenarios or terms used, so they must be crystal clear.

Great tasks are based on real user or customer goals, they're actionable, they point in a certain direction, and they avoid giving clues or describing how to complete the task.

Early on, you generally want to focus on the happy path—your site or product's main flow—to iron out any kinks in the core processes.

What are the most important things that every user must be able to do in your product?

You can use a structure like the following to turn goals into tasks:

> You'd like to [Goal]. A friend/colleague told you about [Site or Product Tested]. How would you go about achieving [Goal] with [Site or Product Tested]?

For example:

> You'd like to buy travel insurance. A colleague told you about SuperInsurance. How would you go about buying travel insurance using the SuperInsurance website?

This task works because it's based on a real user need (buying travel insurance), it points users in a certain direction (using the SuperInsurance website), and it doesn't mention any of the tools, site sections, or functionalities that you are hoping to test.

You can make your tasks even more engaging by making them more personal. For example, you could let participants perform the tasks for themselves.

To make sure that your tasks are clear, test them with colleagues or prospects beforehand. *What do they understand? How does their understanding line up with what you're trying to test?*

Iterate until the tasks are both clear and unambiguous.

7. Conducting User Tests

> "Reactions are hard to fake.
> Feedback is hard to give."

User—or usability—tests can help validate a prototype, find issues in complex workflows, improve the user experience, and capture user feedback.

Combined with interviews, user tests can be a very effective way to learn about your users, prospects, or customers.

There are three main ways to conduct user tests:

1. **Moderated in-person**: Participants come in one at a time in an office, in a lab, or in a coffee shop (in the case of guerilla testing[283]). A moderator helps facilitate the tests.
2. **Moderated remote**: The participant and moderator are in different locations. Screen sharing software like Zoom or Skype is used to help facilitate the tests.
3. **Unmoderated remote**: Participants are either recruited through a platform like Loop11 or UserTesting, or they're directed there to take part in the tests. Users are given tasks by the platform, which records their use of the product. This type of tests can be done quickly, and often for a fraction of the cost of in-person testing.

It's generally a good idea to pick the approach that best matches your budget, the location of your ideal test participants, and how often you want to do user tests. As Erika Hall says: *"Don't use expensive testing—costly in money or time—to discover what you can find out with cheap tests."*

User tests are especially effective when they're included in an iterative design or development process. Iterative processes allow you to test more often with fewer users, making changes between each series of tests.

In famous research, usability thought leader Jakob Nielsen demonstrated that five users could help reveal 85% of all usability issues[284] on a site. However, until you are comfortable with your ability to recruit—and weed out *wrong-fit* participants—you'll probably want to recruit at least one extra participant per series. This will ensure that you can get all the data points you need for your tests.

Your tests will last 30-60 minutes, depending on whether you interview participants before the tests or not. It's usually best to schedule all five (or six) tests on the same day, keeping a buffer of 30-45 minutes between tests.

Pick a neutral location like a meeting room or a quiet space. Make sure that participants know exactly how to get to the facilities, and will have enough time to get there. Stressed participants make mistakes that they wouldn't usually make.

Depending on the complexity of the tasks that you are hoping to test, you may be able to go through three or four tasks in 30 minutes. To make sure the timing works, consider doing a dry run with contacts or colleagues; people who haven't been exposed to your product yet.

Tools like Lookback, Loop11, or ScreenFlow can be used to record both your participants' screens—web or mobile—and their comments.

It's often a good idea to split moderating responsibilities between a facilitator—sitting next to the participant—and a person who is taking notes in another room (or in the same room, but out of the participant's field of view).

It's your responsibility to make sure that participants are comfortable. Let them adjust their seat and device, explore the desktop or homepage before the test begins, and have a leisurely read through the first task.

Explain that your goal is to learn how to improve the site or product, and that their feedback will only be used for this.

To ease the participants into the tests, begin with the simplest task. A quick success will help participants gain confidence.

Often, participants who encounter usability issues are quick to blame themselves rather than the product. Make sure participants understand that you're testing the product, not them. There are no right or wrong answers.

As you go through the tests, make sure that you don't react. Don't help the participants unless there's nothing more that can be learned from an issue.

Keep an even tone. Watch for verbal cues and body language. Ask questions to get participants to open up:

- ***I noticed you did ______. Can you tell me why?*** You can follow up on interesting behaviors observed during the tests to get a better understanding of the participant's reasoning.
- ***Did you notice whether there was any other way to ______?*** You can ask users to understand why users chose one alternative over another.
- ***What do you think of ______?*** You can ask about specific aspects of the interface or product (icons, menus, text, etc). You'll learn about elements that may be confusing to users.

Focus on what participants are doing, more than what they're saying. Take note of contradictions. Keep track of task successes, failures, and partial successes.

Consider asking participants the Single Ease Question (SEQ) after they attempt each of your tasks (Chapter #21).

After a test, consider asking clarifying questions:

- *What were your overall impression of [Product]?*
- *What were the [Best / Worst] thing about [Product]? Why?*
- *What, if anything, surprised you about the experience?*
- *Why didn't you use [Feature]?*
- *I saw you did [Action]. Can you tell me why?*
- *Did you notice that there was any other way to accomplish [Task]?*
- *How would you compare [Product] to [Competitor's Product]?*
- *Can you think of any other product that resembles this one?*

Compare your notes with those of the other note-taker. Create a list of issues. Rank them by importance and frequency. Any issues that caused task failures should be addressed as quickly as possible.

Alternatively, if you weren't testing your own product (Chapter #5), then any problems that you have identified could point to opportunities to improve over the competition.

8. Creating Effective Surveys

"A survey shouldn't be a fallback for when you can't do the right type of research.[285]"

Erika Hall

On the surface, running a survey seems easy. After all, all you have to do is:

1. create an account on SurveyMonkey, Typeform, or any of the bazillion survey platforms on the internet;
2. write questions;
3. publish the survey;
4. share it with the appropriate audience; *and*
5. wait for the answers to come in.

Right?

However, surveys are one of the most dangerous research tools. Creating a survey that is both representative of the views of the target audience *and* captures the right information is a real challenge.

As we've seen in Chapter #12, even a standardized survey like the NPS has its flaws.

Surveys are good for evaluative research; they can help you to understand the composition of a given population, and get a more granular understanding of the patterns within that population (e.g. how many one-time buyers find the product too expensive).

To create a good survey, you need to be very clear on:

- what you are trying to learn;
- the audience you're trying to learn from; *and*

- the sample size that you need in order to be able to rely on the data you're collecting.

With surveys, you are usually trying to reveal hidden patterns, or to sample a large population so that you can better understand its composition and preferences.

If we look back at the Grubhub case study in Chapter #12, we see that Casey and his team did both:

1. They already knew that the average person ordered delivery once or twice a month. They sent a survey to gather more data on delivery ordering patterns.
2. Once the patterns started to become clear, they sent a survey to a larger part of their user base to get a breakdown of its composition.

So, what challenges is your business facing? Where are you making assumptions? What information could help reduce uncertainty?

You should be able to summarize the goal of your survey in one sentence. List out the sub-topics you'd like to explore.

Who would you need to survey to get representative answers to your questions? Prospects? Users? Customers? Random strangers?

Recruiting from your user base should be pretty straightforward at this point. Make sure you target the appropriate segment as precisely as possible. If you need to poll strangers or prospects, consider working with a research recruitment firm, or using ads to target the right folks.

Calculate the sample size ahead of time[286]. This will help you figure out how many respondents you need. A confidence level of 95% means that the survey results have a 95% chance of being representative. This is an accepted standard[287].

The sample size you need—and the confidence level you aim for—will dictate your recruitment strategy and the speed at which you can get results. It's important to consider that only a small percentage of the people you contact will actually take your survey. For example, via email, it's possible that only five percent of the people you invite will complete your survey[288].

Once you know what you are trying to learn, and from whom you're trying to learn, it's time to create your survey.

As a rule of thumb, you should only include questions that will lead to specific actions. If you don't know how the answers will help you advance your business, then you're probably wasting your users' precious attention.

The shorter the survey, the more likely respondents are to complete it, and the more likely your data will be reliable. Try to aim for four or five questions at most. If you need to ask more questions, break up your survey into several steps.

Write clear and short questions using language your audience is familiar with. Ask one question at a time. Don't try to combine two or more questions into one. Avoid loaded or leading questions. Don't ask people to predict the future, or to recall the distant past.

Use closed questions for validation or to collect discrete answers. Those could be:

- **Checkboxes**: best used when several answers could apply.
- **Multiple choice**: best used when the respondent needs to pick an answer within a set.
- **Scales**: best used when you want respondents to rate an item or statement on a numerical scale.
- **Ranking**: best used when you want to understand your respondents' priorities.

For closed questions, be sure to consider all possible options from the respondent's perspective ahead of time. If you're not entirely clear, then add a fill-in option for extra answers.

Open-ended questions help you learn about customer needs that you might not have known existed. They take more time to analyze, but can help reveal deeper patterns and insights. Use them sparingly.

To ensure that your questions are clear and unambiguous, do a dry run with small sample, or with colleagues who haven't yet been exposed to the project. *How does their understanding line up with the information you're trying to collect?*

Think through your question sequencing carefully. It's often a good idea to start with easy questions like 'yes' or 'no' questions. Oftentimes, people will be more likely to complete the survey once they feel they made a commitment.

Once your survey is ready and the questions have been validated, share it with the precise audience you had envisioned. Sharing surveys at large on social media only works if you're hoping to learn from just about anyone.

When you've collected enough responses to meet your sample size requirements, analyze the data. Don't get fixated on any specific data point. Evaluate all patterns independently before making up your mind, or communicating the insights to a broader group.

Unfortunately, survey results often become 'truths' once they have been shared across an organization. It's generally a good idea to try and disprove the results before you go all in on the insights.

9. Defining Your North Star Metric

"Each strategy we had at Netflix—from our personalization strategy to our theory that a simpler experience would improve retention—had a very specific metric that helped us to evaluate if the strategy was valid or not. If the strategy moved the metric, we knew we were on the right path. If we failed to move the metric, we moved on to the next idea. Identifying these metrics took a lot of the politics and ambiguity out of which strategies were succeeding or not."

Gibson Biddle
Netflix Former VP of Product

Throughout this book, we have talked about the importance of setting goals and then measuring progress towards those goals.

At the Idea stage, I recommended using pre-orders to validate market need (Chapter #7).

At the Startup stage, I recommended using the PMF survey or a proxy of customer value (Chapter #10) to focus product iterations.

Well, this type of metric is often referred to as a North Star metric (NSM)—the metric that best captures the value that your product delivers to customers.

NSMs are unique to every organization and change over time. This means that at the Growth, Expansion, and Maturity stages (and possibly before) you need to come up with your own metric.

Thankfully, a lot of the analyses done throughout this book can serve as inputs to help define your NSM. By this stage, you should know what drives what, and should also have a sense of which levers to pull to achieve certain results.

Teams across product organizations rarely agree fully on which drivers matter most. This can lead to teams coming up with their own goals, doing their own research, and prioritizing initiatives that sometimes conflict with one another.

A good NSM helps to create a unified view of priorities. It can help drive team alignment and focus, and move your business forward.

The metric you choose should be a function of inputs that your team can influence. It should be predictive of mid- to long-term growth. For the team, it should be as simple as *move the metric, grow the business*.

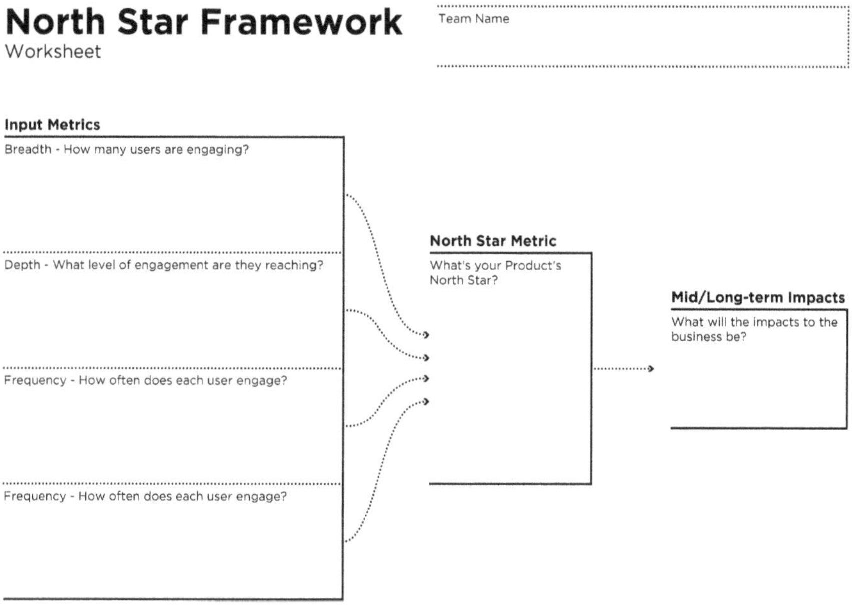

Figure BB.4 - The North Star Framework Worksheet

John Cutler, who co-wrote a full book on the North Star framework[289], says that a good NSM:

- **Expresses value**: It's easy to see why it matters to customers.
- **Represents vision and strategy**: It reflects the company's current product and business strategy.
- **Is a leading indicator of success**: It predicts the future, rather than reflect the past (e.g. leads vs. sales).
- **Is actionable**: Team members can take action to influence it.
- **Is understandable**: It's easy to express, and can be communicated in plain language that non-technical folks understand.
- **Is measurable**: You can track it with analytics or via some other form of reporting.

- **Isn't a vanity metric**: Just because something is measurable doesn't make it meaningful. When your NSM increases or decreases, you have to be confident that the change is meaningful.

Your NSM should change as your strategy changes. As we've seen, it can be a good idea to go from revenue, to value, to the metric that best captures your unique business model.

Over time, Amplitude's NSM evolved from early revenue to Weekly Querying Users (the number of users analyzing data), to Weekly Learning Users (the count of active users who have shared a learning that's consumed by at least two other people in the previous seven days)[290]. The metrics Amplitude chose were indicative of the stage of growth they were at, and their current strategy.

I recommend reading Amplitude's *North Star Playbook* to help you find the best metric for your business.

Once you have a clear NSM, your team should focus on the opportunities that are the most likely to influence its inputs.

For example, if you were to look at Facebook's famous 'Seven Friends in 10 Days'[291]—which meant that if users added seven or more friends in their first ten days, they were extremely likely to keep using Facebook—the opportunities that were worth prioritizing might have included the sign up, onboarding, and invitation flows.

The best way to measure progress is against a goal. Set your NSM, and then use it to move your product forward.

Case Study Learning in Business-to-Business-to-Consumer (B2B2C)

"Every time we add another step to some system, the probability that the system works is reduced."

Peter Bevelin
Author of Seeking Wisdom

Early in his career, Simon Seroussi worked as a product manager for TravelClick, makers of a hotel reservation and booking platform.

As a B2B2C organization, their product had two distinct user groups:

1. **Hotel chains**: the companies paying TravelClick to use their booking engine on their websites; *and*

2. **End users**: the consumers using their booking engine daily to make hotel reservations.

Two completely different user types with different needs, both critical to the success of their organization.

As the customers, hotels made constant feature requests. But although they knew about *their* needs, more often than not, the requests they made with the aim of improving the end user experience failed to improve it.

Their requests were either based on research, what competitors were doing, or gut feelings; it was hard for Simon to tell those apart.

Hotels were not their own customers. Maybe they thought their customers wanted to use the engine in certain ways—but it wasn't always the case.

> *"It's already hard enough to not put your own perception into someone's understanding of a problem. But when it's a customer voicing it to a business, who then voices it to us, we get a completely new different problem. It's very challenging to try and go back to that source."*

Although Simon and his team had access to metrics, they were missing qualitative feedback from the booking engine's end users. Simon wanted to speak directly to the end users, to short-cut the game of telephone.

Because access to their customers' users was limited, Simon had to get creative. As a large company itself, TravelClick had teams and departments that had never been exposed to the booking engine. This meant that there were employees who had never been exposed to the product.

Since just about anyone could use the booking engine to make hotel reservations, internal stakeholders could be used as proxies for user tests.

Simon organized guerilla user tests, asking colleagues to go through different hotel booking scenarios. It took a few rounds, but the tests generated enough insights to significantly improve the experience of their customers' customers.

In B2B2C, you often need to go directly to the end user to learn about their experience. This might require a bit of creativity, but the learnings will help to move your product forward.

---

10. Acting on Customer Insights

> "When people tell you something's wrong or doesn't work for them, they are almost always right. When they tell you exactly what they think is wrong and how to fix it, they are almost always wrong."

Neil Gaiman
Author

It's not enough to learn about user and customer needs. You have to use what you learn.

Once you have discovered what users want, what they like, what their problems are, and why they're using your product, then you need to act on the insights.

Think about it, when you have a negative experience with a brand and take time out of your schedule to inform them, they may apologize and tell you that the product team has been informed—but often you never hear from them again. *Did you have a positive experience?*

It's even worse if you have taken the time to jump on a call with someone from the product team, shared legitimate concerns, and then heard crickets.

Whether or not you decide to act on what you learn, people want to feel heard.

Users will generally be more forgiving (and willing to wait) if they know they're being heard. When we think that other people are trying their best, we tend to be more willing to excuse problems and delays.

Better yet, going the extra mile to help users achieve their goals often makes them stay with you longer[292]. *Can you help users hack things together to get the Job done? Can you help them find the answer elsewhere? Can you go above and beyond to provide great service?*

Zappos support is famous for helping users find solutions even if it means pointing them to their competitors' websites[293]. This proactivity creates a lot of goodwill that ultimately benefits the company.

Keep track of feedback and issues. Be honest and forthright about timelines. Follow up when things move forward.

The team at Canny, a customer feedback management tool, created the following infographic to sum up the process of managing feature requests[294]:

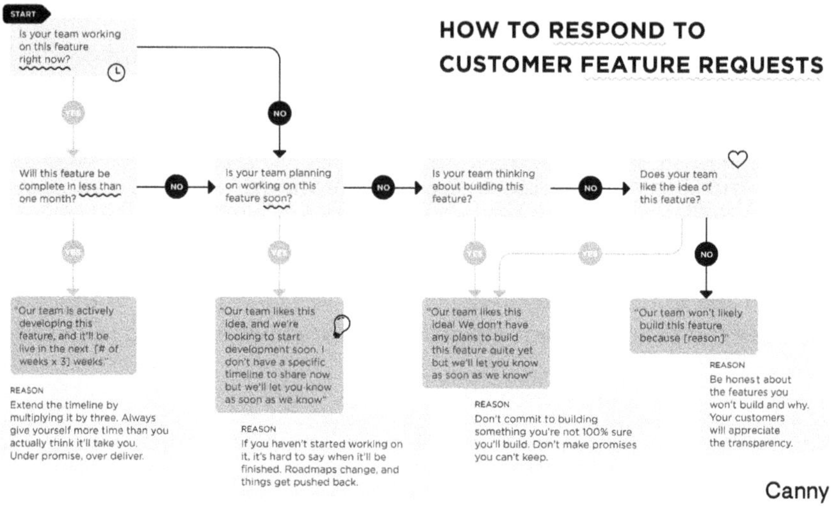

Figure BB.5 - Canny's Feature Request Management Infographic

Manage expectations and make sure your users and customers feel heard.

Ultimately, good customer feedback management is about feeding feedback, insights, and product usage data into the road map.

Case Study
Managing Customer Expectations at Feather

> "Customer satisfaction is the only way to maximize long-term profits."
>
> Hermann Simon

Simon Seroussi learned about the value of saying 'no' at TravelClick. Dealing with different user types—with sometimes conflicting views—had taught him that you can't do everything and you can't please everyone.

Companies have to build the best product they can. Saying 'no' helps them to manage customers' expectations.

He says: *"A lot of companies let customers speak and voice their concerns, but they don't necessarily give them a reply. Whether it's the fact that the feature is going to get built, or the fact that the feature isn't, or that it's going to be addressed through another problem or another solution."*

Now product manager at Feather, a furniture subscription service based in New York, Simon gets to apply this mindset.

Feather's product request board is tied to their kanban board, which is where they follow the progress of the development of new features. Whenever something in the storyboard progresses from icebox to backlog to code review to in progress, the request board gets updated. Users are able to see the progress of their requests in real time.

When a feature gets to QA or the code review stage, or when they're ready to deploy, they know who raised the concern, and can immediately validate with the users if the changes solved their problem.

This allows them to keep their users and customers in the loop, and also to launch better features and product improvements.

This, in turn, helps create better relationships with users and customers. Managing expectations is a good way to avoid creating frustration in the user base.

---

11. Making Customer Insights Actionable

"Innovation is insights put into action."

Stephen Inoue
Investor

As businesses grow, the types and amount of customer data that they generate usually start to grow exponentially.

This creates both a challenge and an opportunity. The better you can make sense of your data, the smarter your organization can become.

It's a good idea to set up processes for categorizing learnings, insights, and customer feedback.

As an organization, it might make sense to dig systematically into every issue raised, and to add context like:

- *How often does this issue happen?*
- *At what frequency?*
- *What kind(s) of users or customers provided the feedback? Are there patterns in terms of roles or personas?*
- *How many people are affected?*
- *How costly is the issue? Can it be quantified?*
- *What are people trying to achieve? What's the Job to be Done?*
- *What's at stake? What happens if the issue goes unresolved?*

The reason why companies rarely do this is because it's very difficult to centralize data in a way that makes it usable.

Companies often use different tools to manage different parts of the customer journey (Zendesk, Intercom, Facebook, etc). This makes it difficult to get a central view of all customer interactions.

For information to be useful and actionable it has to be:

1. easy to access;
2. easy to consume and analyze; *and*
3. *Felt.*

Ultimately, you should start with customer data that you can retrieve. This might include:

- Support tickets
- Social media messages
- Text and video chats
- Email clicks and responses
- Product reviews
- Sales and support calls
- Ad clicks and intent data, etc

Start with information that you're able to collect. You can create a system of records using a CRM, a specialized tool like productboard or Canny, a Trello or Notion board, or a simple spreadsheet. The important thing is to centralize the information and make it easy to query by all team members.

As you'll see in the next case study, companies like Drift have taken this a step further. The information that they collect is fed into a machine learning algorithm which analyzes hundreds of inputs in order to make recommendations.

That data can then be used to make customer experience improvement predictions, and in turn to create a real competitive advantage for the organization.

Sachin Rekhi also recommends creating what he calls a 'feedback river'—an open channel for anyone who is interested to get direct access to primary feedback on the product. It's a strategy that he's used both at LinkedIn and Notejoy, the company he co-founded in 2016.

The general idea is to create a central place where all feedback collected by the company gets funneled. It can be a Slack channel, an email group, or any other place that makes it easy for team members to access the information.

At Notejoy, the feedback river centralizes:

- NPS ratings;
- Account cancellation reasons;
- Search queries in the help center;
- Feature request votes;
- Feature request comments;
- Social media mentions;
- Support tickets; and
- Contact form messages.

You could also imagine:

- Product reviews;
- Bugs and app failures;
- Chat messages, etc.

Consider adding anything that helps you or your team get a feel for the customer experience. As Sachin says: *"What's great about this is that you're continually getting feedback from your customers every single day."* It's instantaneous and constant. Team members can really get the pulse of the product.

Although customer feedback shouldn't be used to *directly* dictate the product road map, it should definitely inform it.

Case Study
How Guillaume Cabane Took Learnings to the Next Level

> "Most companies have hundreds of ad copies. They're paying good money to make people take certain actions, and then they're just destroying the data. It's a crime scene and you're destroying evidence. They should pass it on to the CRM."

Guillaume Cabane

Guillaume Cabane has been working in growth and marketing for the past decade. Along the way, he has helped create sustainable growth at Segment and Mention. He has also created many growth tactics like the Reveal Loop[295].

After years advising Drift's executive team and acting as a reference customer for them, Guillaume agreed to join the company full-time in 2017.

As VP of Growth for the customer-centric organization, he had two main goals:

1. To provide a better experience from marketing to sales to product and beyond; and
2. To drive incremental gains in revenue.

Guillaume was the 50th employee when he joined the organization. At that time, Drift was growing fast and maturing quickly.

Starting out, Guillaume knew that his team would have to make a lot of assumptions. The key for them was to try to make the best guesses possible.

> "In most startups that I talk to in the Bay Area, the success rate of growth teams at the experiment level is about 20%. What that means is that we fail eight times out of 10. Growth teams are expected to fail."

Guillaume knew that the optimal experience for each user would have to be discovered. Instead of assuming that his team could define the optimal experience, he set up processes for soliciting ideas from the entire organization, prioritizing experiments, and aggregating test results.

Ad, content, landing page, email, and onboarding performance data was collected and analyzed by the AI Guillaume had put in place.

By letting machines analyze high volumes of data, they were able to continuously refine their users' behavior profiles; every ad click, email open, and conversion made the profiles better.

The machines did their part, while Guillaume's team handled the creative and delivery processes. He says: *"What I see in marketers is that they say either I know the users, or I don't. And so that's a very Boolean mindset [black or white]. A guess is better than no guess. No guess means that you're then reverting to the default. You're assuming defeat immediately. That's terrible."*

In the end, Guillaume's approach helped contribute to a 5X revenue growth in 18 months. By creating processes to maximize learning from every experiment they ran, Drift managed to become one of the fastest growing technology company in the world.

There's a lot to learn from Guillaume's approach.

Appendix I – Acknowledgments

Solving Product would not have been possible without the generous contributions of the following authors, entrepreneurs, and product and growth leaders:

NAME	EXPERIENCE	ROLE
Alan Klement	Revealed, The ReWired Group	Entrepreneur, Author
Alex Schiff	Benzinga, Fetchnotes, Occipital	Entrepreneur
Alicia Hurst	JW Player, PowerToFly	Product Leader
Andrew O'Shaughnessy	Newsweaver, Poppulo	Entrepreneur
Ashwin Gupta	VWO	Growth/Product Leader
Bob Moesta	Clayton Christensen Institute, The ReWired Group	Entrepreneur, Author
Casey Winters	Eventbrite, Grubhub, Pinterest, Reforge	Product Leader
Claudio Perrone	Agile Sensei Consulting	Entrepreneur, Author
Claus Rosenberg Gotthard	Book'n'Bloom, NoWHEY, Scanclean, Zetako	Entrepreneur
Dan DeAlmeida	Dassault Systèmes, LabVoice	Product Leader
Dan Martell	Clarity, Flowtown, Spheric Technologies	Entrepreneur
Dan Touchette	Bitly, Patch.com, Personio, Rocketrip	Product Leader
Daniel Shapiro	Gigsy, PartnerStack, Points, Microsoft	Product Leader
Daniel Zacarias	Limetree, Premium Minds, Substantive	Entrepreneur
David Cancel	Compete, Drift, HubSpot, Performable	Entrepreneur
Francis Wu	Acquisio, Standout Jobs, TrackTick, Qwalify	Product Leader
Guillaume Cabane	Apple, Drift, Growlabs, Mention, Segment	Growth Leader

Hiten Shah	Crazy Egg, FYI, KISSmetrics, Product Habits	Entrepreneur
Ian Gervais	Cykron, Spry Agency, Statflo	Product Leader
Indi Young	Adaptive Path, Indiyoung.com	Entrepreneur, Author
Jim Kalbach	LexisNexis, MURAL, Razorfish	Author, Product Leader
Jason Stanley	Breather, Element AI, Provender	Product Leader
Jeff Gothelf	AOL, Gothelf.co, Sense & Respond Press, TheLadders.com	Entrepreneur, Author
John Cutler	Amplitude, AppFolio, Pendo.io, Zendesk	Product Leader
Jonathan Laba	BNOTIONS, Kinetic Commerce, Uberflip	Product Leader
Karl Gilis	AGConsult, Kluwer Opleidingen, Netsign	Entrepreneur
Kieran Flanagan	Cybercom, HubSpot, Marketo, Salesforce	Growth Leader
Luke Wroblewski	Bagcheck, Google, Input Factory, Yahoo!	Entrepreneur, Author
Michael Sacca	Brandisty, Crew Labs, Dribbble, Rocketship	Product Leader
Mostafa Elhefnawy	Gym Fuel, HomeStars, Influitive, SnapTravel	Entrepreneur
Nate Archer	Ada, Connected Lab, Myplanet, Strategyzer	Product Leader
Nick Babich	UX Planet	Entrepreneur
Nick Mauro	PointClear Solutions, Sailthru, SevenFifty	Product Leader
Nir Eyal	AdNectar, NirAndFar.com, Sunshine Business Development	Entrepreneur, Author
Nir Halperin	MuzArt.me, Playtika, Yotpo	Product Leader
Patrick Campbell	Gemvara, Google, ProfitWell	Entrepreneur
Rahul Vohra	LinkedIn, Rapportive, Superhuman	Entrepreneur
Sachin Rekhi	Connected, LinkedIn, Microsoft, Notejoy	Entrepreneur

Figure A1.1 - List of Contributors

Sam Ladner	Amazon, Critical Mass, Microsoft, Workday	Author, Product Leader
Samuel Hulick	Cloudability, The Good, UserOnboard	Entrepreneur
Sergey Barysiuk	Coding Staff, PandaDoc	Entrepreneur
Simon Seroussi	Feather, TravelClick	Product Leader
Steve Portigal	Dollars to Donuts, GVO, Portigal Consulting	Author, Product Leader
Thomas Tullis	Bell Labs, Fidelity, UXMetricsGeek.com	Author, Product Leader
Tony Ulwick	IBM, Strategyn	Entrepreneur, Author
Zoran Kovacevic	Func, StudyGrasp, TravelBird, TripActions	Product Leader

Figure A1.1 - List of Contributors

I feel wiser for having had the opportunity to interview these product experts and thank them for their generous contributions.

Other people who have played a key role in the writing of *Solving Product*—reading through drafts, giving ideas, and comments—include Alexandre Cayla, Amanda Robinson, Bruno Raymond, Jean-Bernard Tanqueray, Jean-Philippe Gousse, Kate Caldwell, Louis Beauregard, Louis-Dominic Parizeau, Mathieu Janelle-Gravel, Nathan Rose, Nicolas Cossette, Pavel Okulov, Pedro Souto, Roberto Garbugli, Rock Trembath, Samuel Hulick, Sam Shepler, Simon Vosgueritchian, Vanessa Salvo, and Xavi Creus.

A big thanks must also go out to the various authors, researchers and entrepreneurs mentioned in this book. From Amy Hoy to Bernadette Jiwa and Tristan Kromer, their work helped fuel and inspire the writing of *Solving Product*.

Thanks for helping make this book a reality.

References & Further Reading

To dive deeper into the concepts in this book, I recommend reading:

- *Blue Ocean Strategy*, W. Chan Kim and Renée Mauborgne
- *Crossing the Chasm*, Geoffrey A. Moore
- *Don't Make Me Think*, Steve Krug
- *Hooked*, Nir Eyal
- *How to Measure Anything*, Douglas W. Hubbard
- *Inspired*, Marty Cagan
- *Intercom on on Jobs-to-be-Done, on Marketing, on Onboarding, on Product Management, on Starting Up,* Intercom
- *Interviewing Users*, Steve Portigal
- *Just Enough Research*, Erika Hall
- *Lean Analytics*, Alistair Croll and Ben Yoskovitz
- *Lean B2B*, Étienne Garbugli
- *Lean Customer Development*, Cindy Alvarez
- *Lean UX*, Jeff Gothelf and Josh Seiden
- *Lost and Founder*, Rand Fishkin
- *Marketing*, Bernadette Jiwa
- *Measuring the User Experience*, Tom Tullis and William Albert
- *Mental Models*, Indi Young
- *Monetizing Innovation*, Georg Tacke and Madhavan Ramanujam
- *Obviously Awesome*, April Dunford
- *Practical Ethnography*, Sam Ladner
- *Principles*, Ray Dalio

- *Running Lean*, Ash Maurya
- *Shape Up*, Ryan Singer
- *The Elements of User Onboarding*, Samuel Hulick
- *The Entrepreneur's Guide to Customer Development*, Brant Cooper and Patrick Vlaskovits
- *The Four Steps to the Epiphany*, Steve Blank
- *The Innovator's Dilemma*, Clayton M. Christensen
- *The Jobs To Be Done Playbook*, Jim Kalbach
- *The Lean Startup*, Eric Ries
- *The Mom Test*, Rob Fitzpatrick
- *The North Star Playbook*, Amplitude
- *This Won't Scale*, Drift
- *Traction*, Gabriel Weinberg and Justin Mares
- *Web Form Design*, Luke Wroblewski
- *What Customers Want*, Anthony Ulwick
- *When Coffee and Kale Compete*, Alan Klement
- *Zingerman's Guide to Giving Great Service*, Ari Weinzweig

Appendix II – Next Steps

Thanks for reading *Solving Product.*

Believe it or not, at some point during the writing process, this book was at least twice its current length.

Unfortunately, for the sake of brevity I had to leave out a lot of great stories, techniques, and ideas.

To help you dive deeper into the techniques and ideas covered in this book (and those that got left out), I encourage you to visit the companion website at www.solvingproduct.com.

On it, you'll find tools, lessons, stories, checklists, ready-to-use templates, and articles designed to help you put this book's best ideas to use.

Solving Product is a book that you should come back to time and time again. I hope the website will be too.

Work With Me

Growing a business is hard. Unfortunately, even with the best techniques, case studies, and a full book and website to refer to, you may still have questions.

Maybe the situation you find yourself in is atypical, maybe many techniques could help address the specific challenge, or maybe you'd like to discuss the approach in greater detail.

No matter the reason, I understand quite well that some situations require going *off script.*

Each month, I help several entrepreneurs, product teams, and innovators work through their specific business or product challenges.

If you feel I can help, connect with me at (**solvingproduct.com/coach**. It will be my pleasure to help you and your team work through your specific challenges.

Notes

1. Law of the instrument
   https://en.wikipedia.org/wiki/Law_of_the_instrument

2. The Business Impact of Investing in Experience
   https://www.adobe.com/content/dam/acom/en/experience-cloud/research/roi/pdfs/business-impact-of-cx.pdf

3. Lecture 3 - Before the Startup (Paul Graham)
   https://youtu.be/ii1jcLg-eIQ?t=639

4. The SaaS Funding Napkin
   https://www.dropbox.com/s/etmgz1vbxuys1yw/SaaSNapkin2019.pdf?dl=0

   Note that it used to be possible to raise capital based on an idea, but it's increasingly less likely today.

5. The single biggest reason why start-ups succeed
   https://youtu.be/bNpx7gpSqbY?t=217

6. Research: The Average Age of a Successful Startup Founder Is 45
   https://hbr.org/2018/07/research-the-average-age-of-a-successful-startup-founder-is-45

7. Why Location Does (And Doesn't) Matter For Entrepreneurial Success
   https://www.forbes.com/sites/williamcraig/2015/01/16/why-location-does-and-doesnt-matter-for-entrepreneurial-success/#560226554bf6

8. Stagnation can come from relying on old data. Markets change, competitive positions evolve, expectations rarely stay the same. Are your competitive advantages still relevant? Have customer expectations changed?

9. Jeff Patton OnAgile2017 Q&A
   https://www.agilealliance.org/resources/videos/jeff-patton-onagile2017-qa

10. Startup Genome Report Extra on Premature Scaling
    https://solvingproduct.com/prematurescaling

11. Curb your enthusiasm: Optimistic entrepreneurs earn less

https://www.sciencedirect.com/science/article/pii/S0014292118301582

12. Steve Blank It's Our Research interview
https://youtu.be/d6pRCTV45Zs?t=291.

13. Drift's David Cancel on Whoever Gets Closer to the Customer Wins
https://youtu.be/ITBX3VEb1mQ?t=1398

14. Marketing Technology Landscape Supergraphic (2020): Martech 5000 – really 8,000, but who's counting?
https://chiefmartec.com/2020/04/marketing-technology-landscape-2020-martech-5000

15. Product Zeitgeist Fit and the Next Big Thing
https://www.youtube.com/watch?v=uztjCqlgzsI

16. Good Days for Disruptors
http://sloanreview.mit.edu/article/good-days-for-disruptors

17. Making things people want
https://www.intercom.com/blog/making-things-people-want

18. Startup Genome Report Extra on Premature Scaling
https://gallery.mailchimp.com/8c534f3b5ad611c0ff8aeccd5/files/Startup_Genome_Report_Extra_Premature_Scaling_version_2.1.pdf

19. Don't build a product unless you can validate it
https://pando.com/2014/01/13/dont-build-a-product-unless-you-can-validate-it

20. Double Diamond (design process model)
https://www.designcouncil.org.uk/sites/default/files/asset/document/ElevenLessons_Design_Council%20(2).pdf

21. The Elements of Value
https://hbr.org/2016/09/the-elements-of-value

22. Ep 14: Alex Hillman of 30x500
https://youtu.be/4cjlU2XGjzQ?t=1162

23. Amy Hoy - Sales Safari - La Conf Paris 2013
https://www.youtube.com/watch?v=exMoRoaxKtQ

24. Sam Ladner: Data Exhaust and Personal Data—Learning From Consumer Products to Enhance Enterprise UX
https://youtu.be/7ZSZ3-YnSys?t=577

25. Why you shouldn't ignore your competitors
https://producthabits.com/stop-ignoring-competitors

26. Getting out of recruitment - a HireVoice post mortem
https:
//www.etiennegarbugli.com/getting-out-of-recruitment-a-hirevoice-post-mortem

27. I was wrong.

The HR software market is thriving
https://www.sagepeople.com/about-us/news-hub/hcm-market-guide-gartner

28. Pretotyping - Techniques for Building the Right Product
https://www.skmurphy.com/blog/2012/03/06/pretotyping-techniques-for-building
-the-right-product

29. "Why are you building X when Y exists?"
https://www.indiehackers.com/@pjrvs/why-are-you-building-x-when-y-exists-0e
dc3c5507

30. Copycat Your Competitors to Take the Market
https://hitenism.com/copycat-competitors-take-market

31. FYI's Cofounder on Beta Testing Products and Survey Questions: Exact Questions to Ask Your Users (and Why)
https:
//www.userinterviews.com/blog/beta-testing-products-what-to-ask-and-why

32. https://twitter.com/levie/status/521709282782609409

33. Eager Sellers and Stony Buyers: Understanding the Psychology of New-Product Adoption
https://hbr.org/2006/06/eager-sellers-and-stony-buyers-understanding-the-psy
chology-of-new-product-adoption

34. My Billion Dollar Mistake
https://producthabits.com/my-billion-dollar-mistake

35. Product Habits SaaS Early Access
https://hnshah.typeform.com/to/aRq22o

36. Perspectives and Challenges of Jobs to Be Done: Livestream Recap
https://www.mural.co/blog/jobs-to-be-done-livestream-recap

37. Niche to Win, Baby.
https://500hats.com/niche-to-win-baby-934eba97f28c

38. How to Create a Unique Value Proposition (with Examples)
https://cxl.com/blog/value-proposition-examples-how-to-create

39. How to price something
https://signalvnoise.com/posts/3394-how-to-price-something

40. 9 Things First-Time Founders Get Wrong About The Journey
https://www.saastr.com/9-things-first-time-founders-get-wrong-about-the-journey

41. The Wilderness Period
https://medium.com/craft-ventures/the-wilderness-period-61f009c769ac

42. 4 pricing principles to never forget
https://www.intercom.com/blog/four-pricing-principals-to-never-forget

43. 7 Things I've Learned About Lean Startup
https://medium.com/precoil/7-things-i-ve-learned-about-lean-startup-c6323d9ef19c

44. Shelfware
https://en.wiktionary.org/wiki/shelfware

45. Startup Playbook
https://playbook.samaltman.com

46. From hand to hand combat to a Bond villain - how you evolve as a startup marketer
https://purde.net/2016/04/how-you-evolve-as-a-marketer

47. Do Things that Don't Scale
http://paulgraham.com/ds.html

48. Lessons learned in growing a product
https://www.intercom.com/blog/lessons-learned-in-growing-a-product-business

49. https://twitter.com/davidjbland/status/467096015318036480

50. 5 Phases of the Startup Lifecycle: Morgan Brown on What it Takes to Grow a Startup
https://medium.com/tradecraft-traction/5-phases-of-the-startup-lifecycle-morgan-brown-on-what-it-takes-to-grow-a-startup-50b4350f9d96

51. Startup = Growth
http://www.paulgraham.com/growth.html

52. I hate MVPs. So do your customers. Make it SLC instead.
https://blog.asmartbear.com/slc.html

53. The Inconvenient Truth About Product
https://svpg.com/the-inconvenient-truth-about-product

54. Brennan Dunn, Co-founder of RightMessage
https://www.youtube.com/watch?v=RxlvNB2Xrbs

55. "Your email is unbelievable"
https://newsletters.feedbinusercontent.com/de1/de198c5fcaece1ff99e6c77b40f4fe135646e47f.html

56. Reactions > Feedback
https://medium.com/@jakek/reactions-feedback-dc1ea9a06ce0

57. S4E4-Jeff Atwood: Building Communities & Customer Feedback Loops
https://www.youtube.com/watch?v=G5s-4lx-cFA

58. Designing progress of the high-expectation customer
https://uxdesign.cc/designing-progress-of-the-high-expectation-customer-33078ca8305

59. What I Learned From Developing Branding for Airbnb, Dropbox and Thumbtack
https://firstround.com/review/what-i-learned-from-developing-branding-for-airbnb-dropbox-and-thumbtack

60. Startups Always Have a Chasm to Cross
https://medium.com/@arachleff/startups-always-have-a-chasm-to-cross-61b79215ac05

61. Predictably Irrational » Chapter 8 Keeping doors open
https://www.youtube.com/watch?v=13rfq9dqKPE

62. Product-User Fit Comes Before Product-Market Fit
https://a16z.com/2019/09/16/product-user-fit-comes-before-product-market-fit

63. Using PMFSurvey.com
https://www.startup-marketing.com/using-survey-io

64. Lecture 1 - How to Start a Startup (Sam Altman, Dustin Moskovitz)
https://youtu.be/CBYhVcO4WgI?t=1026

65. Not all good products make good businesses

https://www.intercom.com/blog/good-products-bad-businesses

66. Only 1 out of 26 unhappy customers complain. The rest churn.
https://cxm.co.uk/1-26-unhappy-customers-complain-rest-churn

67. Start Up on the Right Foot — Build a Customer Advisory Board
https://firstround.com/review/start-up-on-the-right-foot-build-a-customer-advisory-board

68. INBOUND 2016: Peep Laja "How to Figure Out What Really Makes Your Website Work For You"
https://youtu.be/516adk1YIPo?t=541

69. AMA: I'm Patrick Campbell (@Patticus), CEO of the team behind Price Intelligently and ProfitWell
https://growthhackers.com/amas/ama-im-patrick-campbell-patticus-ceo-of-the-team-behind-price-intelligently-and-profitwell

70. https://twitter.com/eshear/status/1155180521485242368

71. The best metric for determining quantitative product market fit
https://www.growthengblog.com/blog/the-best-metric-for-determining-quantitative-product-market-fit

72. https://twitter.com/dunkhippo33/status/1153779854614990848

73. Elad Gil: When do you know you have Product Market Fit?
https://www.youtube.com/watch?v=9vOv5TLZKzA

74. 339 Startup Failure Post-Mortems
https://www.cbinsights.com/research/startup-failure-post-mortem

75. The Never Ending Road To Product Market Fit
https://brianbalfour.com/essays/product-market-fit

76. Leading social apps with the highest 24-month usage retention rates worldwide as of August 2015
https://www.statista.com/statistics/523845/highest-retention-social-android-apps

77. Snapchat founder Evan Spiegel twice turned down cash from Facebook's Mark Zuckerberg
https://www.thetimes.co.uk/article/snapchat-founder-evan-spiegel-twice-turned-down-cash-from-facebook-s-mark-zuckerberg-bqf9mphc7

78. The "Toothbrush" Trick Used By Google's CEO To Get Customers To

Come Back
https://medium.com/behavior-design/the-toothbrush-trick-used-by-googles-ceo-to-get-customers-to-come-back-910d81c272b4

79. Is the Product-Market Fit survey accurate?
https://justinjackson.ca/product-market-fit-survey

80. The Startup Pyramid
https://www.startup-marketing.com/the-startup-pyramid

81. https://twitter.com/naval/status/1128346098362281984

82. In research done by Fred Davis in the early 90s, it's been proven that usefulness can predict around 36% of actual product usage. It's effectively 1.5 times more important than ease of use for products:
https://deepblue.lib.umich.edu/bitstream/handle/2027.42/30954/0000626.pdf;jsessionid=0B8A14B8495628E656C70B99D3E08F5F

83. The Revenge of the Fat Guy
https://a16z.com/2010/03/20/the-revenge-of-the-fat-guy

84. PayPal Mafia
https://en.wikipedia.org/wiki/PayPal_Mafia

85. The Sharp Startup: When PayPal Found Product-Market Fit
https://medium.com/craft-ventures/the-sharp-startup-when-paypal-found-product-market-fit-5ba47ad35d0b

86. S5E8-Casey Winters: Turning startups into rocketships
https://www.youtube.com/watch?v=BXmEXa-Nc7g

87. Part 4: The only thing that matters
https://pmarchive.com/guide_to_startups_part4.html

88. How we set up our Team for Continuous Product Discovery
https://uxdesign.cc/how-to-set-up-your-team-to-run-continuous-product-discovery-4ba757cb52e6

89. Momentum: The ultimate startup killer
https://medium.com/@matvogels/momentum-the-ultimate-startup-killer-bf9868f0426b

90. You've Got Product/Market Fit… What About Marketing/Market Fit?
https://sparktoro.com/blog/youve-got-product-market-fit-what-about-marketing-market-fit

91. David Cancel talks with Constant Contact CEO, Gail Goodman
https://soundcloud.com/dcancel/david-cancel-talks-with-constant-contact-ceo-gail-goodman

92. How we transformed HubSpot into a Product Driven Company
https://www.linkedin.com/pulse/20141102175328-25444-how-we-transformed-hubspot-into-a-product-driven-company

93. How to Avoid the Premature Scaling Death Trap
https://www.entrepreneur.com/article/245603

94. Diffusion of innovations
https://en.wikipedia.org/wiki/Diffusion_of_innovations

95. Unpacking the Progress Making Forces Diagram
http://jobstobedone.org/radio/unpacking-the-progress-making-forces-diagram

96. The Mad Scientist Is Back! Here Are 4 Inbound Automation Secrets That Will Make You Rethink Your Growth Strategy in 2018
https://www.drift.com/blog/inbound-automation-whiteboard-lessons

97. How to Get Good at Making Money
https://www.inc.com/magazine/20110301/making-money-small-business-advice-from-jason-fried.html

98. "The Customer Is Not Always Right": Cindy Alvarez with Lean Customer Development (Video + Transcript)
https://girlgeek.io/the-customer-is-not-always-right-cindy-alvarez-with-lean-customer-development-video-transcript

99. SPI 244: Bootstrapping a Startup with Nathan Barry from ConvertKit
https://www.smartpassiveincome.com/download/Transcript-SPI244.pdf

100. INBOUND 2016: Peep Laja "How to Figure Out What Really Makes Your Website Work For You"
https://youtu.be/516adk1YlPo?t=1163

101. Using Thank You Page Surveys To Segment 80%+ Of Your Subscribers
https://rightmessage.com/articles/thank-you-page-surveys

102. Dividing User Time Between Goal And Tool
https://articles.uie.com/dividing-user-time-between-goal-and-tool

103. The Never Ending Road To Product Market Fit
https://brianbalfour.com/essays/product-market-fit

104. Zero to IPO: Lessons From Unlikely Story of HubSpot
https://www.slideshare.net/HubSpot/zero-to-ipo-lessons-from-unlikely-story-of-hubspot

105. A cognitive model of the antecedents and consequences of satisfaction decisions.
https://psycnet.apa.org/record/1981-04315-001

106. 8 Customer Discovery Questions To Validate Product Market Fit For Your Startup
https://www.linkedin.com/pulse/8-customer-discovery-questions-validate-product-market-tomasz-tunguz

107. Zingerman's Guide to Great Service
https://www.zingermans.com/Product/zingermans-guide-to-great-service/P-ARI-7

108. The Spotlight Framework - Making Customer Feeback Actionable
https://davidcancel.com/the-spotlight-framework-making-customer-feeback-actionable

109. https://twitter.com/Austen/status/1064687271557779456

110. Facebook-Google Duopoly Won't Crack This Year
https://www.emarketer.com/content/facebook-google-duopoly-won-t-crack-this-year

111. Is content marketing dead? Here's some data
https://www.profitwell.com/blog/content-marketing-customer-acquisition-cost

112. 4 reasons why the Net Promoter Score is overrated
https://www.reforge.com/brief/4-reasons-why-the-net-promoter-score-is-overrated#MZEBanKXnaPLmdBkiW8YWg

113. https://twitter.com/jmspool/status/941727814365143040

114. The Inventor of Customer Satisfaction Surveys Is Sick of Them, Too
https://www.bloomberg.com/news/articles/2016-05-04/tasty-taco-helpful-hygienist-are-all-those-surveys-of-any-use

115. The One Number You Need to Grow
https://hbr.org/2003/12/the-one-number-you-need-to-grow

116. Goal Setting: Do Less & Accomplish More
https://www.inc.com/logan-chierotti/how-doing-less-allows-you-to-accomplish-more.html

117. Startup Metrics for Pirates
https://www.slideshare.net/dmc500hats/startup-metrics-for-pirates-long-version

118. Note that in McClure's model, Revenue is the last step.

119. The Right Way to Involve a Qualitative Research Team
https://caseyaccidental.com/the-right-way-to-involve-a-qualitative-research-team

120. https://twitter.com/IshIsDeep/status/1208516882556428291

121. Where to play: a practical guide for running your tech business
https://actu.epfl.ch/news/where-to-play-a-practical-guide-for-running-your-t

122. How to Get Good at Making Money
https://www.inc.com/magazine/20110301/making-money-small-business-advice-from-jason-fried.html

123. 9 Things First-Time Founders Get Wrong About The Journey
https://www.saastr.com/9-things-first-time-founders-get-wrong-about-the-journey

124. Innovation Consultant Rene Bastijans on Uncovering Your Product's True Competition
https://leanb2bbook.com/blog/innovation-consultant-rene-bastijans-uncovering-product-true-competitors

125. Why Great Pitches Come From Customers
https://www.linkedin.com/pulse/why-great-pitches-come-from-customers-andy-raskin

126. 7 Lessons Helping Start Pardot, SalesLoft, and Calendly
https://youtu.be/Yc2FkI56qLw?t=1156

127. The power of niche
https://www.campaignlive.co.uk/article/power-niche/1671284

128. The Definitive Guide to User Onboarding
https://productled.com/user-onboarding

129. Slack CMO Bill Macaitis | Marketing the Fastest Growing App in History
https://youtu.be/hZpJMcOBb5U?t=3009

130. You can also use tools like Apify or Instant Data Scraper to

crawl and return all of your client's reviews in a database or an Excel spreadsheet.

131. Why Most Companies Fail At Moving Up or Down Market
https://brianbalfour.com/essays/key-lessons-for-100m-growth

132. How to Acquire Customers: 19 "Traction" Channels to Start Testing Today
https://zapier.com/blog/acquire-customers

133. Bootstrapping Side Projects into Profitable Startups
https://levels.io/bootstrapping

134. How Long Should You Wait for Content Marketing to Work?
https://contentilo.com/blog/how-long-should-you-wait-for-content-marketing-to-work

135. Four Fits For $100M+ Growth
https://brianbalfour.com/four-fits-growth-framework

136. When Freemium Fails
https://www.wsj.com/articles/SB10000872396390443713704577603782317318996

137. Freemium Conversion Rate: Why Spotify Destroys Dropbox by 667%
https://www.process.st/freemium-conversion-rate

138. Case Studies in Freemium: Pandora, Dropbox, Evernote, Automattic and Mailchimp
https://gigaom.com/2010/03/26/case-studies-in-freemium-pandora-dropbox-evernote-automattic-and-Mailchimp/#comment-245266

139. Freemium Conversion Rate: Why Spotify Destroys Dropbox by 667%
https://www.process.st/freemium-conversion-rate

140. Top 10 Learnings about Free Trials with Tomasz Tunguz
https://www.youtube.com/watch?v=tfQNJpnxmMw

141. Hacking Word-of-Mouth: Making Referrals Work for Airbnb
https://medium.com/airbnb-engineering/hacking-word-of-mouth-making-referrals-work-for-airbnb-46468e7790a6

142. https://twitter.com/levie/status/322943602135277568

143. Being Data Driven
https://www.slideshare.net/JacquesWarren/being-data-driven-56145552

144. Principal-Agent Problem: Act Like an Owner
https://nav.al/principal-agent

145. Steve Sasson, Digital Camera Inventor
https://youtu.be/wfnpVRiiwnM

146. Kodak's Downfall wasn't About Technology
https://hbr.org/2016/07/kodaks-downfall-wasnt-about-technology

147. Blockbuster's CEO once passed up a chance to buy Netflix for only $50 million
https://www.businessinsider.com/blockbuster-ceo-passed-up-chance-to-buy-netflix-for-50-million-2015-7

148. Building a Company-Wide Growth Culture: SaaStr Annual 2016
https://www.slideshare.net/seanellis/building-a-companywide-growth-culture-saastr-annual-2016/23-Final_Thought_Focus_on_Value

149. A Simple Tool You Need to Manage Innovation
https://hbr.org/2012/05/a-simple-tool-you-need-to-mana

150. Feature Creep Isn't the Real Problem
https://producthabits.com/feature-creep-isnt-real-problem

151. Why you need customer development
https://www.oreilly.com/content/why-you-need-customer-development

152. Subjective theory of value
https://en.wikipedia.org/wiki/Subjective_theory_of_value

153. Prioritization Shouldn't Be Hard
https://melissaperri.com/blog/2019/10/31/prioritization

154. "95% of your time should be spent iterating on things you've already built. 5% on new ideas This forces focus on actual learnings. Also makes you think REALLY hard about what you want to put that 5% into."
https://twitter.com/mnort_9/status/1013946326315347974

155. The Complete Guide to the Kano Model
https://foldingburritos.com/kano-model

156. How we found Product Market Fit with our Chatbot
https://medium.com/hackernoon/spend-time-with-your-market-if-you-want-to-find-product-market-fit-cd2b0108e572

157. Working Hard Is Overrated
https://www.businessinsider.com/working-hard-is-overrated-2009-9

158. Kano Model — Ways to use it and NOT use it
https://medium.com/design-ibm/kano-model-ways-to-use-it-and-not-use-it-1d205a9cf808

159. Feel free to refer to the following guide if you'd still like to use the Kano survey:
https: //leanb2bbook.com/blog/how-to-find-core-features-product-using-kano-surveys

160. How MaxDiff Analysis Works (Simplish, but Not for Dummies)
https://www.displayr.com/how-maxdiff-analysis-works

161. Kill your darlings—how, why, and when to cut product features
https://www.appcues.com/blog/cutting-features

162. To Kill a Feature
https://www.mindtheproduct.com/to-kill-a-feature

163. KILL A FEATURE. Something Sucks
https://www.slideshare.net/dmc500hats/startup-metrics-for-pirates-fowa-london-oct-2009/17

164. Feature/Product Fit
https://caseyaccidental.com/feature-product-fit

165. Why You Only Need to Test with 5 Users
https://www.nngroup.com/articles/why-you-only-need-to-test-with-5-users

166. How Palantir's Business Model Built A $15 Billion Growth Engine
https://buckfiftymba.com/palantirs-growth-engine

167. https://twitter.com/sgblank/status/573773311756275714

168. Calculate the Total Addressable Market (TAM) Size for the Beachhead Market
http://gsl-archive.mit.edu/media/programs/india-bms-summer-2013/materials/step_4_calculate_the_tam_—-trepreneurship_101.pdf

169. Highlights
https://www.gethighlights.co

170. Expose the price of new features

https://basecamp.com/gettingreal/05.4-hidden-costs

171. Strategic Debt Is the Silent Killer of Startups
https://ganotnoa.com/strategic-debt-is-the-silent-killer-of-startups

172. The Bowling Pin Strategy
https://www.businessinsider.com/the-bowling-pin-strategy-2010-8

173. Newsweaver rebrands as Poppulo and creates world's first dedicated internal comms platform
https://www.poppulo.com/blog/newsweaver-rebrands-as-poppulo-and-creates-worlds-first-dedicated-internal-comms-platform

174. Box founder Aaron Levie is a rare thing in Silicon Valley - he's funny
https://www.telegraph.co.uk/finance/newsbysector/mediatechnologyandtelecoms/digital-media/10324051/Box-founder-Aaron-Levie-is-a-rare-thing-in-Silicon-Valley-hes-funny.html

175. Stars of SXSW: Dave McClure on Lean Start-up Investing
https://www.inc.com/howard-greenstein/lean-start-up-investing-with-dave-mcclure-of-500-startups.html

176. Customer feedback strategy: How to collect, analyze and take action
https://www.intercom.com/blog/customer-feedback-strategy

177. When Amazon Employees Receive These One-Character Emails From Jeff Bezos, They Go Into A Frenzy
https://www.businessinsider.com/amazon-customer-service-and-jeff-bezos-emails-2013-10

178. https://twitter.com/levie/status/454493624659476480

179. According to The Jobs To Be Done Playbook author Jim Kalbach, a good rule of thumb is to have at least twice as many respondents as the desired outcome statements.

180. A Critique of Outcome-Driven Innovation®
https://ams-insights.com/wp-content/uploads/2016/06/A_Critique_of_Outcome_Driven_Innovation.pdf

181. Usually $150 to $250 or more per song.

182. Lew Cirne of New Relic: Scaling Even Faster the Second Time
https://www.youtube.com/watch?v=i6tmnZ7ElK4

183. "7 out of 8 corporate startups do not generate business impact."
https://innovation-3.com/scaling-up-book

184. Steve Jobs 1997 Interview: Defending His Commitment To Apple
https://youtu.be/xchYT9wz5hk?t=27

185. Why 37signals Refocused on a Single Product: Basecamp
https://www.inc.com/magazine/201403/jason-fried/basecamp-focus-one-product-only.html

Interestingly enough, in 2020 they changed back their strategy and launched an email service called Hey.

186. Lost and Founder: A Painfully Honest Field Guide to the Startup World
https://www.penguinrandomhouse.com/books/547217/lost-and-founder-by-rand-fishkin

187. Followerwonk Is Moving On to a New, Loving Home
https://moz.com/blog/followerwonk-news

188. How launching new products for existing audiences can help grow your company
https://gopractice.io/blog/products-for-existing-audiences

189. Search Engine Market Share United States Of America
https://gs.statcounter.com/search-engine-market-share/all/united-states-of-america/#monthly-200901-202001

190. Try More Things
https://evhead.com/try-more-things-f5c743e73a98

191. Why we released a better product for free (& maybe you should too)
https://www.profitwell.com/blog/why-we-released-a-better-product-for-free-and-maybe-you-should-too

192. Patrick Campbell Founder of ProfitWell Shares Why He Chose Scale over Lifestyle
https://growandconvert.com/marketing/profitwell-patrick-campbell-scale

193. 2016 Letter to Shareholders
https://blog.aboutamazon.com/company-news/2016-letter-to-shareholders

194. Traditional company, new businesses: The pairing that can ensure an incumbent's survival

https://www.mckinsey.com/~/media/McKinsey/Industries/Electric%20Power%20and%20Natural%20Gas/Our%20Insights/Traditional%20company%20new%20businesses%20The%20pairing%20that%20can%20ensure%20an%20incumbents%20survival/Traditional-company-new-businesses-VF.ashx

195. https://twitter.com/lukew/status/908352707420758016

196. What Is the Product Life Cycle? Stages and Examples
https://www.thestreet.com/markets/commodities/product-life-cycle-14882534

197. From Darkroom to Desktop—How Photoshop Came to Light
https://web.archive.org/web/20070626182822/http://www.storyphoto.com/multimedia/multimedia_photoshop.html

Fun fact: Photoshop wasn't created by Adobe.

198. Your product is already obsolete
https://www.intercom.com/blog/your-product-is-already-obsolete

199. Startupfest 2015: SEAN ELLIS (GrowthHackers.com)
https://www.slideshare.net/startupfest/startupfest-2015-sean-ellis-growthhackerscom-how-to-stage

200. An alternative is EVELYN, developed by Darius Contractor at Dropbox:
https://bit.ly/evelyn-airtable

201. How to Scale Personalization: with Guillaume Cabane
https://www.youtube.com/watch?v=O3MMK6Z_E-c

202. The Rudder Fallacy—Adopting Lean Startup Principles
https://www.linkedin.com/pulse/rudder-fallacy-adopting-lean-startup-principles-tristan-kromer

203. The Origin of A/B Testing
https://www.linkedin.com/pulse/origin-ab-testing-nicolai-kramer-jakobsen

204. What Are Clinical Trial Phases?
https://www.youtube.com/watch?v=dsfPOpE-GEs

205. INBOUND 2016: Peep Laja "How to Figure Out What Really Makes Your Website Work For You"
https://youtu.be/516adk1YIPo?t=214

206. Like these:
https://www.optimizely.com/sample-size-calculator

https://www.evanmiller.org/ab-testing/sample-size.html
https://abtestguide.com/calc

207. 4 Pillars of User Driven Growth
https://youtu.be/iz34CTOEUBQ?t=245

208. Lean Startup Comes Home
https://medium.com/precoil/lean-startup-comes-home-8f205993da40

209. Lean Startup Comes Home
https://medium.com/precoil/lean-startup-comes-home-8f205993da40

210. NatWest in "off-brand and disruptive" beta-testing for new services
https://www.designweek.co.uk/issues/2-8-march-2015-2/natwest-in-off-brand-and-disruptive-beta-testing-for-new-services

211. Shape Up: Stop Running in Circles and Ship Work that Matters
https://basecamp.com/shapeup

212. Letter to Shareholders - EX-99.1
https://www.sec.gov/Archives/edgar/data/1018724/000119312517120198/d373368dex991.htm

213. MeasuringU: What Is A Good Task-Completion Rate?
https://measuringu.com/task-completion

214. Comparison of three one-question, post-task usability questionnaires
https://www.researchgate.net/publication/221514412_Comparison_of_three_one-question_post-task_usability_questionnaires

215. MeasuringU: 10 Things To Know About The Single Ease Question (SEQ)
https://measuringu.com/seq10

216. 7 Basic Design Principles We Forget About
https://www.laroche.co/blog/7-basic-design-principles-we-forget-about

217. Jakob's Law
https://lawsofux.com/jakobs-law

218. Scott Cook, Intuit
https://www.inc.com/magazine/20040401/25cook.html

219. Diary Studies
https://www.userinterviews.com/ux-research-field-guide-chapter/diary-studies

220. How To Get Results From Jobs-to-be-Done Interviews
https://jobs-to-be-done.com/jobs-to-be-done-interviews-79623d99b3e5

221. What is Customer Research? Top Findings and Benchmarks
https://www.profitwell.com/blog/customer-research-benchmarks

222. Andon (manufacturing)
https://en.wikipedia.org/wiki/Andon_(manufacturing)

223. Amazon Andon Cord - what it is and how to react
https://blueboard.io/resources/amazon-andon-cord

224. Based on the book and research by Lisa Bodell
https://www.youtube.com/watch?v=n4Li9KjFc1w

225. Jason Fried (Basecamp) and Derek Andersen at Startup Grind Global 2016
https://youtu.be/ft-q9s2uxlQ?t=1186

226. Why Reading About Your Competitors Will Hurt Your Business
https://www.inc.com/magazine/201511/jason-fried/taking-an-industry-detox.html

227. Six Hours of Phone Calls
https://rework.fm/six-hours-of-phone-calls

228. Basecamp now has a totally free version to help you manage personal projects
https://www.theverge.com/2019/11/14/20965543/basecamp-free-version-manage-basic-personal-projects

229. Basecamp is hiring a Head of Marketing
https://m.signalvnoise.com/basecamp-is-hiring-a-head-of-marketing

230. Clearbit Enrichment
https://clearbit.com/enrichment

231. How Showmax Runs a Growth Team Across 70+ Global Markets
http://barronernst.com/how-showmax-runs-a-growth-team-across-70-global-markets

232. The Hypergrowth Curve: How to Navigate the 3 Stages of Massive Growth

https://www.drift.com/blog/hypergrowth-curve

233. Going Freemium - One Year Later | Mailchimp
http://pricing-news.com/going-freemium-one-year-later-Mailchimp

234. On Surveys
https://www.linkedin.com/pulse/surveys-erika-hall-1

235. Which of the following methods do you prefer to use when you pay for a product you have bought online?
https://www.statista.com/statistics/434294/e-commerce-popular-payment-methods-france

236. Brazil payments guide
https://www.adyen.com/knowledge-hub/guides/global-payment-methods-guide/local-payment-methods-in-latin-america/brazil-payments

237. Indonesia payments guide
https://www.adyen.com/knowledge-hub/guides/global-payment-methods-guide/local-payment-methods-in-asia-pacific/indonesia-payments#paymentmethods

238. Argentina makes sweeping changes to tax laws, followed by regulations implementing recently enacted tax reform
https://globaltaxnews.ey.com/news/2020-5025-argentina-makes-sweeping-changes-to-tax-laws-followed-by-regulations-implementing-recently-enacted-tax-reform

239. Your Largest Bucket of Churn (and How to Prevent it)
https://www.profitwell.com/blog/reducing-delinquent-churn-dramatically

240. Not by sales.

241. The 11%+ Reason You Need To Localize Your SaaS Pricing
https://www.profitwell.com/blog/the-11-reason-you-need-to-localize-your-saas-pricing

242. How to Reduce Customer Churn w/ Bullet-Proof Retention
https://www.profitwell.com/blog/how-to-reduce-churn-by-building-a-bulletproof-retention-process

243. We Studied 6,452 SaaS Companies. The Findings Will Make You Grow.
https://www.chargebee.com/blog/saas-business-growth-findings

244. Reinventing Voice-of-Customer for B2B: 12 New Rules
http://lightningreleases.com/reinventing-voice-of-customer-for-b2b-12-new-rules

245. Managing Price, Gaining Profit
https://hbr.org/1992/09/managing-price-gaining-profit

246. Data shows our addiction to acquisition based growth is getting worse
https://www.priceintelligently.com/blog/saas-growth-focused-too-much-on-acquisition

247. Pricing benchmarks
https://www.profitwell.com/pricing-growth-benchmarks

248. Value metric benchmarks
https://www.profitwell.com/benchmarks-for-value-metric-pricing

249. It's Price Before Product. Period.
https://firstround.com/review/its-price-before-product-period

250. https://twitter.com/davidjbland/status/302138756813684736

251. How Startups Should Do Customer Discovery
https://thinkgrowth.org/how-startups-should-do-customer-discovery-51b151724a01

252. Why Startups that Survive are "Learning Organizations"
https://www.nfx.com/post/learning-organizations-survive

253. https://twitter.com/mulegirl/status/1178790260441927681

254. Customer feedback strategy: How to collect, analyze and take action
https://www.intercom.com/blog/customer-feedback-strategy

255. Why radical truth and radical transparency are keys to success
https://www.youtube.com/watch?v=7KqyXF9f1dc

256. Leadership Principles
https://www.drift.com/principles/

257. The Hypothesis Prioritization Canvas
https://jeffgothelf.com/blog/the-hypothesis-prioritization-canvas/

258. Knowns vs Unknowns — Are you building a successful company or just typing?
https://medium.com/lightspeed-venture-partners/knowns-vs-unknowns-78b0da5ca887

259. "There are things we know that we know. There are known unknowns—that is to say, there are things that we now know we don't know. But there are also unknown unknowns—there are things we do not know we don't know." - Donald Rumsfeld, Former US secretary of Defence

260. What is Customer Research? Top Findings and Benchmarks https://www.profitwell.com/blog/customer-research-benchmarks

261. What is Customer Research? Top Findings and Benchmarks https://www.profitwell.com/blog/customer-research-benchmarks

262. 42% of Companies Don't Listen to their Customers. Yikes. [New Service Data] https://blog.hubspot.com/service/state-of-service-2019-customer-first

263. What is Customer Research? Top Findings and Benchmarks https://www.profitwell.com/blog/customer-research-benchmarks

264. Why Great Pitches Come From Customers https: //www.linkedin.com/pulse/why-great-pitches-come-from-customers-andy-raskin

265. Definition of Done https://www.agilealliance.org/glossary/definition-of-done/

266. What is the least intrusive/least threatening question to ask a prospective employer that will yield the most information about the culture? https://twitter.com/johncutlefish/status/1206137769908531201

267. Product discovery & re-imagining organizational change https://gamethinking.io/podcast/306-teresa-torres

268. Setting up to fail https://en.wikipedia.org/wiki/Setting_up_to_fail

269. The question index for real startups https://mycourses.aalto.fi/pluginfile.php/1136837/mod_folder/content/0/Kromer%2 02019%20JBVI.pdf

270. Steve Blank It's Our Research interview https://youtu.be/d6pRCTV45Zs?t=429

271. Sensemaking https://en.wikipedia.org/wiki/Sensemaking

272. "I don't give a fuck if you like or use personas. Just don't make up some random shit, call it "personas", and then say it doesn't work."
https://twitter.com/MrAlanCooper/status/909897368216117249

273. Journey Mapping 101
https://www.nngroup.com/articles/journey-mapping-101

274. A Three-Step Framework For Solving Problems
https://uxdesign.cc/how-to-solve-problems-6bf14222e424

275. Instead of Gap Thinking, Present Thinking
https://twitter.com/cyetain/status/971753487586521088

276. Defensibility creates the most value for founders
https://techcrunch.com/2016/09/15/defensibility-creates-the-most-value-for-founders

277. https://twitter.com/pc4media/status/1143153932992225280

278. What Building 5 Products in a Year Forces You to Do
https://youtu.be/ZGUsXomel_w?t=1467

279. Airbnb: The Growth Story You didn't Know
https://growthhackers.com/growth-studies/airbnb

280. The Spawn of Craigslist
https://thegongshow.tumblr.com/post/345941486/the-spawn-of-craigslist-like-most-vcs-that-focus

281. How to Find Anyone's Email: 12 Little-Known Tricks
https://www.yesware.com/blog/find-email-addresses

282. Steve Portigal - Great User Research for Non Researchers
https://youtu.be/x-_1r5uKqlA?t=713

283. A Guide to the Art of Guerrilla UX Testing
https://medium.springboard.com/a-guide-to-the-art-of-guerrilla-ux-testing-69a1411d34fb

284. Why You Only Need to Test with 5 Users
https://www.nngroup.com/articles/why-you-only-need-to-test-with-5-users

285. On Surveys
https://medium.com/mule-design/on-surveys-5a73dda5e9a0

286. You can use a calculator like this one:
https://www.surveymonkey.com/mp/sample-size-calculator

287. Confidence interval
https://en.wikipedia.org/wiki/Confidence_interval

288. Assuming a 30% open rate, and a 5% click rate.

289. North Star Playbook
https://amplitude.com/north-star

290. We're Evolving Our Product's North Star Metric. Here's Why.
https://amplitude.com/blog/evolving-the-product-north-star-metric

291. Spenser Skates, Finding Your Mobile Growth, LSC15
https://youtu.be/zRSMo7Dt2PY?t=72

292. How Zappos Wins at Customer Service Every Day
https://etailwest.wbresearch.com/zappos-customer-service-ty-u

293. Uncommon Service: The Zappos Case Study
https:
//www.inc.com/inc-advisor/zappos-managing-people-uncommon-service.html

294. Managing customer expectations for new feature requests
https://canny.io/blog/managing-customer-expectations

295. Automated Outbound Sales
https://clearbit.com/books/data-driven-sales/automated-outbound-sales

Index

C

D

E

F

G

H

I

J

K

L

M

N

O

P

Q

R

S

W

Y

Z

Also by
Étienne Garbugli

Étienne's books focus on leveraging customer insights to build and grow businesses.

Lean B2B: Build Products Businesses Want

Lean B2B consolidates the best thinking around Business-to-Business (B2B) customer development to help technology entrepreneurs quickly find traction in the enterprise, leaving as little as possible to luck.

The Lean B2B methodology is used by thousands of entrepreneurs & innovators around the world.

Find Your Market

Find Your Market helps founders and innovators find the right market for their innovations.

It shows them how to evaluate whether their product is aimed at the right market or customers, how to identify promising market opportunities derived from the unique strengths of their technology, and how to lock in on the best market opportunity.

About the Author
Étienne Garbugli

Étienne works at the intersection of Tech, Product Design and Marketing.

He's a three-time startup founder (Highlights, Flagback and HireVoice), a five-time entrepreneur, and a customer research expert.

In 2014, he published the book Lean B2B. The Lean B2B methodology helps thousands of entrepreneurs and innovators around the world build successful businesses.

www.ingramcontent.com/pod-product-compliance
Ingram Content Group UK Ltd.
Pitfield, Milton Keynes, MK11 3LW, UK
UKHW030648140425
5458UKWH00027B/204

9 781778 074066